The Big Hurt

ALSO BY ERIKA SCHICKEL

You're Not the Boss of Me: Adventures of a Modern Mom

The
Big Hurt

A Memoir

Erika Schickel

hachette
BOOKS

New York

Copyright © 2021 by Erika Schickel

Cover design by Terri Sirma
Cover photograph: Photograph of Erika Schickel in Patti Smith shirt c. 1980 © Rhea Smith
Cover copyright © 2021 by Hachette Book Group, Inc.

Hachette Books
Hachette Book Group
1290 Avenue of the Americas
New York, NY 10104
HachetteBooks.com
Twitter.com/HachetteBooks
Instagram.com/HachetteBooks

First Edition: August 2021

Published by Hachette Books, an imprint of Perseus Books, LLC, a subsidiary of Hachette Book Group, Inc. The Hachette Books name and logo is a trademark of the Hachette Book Group.

The Hachette Speakers Bureau provides a wide range of authors for speaking events. To find out more, go to www.hachettespeakersbureau.com or call (866) 376-6591.

The publisher is not responsible for websites (or their content) that are not owned by the publisher.

Print book interior design by Marie Mundaca.

Library of Congress Cataloging-in-Publication Data
Names: Schickel, Erika, author.
Title: The big hurt : a memoir / Erika Schickel.
Description: First edition. | New York: Hachette Books, 2021.
Identifiers: LCCN 2020046240 | ISBN 9780306925054 (hardcover) | ISBN 9780306925047 (ebook)
Subjects: LCSH: Schickel, Erika. | Actors—United States—Biography. | Journalists—United States—Biography. | Essayists—United States—Biography.
Classification: LCC PN2287.S334 A3 2021 | DDC 791.4302/8092 [B]—dc23
LC record available at https://lccn.loc.gov/2020046240

ISBNs: 978-0-306-92505-4 (hardcover), 978-0-306-92504-7 (ebook)

Printed in the United States of America

LSC-C

Printing 1, 2021

For CJ Dallett
and all the others

Native Moments! When you come upon me—ah, you are here now.
Give me now libidinous joys only!
Give me the drench of my passions! Give me life coarse and rank!
To-day, I go consort with nature's darlings—to-night too;
I am for those who believe in loose delights—I share the midnight orgies of
  young men;
I dance with the dancers, and drink with the drinkers;
The echoes ring with our indecent calls;
I take for my love some prostitute—I pick out some low person for my
  dearest friend,
He shall be lawless, rude, illiterate—he shall be one condemn'd by others
  for deeds done;
I will play a part no longer—Why should I exile myself from my
  companions?
O you shunn'd persons! I at least do not shun you,
I come forwith in your midst—I will be your poet,
I will be more to you than to any of the rest.

—Walt Whitman, *Leaves of Grass*

The Big Hurt

Los Angeles, Summer 2009

I knew he was waiting for me, stretched out on his long leather couch, the back of his wrist pressed to his third eye, his elbow a pale antenna, searching for my signal.

I stepped on the gas. It was all too easy to drive away from my life and the book I was trying to write about what happened to me in high school. I turned north on Rossmore and the Ravenswood came into view. The 1930s Art Deco landmark announced itself from a half mile away in red vintage neon. The *N* and the *D* in the sign were burned out, so it read the RAVE SWOO, and I thought that was the perfect name for what Sam Spade did in that old building, beneath those sputtering neon tubes: rave and woo.

Spade never suffered writer's block. Books poured out of him. "Imitate the virtue you wish to achieve," he told me, which meant, sit down and work. I knew what that looked like. It looked like my father, hunched over his IBM Selectric, cigarette ash between the keys, cold coffee in his mug, firing off movie reviews and film biographies like a turret gunner.

It wasn't work I was afraid of. It was the story itself. The story of what happened to me in high school. Every time I probed it for some hilarious anecdote about my "bad girl" past, it spat venom at me. It hissed truths at me that I didn't want to face, much less describe on the page.

The whole thing was terrifying, and running into the arms of a predator I barely knew felt like a safer plan, or at least a familiar one. My interest in my painful past was no match for the fascination of the present with Sam Spade.

The electric crackle over the building's intercom evoked a Pavlovian response in my cunt. All I wanted these days was *this* moment, the moment when I was about to see him again: Sam Spade, author, lothario, famously sober, son of a murdered woman.

The Ravenswood had an ancient sarcophagus of an elevator that moved too slowly, so I took the wide, smooth stairs two at a time, the wrought-iron railing slipping beneath my damp palm. The halls were dimly lit and reeked of microwaved meats and Bubba Kush. As I approached the third floor, the smell shifted. A distinct twang of coffee crept in. As I walked down the hallway to Apartment 301 the smell intensified, and other notes were added: leather, oatmeal, sweat. The smell of Spade surrounded me before I was even within knocking range of his door. I paused for a moment to deeply inhale the sweetly bitter tang of him.

It had only been a month since my first visit to his apartment. "It's a brood den," he had said when he opened the door to me. The décor was death chic. The walls were painted scab red. An animal hide lay on the floor. His coffee table was a hewn slab of tree mounted on a hospital gurney. On the kitchen wall was a framed vintage morgue photo of a murdered woman. She looked like a sleeping hippie, but she had died thirty-five years before Woodstock and hers was a dirt nap. Every wall had photographs of stiffs, crooks, DOAs, and in the bathroom, a black-and-white photo of 1940s cops in a men's room, standing at a long sink, washing their hands of it all. Sin and absolution. This was the home of a Lutheran.

Spade's office had two more dead people on the wall, the Black Dahlia and his redheaded mother, perched on a fence in jodhpurs. But in general, this room was more alive. It was brightly functional in a way the other rooms were not. There was a stair climber in the corner, upon which Spade performed his daily exertions— staggering ever forward, sweating and panting, the digital read- out giving him illuminated proof of his virility and endurance.

Occupying the center of the room was an enormous desk upon which he wrote enormous works of historic political murder fiction. The desk was bare but for a blotter and a gooseneck lamp. He pointed to the lamp. "I used to have a Post-it note stuck to the shade that read, 'No sports cars. No married women.'" We laughed. He had an M5 parked in the basement. My husband thought I was at yoga.

The office window looked out over the community pool. The building was tenanted by Hollywood hipsters and their purse dogs. They gathered around the pool on weekends, playing house music, clad in scanties that showed off their tattoos. Spade watched them like a bird of prey from his third-floor aerie, observing interracial shenanigans through the slats of his Venetian blinds. He told me he had called the cops once and had a black guy arrested because he just didn't like the man's looks from a distance. When I expressed horror at this, he said no, he didn't really do that. Later, when we fought, that was one of the stories he would change to either infuriate or placate me. But I didn't know any of that yet. I just looked out at the pool and saw my kids splashing in it some sunny Saturday in a happy, impossible future.

Spade showed me his bedroom. The walls were a soft blue. Heavy, lined dupioni drapes blocked out the day. There were a zebra-stripe rug and a manly club chair upholstered in what looked like herringbone suiting material. His headboard was covered in a wool felt, piped and buttoned, masculine, adult. The bedspread was a satiny matelassé. Over the headboard a portrait of Beethoven scowled down at us. The overall effect was one of louche asceticism. This was not a room in which people made love, it was the room where Spade masturbated. On his nightstand sat the Bible and an 8x10 framed photograph of his second ex-wife—"the Cougar Woman," as he called her—a prim, furious, little mid-lister with a pixie cut and a razor-edged tongue. The Cougar was still his best friend and daily telephone confidante.

"Look at this," he said. "Are you ready?" He opened a door to reveal a cedar-lined closet with evenly spaced hangers holding perfectly draped suits. They were all cashmere and custom-made; windowpane, Glen check, chalk-striped. Everything about him was fierce and dark and masculine and sexy and weird.

I should have known better. I should have picked up my purse and walked out, and I have no excuse, other than I was fooled by the three plush alligators on his bed.

"This is Al," Spade said, showing me the biggest gator and wiggling him at me. He was velvety-soft, with felt teeth. He picked up the two smaller alligators next to Al and waggled them at me. "This is Gertie, Al's wife. Al is jealous of Gertie because she has a bigger tail than him. And this is their daughter, Betty." He had made a small nuclear family there on his bedspread, with a mommy and a daddy and an only child. Spade looked me in the eyes with the seriousness of a first grader and said, "I believe that stuffed animals have souls." That is when I went all in with him.

These past four weeks after that we had toed a shaky line. As long as our bodies stayed in separate corners, we could continue our endless flirtation. Every visit was a negotiation. We constantly discussed the boundary and where it was that day and whether it could be moved a fraction of an inch. We kept our activities to the dining-room table at first, with my manuscript—our alibi— sitting between us like a chaperone. He had read it all and returned it fringed in sticky notes that said things like "Strong idea; wrong context" or "Describe in Overview Narrative," mixed in with more colorful commentary: "Fuck Holden Caulfield, he's an un-hung fag!"

We held the vertical line like the good WASPs we were, but the horizontal beckoned. Slowly and inevitably, the boundaries began to crumble. We wondered whether it wouldn't be more comfort-able to work in the living room, side by side on the sofa. After a few days of this, we discussed the pros and cons of lying down next to each other on the sofa so that we might rest. We needed to know what it felt like to lie next to each other, and, after all, it was just a sofa, not a bed. In our cockamamie construction that seemed acceptable, and so it came to pass, on a late summer afternoon, that I first lay my head down on Sam Spade's chest and felt I had finally found home.

All of it was adultery and none of it was ever enough. Soon we were crossways on his satiny bedspread, the afternoon rolling out from under us. Los Angeles surged outside his windows, a rodeo bull-run three stories below. The bellow of late-afternoon traffic from Rossmore soared up through his open windows and came in on the breeze as a caress.

We had not yet kissed, but we imagined each other's bodies in excruciating detail. We explored every available surface of our lives, where we came from, what we believed in, who we had fucked, how our paths had crossed and missed and finally led us to each other. In his gaze I was transformed from a depressed, perimenopausal housewife into his femme fatale. I knew it was too good to be any good for me, but I just wanted a little taste of it. I wanted, at long last, to be tasted.

"Baby, we're doomed," he would joke. "We're going to end up in the Green Room at Big Q." But the danger was real for me. I had children. Lives were at stake.

Then he would do that thing with his hand, little spider push-ups on the top of my head, and he would ask me, his baritone rolling up through my ribs, "Do you feel loved? Do you feel seen? Do you feel acknowledged and understood?" No one had ever asked me these questions before. I was surprised by his sweetness. No one had ever been willing to lie still with me for as long as I needed, but Spade needed my embrace as much as I needed his. He stirred something deep and yeasty in me. With him I felt warm and fed and known and loved and... "This is the sweetest shit ever," we would purr together, stoned on dopamine and projection.

In the warmth of his gaze, my ego underwent a superbloom. I felt vigorous, electric, charged with sex and specialness, and all I wanted to do was fuck the man but he wouldn't even let me unbutton my blouse. What was between us was far too important for the cheapness of infidelity, he said. We were Beethoven and his

Immortal Beloved. We would not besmirch our love with a tawdry affair. He insisted our bodies couldn't join until we were "free and clear," which, I was to learn later, was a prerequisite meant only for me.

We were both on the lam from ourselves, and broken by the loss of our beautiful, brilliant redheaded mothers. His had been murdered and mine had thrown me away at fourteen. In order to tell my story I would have to account for her. The more I came to understand what happened to me in high school, the more I wanted to disappear into his story and abandon my own.

Spade was a master of complex narrative, and our excuse was I was here to learn from him. He would be my teacher. The problem was, I was a proven teacher-fucker. Rather than tell the truth about my past, it would be easier for me to sacrifice my reputation, my career, my marriage, my closest friendships, my children, and my identity to become his lover.

So that is what I did.

PART I

THE OKEY-DOKE

Los Angeles, April 2007

E very April the solitary writers of Los Angeles cast off their house pants, don their statement jewelry, and cavort for two glorious days at the L.A. Times Festival of Books, or the LATFOB as it is locally known, held, in those days, on the campus of UCLA. The festival's Green Room was a literary hive where authors, editors, publicists, and personalities buzzed around one another, making endless passes at the complimentary and bottomless buffet before they flew off to their various panels.

It was the most exciting place in the world to me. I was part of a small but fruitful literary community in L.A. All us locals knew one another. We blurbed one another, bantered on book panels together, and presented each other with prizes. At the helm of it all was my friend and mentor Jack Margolin, who had just been made the book editor at the local paper. His wife, Diana, was my best friend. We had all met at our kids' preschool and formed a deep bond in the early aughts. Our collective four tweenaged children, who had grown up together as ersatz siblings, loved the festival as much as we did. They were free-ranging out there, stuffing publishing swag into their free tote bags, feeling large and in charge, the older kids keeping an eye on their little sisters.

I was there because I had just published my first book that winter, a collection of down-and-dirty parenting essays, written in a witty, voicey way that had gotten me dubbed by one reviewer as "Erma Bombeck in leather." This book festival felt like my coming-out party.

I swanned around, my lanyard flapping in my downdraft as I raced to panels, handing out postcards for my book like a blackjack dealer, working the schmooze relentlessly. I introduced myself to my literary heroes, glad-handed my colleagues, and felt acknowledged and accepted by my peers. I could not have felt more plugged in to my community, my family, or my career that day.

Not only was my ambition being rewarded, but I was carrying on a family tradition by being a professional writer. Every branch of my family tree going back to the *Mayflower* bore writers: critics, novelists, sitcom writers, memoirists, diarists, and sermonizing pastors. The biggest apple on our tree was my father, Richard Schickel, legendary film critic and the author of thirty-seven books. He was sitting next to me, tucked into a tuna sandwich, when my friends Diana and Dagmar came and found me.

"Hey, we're going to go introduce ourselves to Sam Spade," Diana said. "Want to come?"

"Oh *hell* yes," I said, abandoning my plate and my father, who *tut-tutted* at me.

"Oh fine, just leave the old man here to go meet the famous person." Dad sighed as we left. This was just his shtick, being a kind of put-upon curmudgeon.

"I'll be right back," I called over my shoulder.

Sam Spade was a writer of crime novels and historical fiction. He was perhaps Los Angeles's most notorious living literary son, and the author of several noir classics that I had never read. He was a lone wolf with a bad reputation among the locals as a lothario. He was also currently dating a woman I knew, another writer, who was probably somewhere in the room. Yes, I definitely wanted to meet him.

Among the slouchy, Dockers-clad Green Room crowd Spade stood out like a golem in a seersucker suit. He was six-foot-three, had a big shiny pate, and sported a bow tie and a silk pocket square. He was eyeballing the room with pursed lips. He drew himself up and sucked in his gut when he spotted the three of us heading his way. I was prepared to meet a loose-limbed hepcat, but instead I was confronted by a Lutheran choirboy with starched manners and a fiercely direct gaze.

Dagmar made introductions all around. Each time he was introduced to one of us he said, "Sam Spade; it's a pleasure to meet you," as though we hadn't just heard him say it, or didn't know who he was. I could tell he took pleasure in saying his own name.

Diana mentioned that her husband, Jack, was the book editor as a way of breaking the ice, but Spade was unimpressed. I stood there, suddenly unsure of my own puny bona fides, so I simply told him my name and shook his hand.

"Ms. Schickel." He repeated my surname back to me formally, crisply, as if he were introducing me to myself. His handshake was big and possessory. "Sam Spade; it's a pleasure to meet you. Are you in any manner related to the film critic Richard Schickel?"

"Yes, that's my father. He's here." I looked to where I had left Dad sitting but he had wandered off, probably out for a smoke. I was used to people being interested in me because of my father.

"I really dug his stuff back in the '80s. And you are, I presume, a writer as well?"

"Yes, I'm on the 'Momoir' panel at three p.m."

"Ah," he said, and swept his eyes over the expanse of the Green Room. There was something fiercely present about Spade—an utter lack of bullshit—that felt wrong for the room.

We attempted some small talk, which was clearly not Spade's métier, especially when he clearly had other matters on his mind. "Are you acquainted with Maggie Barlow?" Spade asked our group. We were, and he asked if we had seen her, but we hadn't. Maggie was the friend he was dating. I hadn't seen Maggie since the day before, when I had sat with her for a minute and asked her how it was going with him. She had laughed nervously and said, "He's pretty intense. Actually, he's kind of freaking me out."

Standing in front of Spade, I could see the problem. Spade was like a pit bull tied to a parking meter, alert and quivering, ears cocked, ready to bite anyone who wasn't his owner.

We said our goodbyes and took our leave. As I walked away I glanced back. He had sat back down, but his eyes were darting around the room, and his jaw was moving sideways. There was something so utterly raw and inside-out about him, something so deeply vulnerable that I was caught off guard and an odd thought occurred to me: *If that man knew who I really was, he would come right over here and get me.*

That one little thought made something wink on inside of me, an ember of excitement from a fire that I thought I had banked long ago.

I got a grip on myself and went to look for my father.

Los Angeles, Winter 2008

I was living a life of pure privilege. I had a solid, nearly twenty-year marriage, a home in a decent neighborhood, with a vintage trailer parked in the leafy backyard for me to work in. I had two thriving children, still in the dream stage of latency, in school full-time and out of my hair most of the day.

My husband was off working with my father in the small production company that my father owned. My father wrote and produced documentaries about film history, directors, and stars. My husband, Paul, was his co-producer, and their office, Lorac Productions, was not five miles from our home. It was a cushy job that gave Paul leeway to be around the house and help with the kids when necessary.

I was fully set up to start my second book, and it was time to get to it.

I was going to write a full-length memoir called *Unsupervised,* my coming-of-age story set in a progressive, bohemian boarding school from 1978 to 1982.

I thought my book would be a pastiche of stories, sneaking out of dorms, rolling around in the tall grass with boys, smoking dope out of apple pipes in the woods, ice-skating on quaaludes. It would be a funny bad-girl story that would bring back all the richness of that weird time and place. Featuring a colorful cast of characters, it would be hilarious, and a Gossip Girl would play me in the movie adaptation for which I would be paid a wheelbarrow full of money, the end!

The problem was, the story wasn't funny, and the more I rummaged through the memories I had put away three decades ago, the sadder it became. This wasn't the story of a rebellious bad girl, this was the story of an abandoned child. Worse, the climax, my expulsion from boarding school, which I had imagined writing as a kind of sex-capade gone awry, was neither fun nor romantic.

I was forty-four years old, I had two daughters nearing the age I had been when my family got rid of me. The idea of abandoning either of them in any way was revulsive and unimaginable to me.

What if every decision I had made since 1982 was built on the faulty premise that I was a "bad girl"? What if all along I had just been a very hurt girl trying to survive in a predatory world?

My story wasn't comedy, it was tragedy. The minute I understood that, I stopped writing.

Los Angeles, April 2008

Every year I would wangle a Green Room guest pass to the book festival for my friend Mark Netter and his two boys, so Mark could drink in the rarefied literary air while his kids drank down a thousand complimentary Cokes.

Mark spotted Spade sitting at a table nearby. I had told him about meeting Spade the previous year. "Holy shit, there he is! Introduce me to him!"

Mark had read everything Spade had ever written, whereas Spade's famous first memoir still sat unread on my bookshelf at home. It wasn't as though I wasn't curious. Whenever I had stumbled across him in my mind over the previous twelve months I would feel that flicker of interest, which I would shake off. He was good right where he was on the periphery of my mind, no nearer.

"I can't." There were protocols of cool in the Green Room, chief among them being no shameless fawning over the famous writers. "He won't even remember me."

"Riko, do this for me, please?"

I braced myself for an awkward reintroduction, but to my surprise, as we approached Spade, his eyes drew an immediate bead on me and he rose to pointed attention. This year he was dressed more casually, in a crisp, pink polo shirt and white jeans, but his carriage was the same. His hands were clasped tightly in front of his groin, his gut was sucked in, his chest puffed out. He extended a firm hand at the end of a ramrod arm and looked at me point-blank.

"Ms. Schickel, it is a pleasure to see you again."

I was stunned that Spade remembered both me and my awkward, Germanic last name. I stammered out introductions, and Mark got right down to asking Spade about his views on the second-gunman theory, which kept the conversation afloat while I quietly observed the great author.

I didn't see the yearning choirboy this time. I saw a man just exiting middle age, extraordinarily self-possessed, intense, focused, entirely in control of the conversation. He was undeniably hand-some, but not classically so. His features seemed carved from granite. His lips had a rudeness to them that I found simultaneously ugly and seductive. His bald skull, mounted atop a long neck, was both noble and buzzard-like. He had warm, intelligent, brown eyes. He was rigorously polite and acutely attentive, but there was also something jittery and off-centered about him, a sense of something barely contained.

Mark's boys interrupted us, needing the bathroom—the many free Cokes had taken their toll. Mark dutifully excused himself and I was left standing side by side with Spade. We looked out over the Green Room. Spade's long arms hung at his sides. He was taller than I remembered, bigger. Not just in size, but in the amount of space he seemed to occupy.

He politely asked me what I was working on. I gave him a thumbnail portrait of my book that was currently going no-where, though I tried not to say so to Mr. Spade. I immediately felt self-conscious and dumb. Even when they are going well, memoirs are difficult to talk about, and no matter how I spun it, my life felt ridiculously inconsequential beside his epic one. Spade let me speak without interjection or interruption until I redirected the conversation back to him. "What are you work-ing on?"

"I have just completed a novel that will be published in the fall by Alfred A. Knopf."

He told me the title, which he said he had gotten from an A. E. Housman poem. Then, suddenly he began to recite the poem, something about clay and breath. He had a lazy way of rushing his words together and dropping his voice at the end of his sentences, which made him hard to understand over the thrum of the room. I didn't want to miss a single word, but I only caught the end:

Up, lad; when the journey's over
There'll be time enough to sleep.

"Wow, that sounds like a call to adventure," I said, as though I were reading from a party-talk handbook.

"It is the final volume of my breathtaking trilogy," he said. "It's about lonely, haunted men, their moral and spiritual exhaustion, their never-ending search for 'The Woman,' and their hellish transit with history."

It seemed Spade only spoke in declarative sentences. He didn't mumble or slur; he never said "it's like" or otherwise spackled his conversation with lazy placeholders. Everything about him was intentional. What could I possibly have to say that would interest him? But it didn't matter, because he was still talking.

"In addition to my forthcoming work I am currently concluding work on my second memoir, the first two parts of which have already been serialized in *Playboy* magazine." We were careening dangerously toward a moment where it would be revealed I'd never read his first memoir, or anything else he'd written for that matter.

"What's your constraint?" I said, using some newly acquired memoir-writer lingo. He ignored the question.

"I'm a career yearner. Women rule me. Of course, some of the material was covered in my first memoir, but this book more specifically parses my search for atonement in women."

Everyone in L.A. knew that Spade was a big-league, serial pussy hound. L.A. County was a veritable body dump of his exes. Maggie had bolted out of town not long after last year's book fest, taking a teaching gig in a faraway state. An editor I knew was still haunted by a brief fling she had had with Spade back in the '90s. There were literary ladies stretched from Santa Monica to San Francisco whom he had famously romanced, rolled, and rooked over the years. I didn't know much more about his pursuit of women, other than it had left a high body count.

"As always, the book is about my dead mother." He said this casually, and why not? Everyone knew about Spade's dead mother. One need not have read his first memoir to know his mother had been raped and murdered when he was ten years old. It remains an unsolved crime, forever a part of Literary L.A. lore, referred to in countless articles I had read in local press over the many years I had lived in Los Angeles.

Spade gestured, and his pale wrist caught my eye. His fourth and fifth fingers stood delicately apart from the other three. It was a hand so faultless, so unaware of itself and almost innocent, I felt his mythos transform into pathos. Here was the lost boy himself. I felt my heart squeeze a bit. *This is a dangerous dude*, I reminded myself.

"This sounds like a great book. Do you have a title?" I interjected, trying to stay in the conversation.

"Yes," he said, allowing for a drama-building beat. "It's called *The Big Hurt*."

I felt an odd narrowing, as though an aperture inside of me was tightening, bringing my whole life sharply and startlingly into focus. This man was just as vulnerable as I. Spade was a sheep in wolf's clothing. I knew this man.

An idea disengaged from the morass of thoughts tumbling through me and floated upward with helium clarity presenting itself as a simple and indisputable truth: *I am going to be in his book.*

"*The Big Hurt*," I repeated. "Great title. It sounds like it's been used before, but I can't think where."

"You cannot copyright a title. That said, Toni Fisher had a bubblegum hit with it in 1959." He sang a few bars of the song to me in a cracked, tuneless falsetto. "Otherwise, the title hasn't been used."

"I guess I'm also thinking of *The Big Sleep*."

"Yes. There's also *The Big Love*, the story of Errol Flynn's affair with the fifteen-year-old Beverly Aadland, written by her mother, Florence Aadland." Spade appeared to be encyclopedic.

There was something about the way he stood on the balls of his feet, something about his low-slung jeans, his impudent mouth, his *fuck this* attitude alongside his geeky intellect that felt deeply familiar and oddly stirring. I remembered this guy. Spade was the sixty-year-old version of the boys I had found irresistible in high school: brilliant, misunderstood, full of shit, and deeply sexy in a way that only I could appreciate. I felt a low gyration start in my hips that I hadn't felt in years.

But that wasn't me anymore. I had put in twenty years of monogamy, attachment parenting, school volunteering, knitting, gardening, and roasting free-range chickens, and I was a different person now. I had planted water-wise gardens and served on the PTA and brought orange slices for the soccer team, and so I would never... *Wait a minute, now*... My old inner fuckup was wide-awake and freshening up her lip gloss: *It's not illegal to just talk to the dude.*

Okay, fine. We're just talking.

Then she flipped her hair for him.

Half of me went home to my family that night to check homework and see to it that children brushed and flossed before bed. But another part of me was already sneaking out of the dorm, spring was in the air, and once again I was in bloom.

Possibility swelled inside of me like a sponge absorbing the moisture of the moment—the man, the feeling that an epic story had just been hatched. It replaced my own small meandering, domestic tale of disaffection and decay and set me loose on a tide of romance. It was a perfect storm, and Spade was the perfect pirate.

Los Angeles, Fall 1988

I met my husband on my first day in Los Angeles. I had moved from New York and was living with my stepsister, Ali, in a Hollywood bungalow. Her boyfriend Allen played bass in a local band, and my second night in town Ali took me to a gig. Even though Paul was the lead guitarist, he was so unassuming he barely registered with me at first. I was wrapping up a messy relationship I had left back in New York, and wasn't really looking for a new boyfriend. But a few months later, after a couple of failed romantic wingdings, Ali told me she and Allen thought Paul and I would make a great couple. Nobody had ever said anything like this to me. I was so surprised that Ali, who knew me in high school, would think to fix me up with this decent, sober fellow. I decided to go to the gig and take another gander at the guy.

Raji's was a dark, sticky rock club on Hollywood Boulevard. Onstage Paul was just as unpresuming as he had seemed when I first saw him. He played his guitar diligently, executing beautiful, meticulous riffs with a look of agony on his face. His swooshy, shiny blond forelock fell across his face as he soloed, but Paul didn't have any bad-boy Axl Rose swagger. He clearly hated the spotlight. He grimaced when he sang backup vocals. I was intrigued.

When the gig ended I lured Paul into a deep, dark booth, and we talked together for a couple of hours about whatever it was that people talked about in 1988—XTC, Iran/Contra, I don't know, I just remember watching Paul's broad-knuckled hands as he worried the label off his beer bottle, rolling the scraps of paper into perfect curls that he arranged in a geometric pattern on the table between us.

Paul was born in Ames, Iowa, to a couple of Oklahomans, and spoke with a soft twang that was completely genuine and adorable. His family moved to Southern California when he was five, so he grew up surfing and playing in garage bands. Then he went to law school. He was a magical mix of cool, sweet, and smart.

We both worked in Santa Monica, he as a paralegal, and I as a clerk in a children's bookstore. We began meeting at Douglas Park on our lunch break to watch the lawn bowlers, feed the ducks, share every detail from our brief lives up to that point. I told Paul my Buxton story like it was a party joke. I expected him to recoil from me, but he didn't even bat an eye. He was gently empathetic and nonjudgmental about my scandalous past. Nothing I said seemed to slow or lessen his deepening admiration for me.

Paul lived in a small bachelor apartment in West Los Angeles. He had been single for a while, and the twin-size mattress in his bedroom spoke of his faded romantic hopes. His closet was impossibly tidy, and I would lie in his twin bed and watch him get ready for work in the morning, carefully tapping talcum powder into his loafers before he put them on. How could anything bad happen with such a man?

Paul had two big feet firmly planted in the manly arts, and a heart as clean and wide as a prairie. But there was also a sadness and reticence to Paul that was undeniable. He lived in anticipation of regret. He fretted over money, guitar necks, wheel alignments, and tax receipts. He was bound by the mundane cares of the practical world in a way I didn't understand. I had been raised by impractical people who had never fettered me with any working knowledge of the world. Paul taught me to turn off the air-conditioning before I turned off my car engine. He explained grades of sandpaper and showed me how to Zip-Strip used furniture. In return I thought

I would rock his world with sex and fun and lofty ambition and spark him into joy. It seemed like a good trade: stability for passion. I was possessed by the fatuous notion that I would be able to love and fuck him into the fullest expression of himself.

Paul was the eldest of three siblings, with whom he shared reasonable holidays. His parents were straightforward, honest scions of the Dust Bowl who lived by the adage "Let's save it for good!" This strange saying, I soon came to understand, had two meanings: Let's save this fancy tablecloth/pair of good shoes/wool blanket/used wrapping paper for a better occasion than this one. The second meaning was similar, but more long-standing—let's save it forever, not use it. Let's pass that nice waffle iron or that complete set of Encyclopedia Britannica from 1943 down to your grandkids and then hopefully nobody will ever need to buy anything new *ever, ever, ever again.*

My family, on the other hand, lived by the adage "Let's give it the old heave-ho!" My parents threw away houses full of furniture, clothes, keepsakes, toys, and anything else that would impede our progress into our bright and infinite futures. Left on the road some- where between New York City and Los Angeles were my Peggy Nisbet and Madame Alexander dolls, my British Airways poster of the Beefeater I had met at the Tower of London, nearly every scrap of artwork I had ever glued or woven, my pen-pal letters from film director Bill Wellman—all tossed out as my parents streamlined their lives over and over again.

Paul's parents lived in a house near San Diego that felt like an archaeological dig. Every closet and cabinet held strata of family memories and mementos—antiques and hand-sewn baby clothes laid between layers of yellowing tissue paper and crumbling newsprint. There were daguerreotypes of thin-lipped, brush-cut ancestors named Wyatt and Earl, letters addressed to farmhouses that had long ago been swept away in the dirty winds of the Dust Bowl.

I had come from a disposable family, but Paul and his family felt permanent. The Franklin familial relationships were neither strained nor complex. Paul and his siblings rolled their eyes at their mother's obsessive-compulsive hoarding, but I was entranced. I followed my future mother-in-law into the back bedroom to watch her extract the contents of an armoire. The smell of mothballs was an aphrodisiac for a girl who hadn't had a home since she was fourteen years old, and Paul's mother, Vivian, known to the family as Mama V, was validated by my interest. She would pull out ornate costume jewelry and cloche hats made of velvety felt, lingerie, and eveningwear. Her mother, Mama Grace, had worked the sales floor at Bullock's Wilshire in the 1930s and had spent most of her earnings on clothes. There were bias-cut satin cocktail dresses in dove gray and teal, there was a pink chiffon, a crinoline sundress covered in tea roses, elbow-length opera gloves, and sparkly brooches. The sense of continuity within this family was breathtaking. I felt like Cinderella slipping on a sensible glass Dansko clog, and Paul was the handsome prince kneeling at my feet, asking me to marry him.

Holidays were celebrated with practical gift-giving and festive meats served on the good china. The Franklins never wrote one another long, angry, impassioned letters that dug up the past, they never went to therapy together or wrote thinly fictionalized books about one another or wife-swapped or name-dropped. The sweet, heartwarming rum-and-Cokes everyone drank together before dinner never turned anybody sour or cynical. I never once heard a door slam.

Paul was unimpeachable. He was a kind, steady, decent man. Ours would be a plain marriage. If I married Paul I could stop being Erika-the-fuckup and instead be the wife of a genuinely good person. We would have children together and he would be a loving, present father and I would be the mother I had always wanted. That dream, that I could be better than my own parents, was a prize so glittering I had never even considered putting myself in the running for it before. But Paul made all of it feel possible.

In fact, I would show them. I would flip my family the bird

by squandering my culture-making potential and disappearing into quiet domesticity. Not only that, I would never, ever divorce.

I planned my wedding with the help of my father's second wife, Carol. My mother, still in New York, sent me $500 for a wedding dress. I found two within my budget. One was in a resale shop. It was long, fishtailed, and satiny, and fit me like a glove. It had a train and hundreds of tiny silk leaves hand-stitched all over it that fluttered when I moved. It made me look like a magical mermaid.

I found the other dress in a vintage shop. It was an Edwardian-era Irish-linen tea dress, simple and a little sacklike. It looked a lot like the Laura Ashley graduation dress I never had the chance to wear nine years before. I sent Polaroids of both dresses to my mother and sister and they voted unanimously for the leaf dress. In the end, I chose the linen. I wasn't going to look like some swooshy, sexy beast on my wedding day. The point of this wedding was to expunge the record. I was going to look like Thérèse Bernard, the girl in the Renoir picture postcard I had been carrying around since my freshman year. This wedding was my reinvention of myself.

I married Paul Franklin on the first day of June 1991. The ceremony was held beside my uncle's pool in the Pacific Palisades. I wore flats so that in the photos I wouldn't tower over my modest groom. My two-year-old nephew-in-law fell in the pool and was rescued by his dad. My mother dressed entirely in black and kept her mirror sunglasses on all day and into the evening. Paul's father, "Pops," played the flugelhorn with his jazz band and everyone danced on a square of parquet laid out on the patio. As darkness fell my teenage cousins broke out their synthesizers and began to perform their own stuff. The party devolved. Everyone went home tired and a little bit hungry from the budget hors d'oeuvres I had served.

I escaped with my groom to a nearby bed and breakfast, where I slipped into Paul's grandmother's vintage ivory, bias-cut silk nightgown, drank a glass of complimentary Champagne, and passed out. It didn't matter to me that, technically speaking, I wasn't *madly* in love with Paul, for madness was exactly the thing I was renouncing by marrying him. I loved Paul, yes, deeply, absolutely; he was my best friend and the best man I knew. He would never leave me. That I was sacrificing *Eros* to *philia* didn't bother me at all. I was grateful to be done with Eros. Fuck passion. This time I was going for the okey-doke. I was taking the veil, and in so doing, I was drawing a curtain over every screwed-up thing I had ever been before. I was putting the dirty, bad girl I had once been behind me forever.

Los Angeles, Spring 2009

Every day Netter would call me up and ask, "Are you writing the book?" I would offer him excuses: I was busy with the kids, I had to write a book review, I wasn't feeling well, I would start next week. I had some pages but I knew they were just a tepid dry run. I would go out to the trailer and look at Facebook. Facebook was relatively new, and I found it irresistible. I loved looking into people's lives, curated though they were. All of my writing colleagues were there, not writing, same as me, which was comforting.

One day one of those Facebook procrastinators turned out to be Sam Spade himself. He appeared in a friend's friend list. The last place I ever expected to see him.

His profile picture was his black-and-white author photo. His chin rested on his two balled fists, his mouth set in a pugilistic purse, his eyes full of soul. I thought, *Ah, there is my man.*

Spade was no longer on the periphery of my thoughts; he had become a full-time obsession. I finally read his memoir—the story of him working with a detective to solve his mother's long-cold murder case. I enjoyed it as literature, but I was reading it specifically for clues as to whether this was, indeed, my man. I lapped up the police procedural, which was simultaneously unsparing and tender. The book depicted two relationships: Spade's dark, yearning, uncomfortable love for his mother, and the much cleaner, more compassionate relationship with the detective he worked with. Both of these stories were dark, threaded through with obsession and deep, painful loss.

At one point he described his ideal woman: red-headed, middle-aged, wholesome, and punctual. No rocker chicks, definitely no tattoos or piercings, ten extra pounds straining a skirt seam would be a bonus. Of course I knew he was describing his mother, but he was also describing me. I was always on time! I loved a stretchy skirt! I hated tattoos! I felt the cord between us tightening. He might not know it, but I did. Our clash was coming. I knew it with more certainty than I had ever felt about anything in my life.

This certainty, this strange imaginative dance I did with Spade, sustained me for months. When I became so sad, so lonely, so horny that I couldn't bear it, I broke him out, turned on his penetrating gaze in my mind's eye, and felt a surge of power. There was a larger purpose at work. It kept me buzzed as I went about my days.

In all my feverish fantasies I had never once imagined friending him on Facebook. I scoured Spade's page for personal details, but it was little more than a vehicle to flog his next big novel. His wall was an endless scroll of friend requests and additions, people saying, "Thanks for the add, Dog!" After all this, here he was, mine for the friending.

I let my cursor hover over the Add Friend button for a long time. I knew if I clicked it there would be no turning back. He would find me and come for me. It was a very, very bad idea. I got up and did a couple of laps around my backyard to clear my head.

I did not want an affair. I would never do anything to harm my family. It's not that I hadn't had crushes, but I had recovered from all of them. All the years of my marriage I had never seriously considered rocking the boat. My boat, after all, was a lifeboat. The marriage kept me and my children safe and dry. Only a crazy person would invite someone like Sam Spade in to capsize her life. All of these thoughts ran through my head as I pulled weeds, turned the compost, shoved garden chairs back into place, tossed the kids' yard toys into the toy bin. I knew he knew I was out here. I knew he only needed the tiniest provocation.

I went back into the trailer and friended him.

I awoke the next morning to a private message from Sam Spade that made me gasp. It was four stanzas of fervid, erotic imagery and rampant alliteration. Each stanza ending with the line, "My brave bride, I brace at thy breasts."

He spoke of his tumescence and of being "tantrically tantalized." He described me as a tigress, but also as being "lithe, leonine and luminous." The whole thing was hilarious and ridiculous. No, it was infuriating. How dare he? Didn't he know I was married?

It made me blush, laugh, get up from my desk, and pace back and forth in my trailer like a caged... *Tigress? What the fuck?* Did he actually write this? Could he be serious? And what business did he think he had with my breasts? It was presumptuous. It was embarrassing. It was thrilling.

I didn't know how to respond. I didn't want to encourage him, nor did I want to send him packing. I finally answered back:

Jesus Spade,
You are one illustrious alliterator. Should I presume you penned this purple prose for my particular person?
According to this passionate screed I am both tigress and leonine—which gives me... paws.
Breasts braced by brassiere, the rest in shock,
Schickel

He wrote back. I wrote him back. My days became shaped around letters. Waiting for them, writing them. Spade dazzled me with gritty truths about himself, generous observations of me, dubbing me "a groove and a gas," which seemed premature, as he barely knew me, but I needed the compliment too much not to take it.

Spade was a Luddite who had neither computer nor typewriter.

His home tech included a landline and a fax machine. At first he would go over to his assistant's house and have her connect him to Facebook Messenger on her computer, and he would slowly hunt-and-peck out his replies, having never learned to type. But soon that became too burdensome and she found us a program that could send faxes to computers, and we were off to the races. He furiously block-lettered his words on white lined notebook paper with enough pounds of pressure to make the back of the page read like Braille. He then fed the raw pages straight into his growling fax machine, which would deliver a scan of the letter to my secret email account, which I then filed into a folder on my desktop labeled, innocuously, "Bad Dog."

Technology may have radically changed the mode of the epistolary love affair in the three decades since my first such engagement, back in high school, but all the semantic principles were still at work: grand declarations, flowery prose, fevered confessions, tender absolutions. Never mind that we had only met and spoken to each other in person twice.

Something in you makes me want to offer you wild-ass shit in a whole-sale manner, he wrote. He spoke of emeralds, and dressing me in a charcoal-gray flannel chalk-stripe suit, the hemline well below the knee, practically meeting the high black boots he would have me walk all over him in.

It was so grandiose, so nuts, so lavish, and so inappropriate. He made me feel both alarmed and aroused. He presumed to know me, which I found affronting. He presented me with a version of myself that was a million miles away from who I truly was. Or was it? Dark desires verging on kink had shadowed me my whole life and I felt a deep stirring. I had never imagined being the femme fatale in anyone's noir fantasy, much less Sam Spade's Oedipal ideal. The idea of being a woman with dark secrets, tall boots, and sexual power sounded a lot better than being a woman with gnawing self-doubt, skin tags, and a carpool.

Some part of my brain understood that I was succumbing to an epic midlife crisis. I had read and lived enough to know that these kinds of stories always ended in betrayal and heartbreak. Madame Bovary I was not. In those rare moments of sanity, I saw what a cliché I was being, and I tried to hold the line while still keeping Spade hooked on it. I didn't want him to think this was going to turn into some crazy affair. He begged for my phone number, but I withheld it, which made him write to me more.

I am going to bring you to God, he wrote. Spade referred to himself as "a Tory mystic," which I later came to understand meant a Lutheran with a spotty Sunday attendance record and a savior complex.

But at the time his moral certitude was a bright lure. In all my liberal atheist lifetime I had never met someone like him. He claimed a close, personal relationship with the Divine, whereas in my atheist circles we snickered at faith unless someone was twelve-stepping, in which case we kept respectfully mum.

My familial atheism had worn thin: the study of the Sunday book section, the endless genuflection before glittering screens, and the wafer-thin reasoning that "everything happened for a reason" suddenly felt like sheer twaddle. I lacked higher purpose, and here was Spade to serve some up.

For all his fervor, Spade never preached at me. He was far more likely to quote the poetry of Anne Sexton than the Bible, and he did so prodigiously. It wasn't long before he declared we were divinely ordained, and I had never felt so deeply called to another human being. He offered me a big belt of God with a humanist chaser and it went down smooth as Ovaltine.

Then he offered to help me with the book. Sam Spade, literary legend would be my personal tutor. He would teach me his proven formula for writing a big, complicated book. But I would have to do it his way. "Yes, yes," I swore to him, "please, just tell me what to do."

He began with this edict: *Do your work. Tell the truth. Don't smoke dope.*

★   ★   ★

I believed that if Spade and I stayed safely to the sacred written word, we could achieve these lofty, spiritual ends without ever actually having sex. We called it "the Task." The Task was our chaperone, our cover. We had official literary business to attend to.

Once our permission structure was in place, I gave him my phone number.

There followed many nights of whispered phone calls out in my trailer. We talked about God and art and the meaning of what seemed our ordained connection. Often, when I got excited, or carried away, he would shush me and say, "Be soft with me."

Not all of his observations of me were flattering. He told me I had a harsh affect, that I was flip and defensive and he didn't like it when I was being a "cool girl." He didn't want me to be glib, or wry, or too fired-up, even though I had always been told those were some of my best qualities. All that grated on him. He told me I was more profound than how I presented myself, that I should still myself to silence and brood on who I was and what we meant together.

One night, he called me from a hotel room in San Francisco, where he was attending a wedding. He had worn a kilt and made a speech, then bugged out as soon as the dancing started. He was telling me about how he had waited all day and night to call me. Then he blurted out, "I love you."

"No, you don't," I blurted back. "You barely know me." We hadn't had so much as a cup of coffee together yet. He was jumping the shark on this romance. It was way too early for "I love you." It was such a startling miscue that I hung up on him, spooked and affronted. I pulled back from him for a few days and refocused on my family and friends. But before long, Spade and I were back on the phone.

With or without the phone calls, the letters kept coming. Sometimes two or three in a day. They had recurring motifs and lines: *this is the sweetest shit ever, I want my mouth on your vagina, Erika Schickel, Erika Schickel, Erika Schickel, I can't stop saying your name.* I loved his name—its twang and alliteration. I rolled its vowels and syllables around on my tongue like an Everlasting Gobstopper, a secret meal upon which I feasted endlessly.

Through all of this, we had not yet met in person. I wasn't ready. It wasn't right. What were we doing? This had to stop. I cycled through resistance and release over and over.

One midafternoon in early June I was pulling weeds on my patio when he called. "This is ridiculous," he said. "Meet me at Le Pain Quotidien on Larchmont in half an hour."

"Okay, but do *not* bring flowers," I said, and hung up.

I decided I would wear what I was already wearing: brown hiking pants, a bright-hued camisole, and what I called my "fuck-me Crocs," a pair of black plastic injection-molded platform Dr. Scholl's that I wore both out to drinks and for turning the compost. I would not dress up for him. He would have to take me as I was. Besides, I reasoned, this was not a date or a seduction. This was coffee at Le Pain Quotidien at two p.m. on a Tuesday with a friend, a colleague. We were going to discuss how he would help with my book. He was a master of plot. This was a fantastic career opportunity. Whatever had been happening between us on the phone lately need not even be mentioned, I thought as I put on lipstick. Shit. I wiped off the lipstick, grabbed my purse, and got in the car.

He was waiting at the back of the restaurant. When he saw me he stood at fierce attention and watched as I crossed the room. He wore wheat-colored jeans and a crisp, pink, half-placket, short-sleeved shirt. It was a kind of shirt not to be found on any of my T-shirted peers. I was surprised that I felt so moved by the sight of him: tremulous, eager, a little scared. It was the same Spade I saw at the book fair in 2007, a lost boy.

What were we to do but hug? Why wouldn't I reach my arms up and wrap them around this man's neck? Why wouldn't his hand sweep down the length of my back in response? So we hugged, and our bodies pressed against each other and aligned for the first of what would become many thousands of times. The scent of his neck was a pheromone punch in the face.

We broke the embrace and he presented me with a bouquet of late-season peonies.

"Fuck you." I set them aside. Flowers were one of his signature moves with women. He had written about it. He had been warned.

"Hey, it's a joke. Laugh!"

I placed a fat, brown accordion file on the table between us. We needed to stick to the script. I was here to give him my manuscript. He pushed the file to the side with the flowers.

We sat across the distressed wood table, our four long legs stuffed awkwardly beneath. Strains of piped-in Mozart and the wheeze of milk being frothed filled the silences between us.

I was nervous, but he didn't seem to notice. He was aquiver with the moment—pure ardor, barely contained. His intensity made me feel girlish and vulnerable. Every word and gesture I ventured was clearly being read, recorded, and processed by the supercomputer within his shiny noggin. I was being *seen*, and it felt like a switch had been flipped in me. I felt juiced and static with energy.

Spade placed his long, caramel-colored forearms on the table, his proud chin hovering over impossibly tender wrists. He looked at me expectantly. What was I to do but give him my forearms in return? We threaded our arms between our coffees, pushing the raw sugar and Himalayan sea salt aside with our elbows.

What we said that day didn't matter, we just wanted to hold each other's forearms and stare into each other's eyes. His were deep brown flecked with gold. I tried to take in the full reality of him, but his face was constantly changing. He was older than he had been in my imagination, but also more handsome. When his face relaxed, he was even-featured. His mouth, un-pursed, was wide and sensual. His frame larger than I remembered. We had already spent so much time talking on the phone, we both knew the real conversation here was between our bodies.

He was soft and sweet and curious with me, never once interrupting when I spoke. He told me I was lovely several times, apropos of nothing. His gaze was photosynthesis. I felt myself orient toward him and green shoots unfurled inside me.

Our waitress came to refill our cups and fawned over us, telling us we were a handsome couple. We didn't set her straight on our couplehood. It felt good to look good together. To her we must have seemed like a pair of adorable late-in-life lovebirds. Now I know that we were just a pair of seasoned, broken romantics crafting a cosmology that would serve our own selfish, deluded ends.

We talked until my parking meter ran out. I excused myself and went outside to pump more quarters into the meter, buying us a little more time together before I would have to return to reality. On my way back to the restaurant I snagged my fuck-me Croc on a crack in the sidewalk and I fell, scraping my shin bloody. I came back in with a rivulet of red streaking toward my ankle. I was embarrassed by my klutziness. He was delighted by it. He gently pressed an unbleached paper napkin to my leg.

We sat for another hour, talking about ourselves until the reality of three p.m. asserted itself and pulled me to my feet. I had kids on their way home from school. Spade paid the check and we left the café.

A pit bull was chained to a parking meter outside the restaurant. It had a head like a cinder block and a dopey grin. "Look at that dog. Now, *that's* a dog." Spade beelined over to the beast and started talking to it. "Hey, baby, you look *good*." The dog was impassive, only interested in seeing his owner. Spade cocked his thumb at the dog. "You know this guy is a real lawn-shitter." The remark made me bark out a laugh. Encouraged, he went on. "Yeah, he's a leg-humper, a cat-chomper, and a toilet-drinker." I was yukking on the sidewalk next to him as he free-flowed this spontaneous dog jive, and I realized this was the first time, in the many hours we had spent talking and writing, that Spade had actually made me laugh out loud.

I had begun to worry that Sam had no sense of humor. He mostly spoke in hushed, reverential tones about himself, or me, or us. While it appealed to my romantic vanity, his unrelenting seriousness and solipsism often made me uncomfortable. I came from a family of comedy writers; I needed him to be funny if I was going to love him. And here he was, finally putting me in stitches with this silly dog riff. I had no idea that this was a well-rehearsed shtick he performed compulsively, with every dog he met.

When we got to my car there was a ticket on my windshield. He snapped it up and stuffed it into his back pocket. He wouldn't hear of me paying it. "I'm having a good year," he said, snapping his fingers. We hugged goodbye. He didn't grope me or try to kiss me. He was a model of probity. I got in my car and drove away scabbed, sweaty, wet, and hooked.

Los Angeles, 1995–2004

B oth times I told my father I was pregnant, he was pissed about it. Motherhood was not part of the brilliant future he had hoped for me. But the truth was, my future wasn't turning out to be all that brilliant.

I was still, at that time, going after an acting career. I had gotten some Hollywood "heat" playing the lead in an AFI senior thesis film. An agent signed me and I got a couple of small day-player parts on *Murphy Brown* and the *Dragnet* rehash. But at that point, in the winter of 1994, my biggest credit was playing a twisted, horny, Oedipally fixated psychiatrist in Troma Films' *The Toxic Avenger Part II*. I had not covered myself in glory.

At my baby shower, my sister-in-law, Kim, asked my father what he wanted his grandchild to call him.

"Mr. Schickel," he said in a disgruntled voice, keeping his eyes focused on his potato salad. This was his schtick, being put out by being made a grandpa at the tender age of sixty-two.

"How about GP?" Kim offered. "You know, short for Grand Pa? You'll sound like a studio chief."

This assuaged his vanity and thus my father became GP to all four of his grandchildren.

My sister Jessica and I had found our way back to each other in the early 1990s, after a childhood spent largely apart. When we finally got to know each other, it was like discovering I had a missing twin. We laughed at the same things in the same way. We matched each other in our banter and overthinking, we had similar taste in bad men, we didn't have to explain our hurt to each other, we could just have someone who already knew. I had been dealt a lucky card in my little sister, and I didn't figure it out until I was almost twenty-four years old.

There were a few felicitous years where Jess lived in Los Angeles, and we were able to spend as much time as we wanted together, which was a lot, but then she went and married a boy from Chagrin Falls, Ohio, and moved to the Midwest in the mid-'90s to raise her own family.

That left me in L.A. with Dad, and our lives were deeply entwined. He lived five miles away in his house on Dicks Street in West Hollywood, and my husband worked with him. Dad and I had regular dinner and movie dates together. The more I published, the more collegial our relationship became.

My father was a loving, if distracted, GP. As with me and my sister, he took greater interest as my two girls grew up. Dad never missed a school play, a family barbecue, or a chance to hang out with Jack and Diana Margolin, who were also on our permanent invite list. This was my family, my tribe.

My mother, recently widowed from her second husband, was living in his rent-controlled apartment in New York. Between distance, poverty, and bouts of estrangement, she did not get to spend much time with my family, and when she did, it was tense. Seeing my mother with my children threw into sharp focus memories from my own childhood that time had blurred. She was with them exactly as she had been with me; highly conditional and given to anger. Every time my kid whined I could see her stiffen and I remembered as a child, how she would stop me mid-whine and say, "Whatever it is, the answer is no." If Mae begged for mac 'n' cheese, she would say, "In my day children ate whatever the adults were serving." When five-year-old Grace expressed her concern about smoking, passing on some of the anti-smoking propaganda she had learned in school, my mother said, "Children do not get to tell adults what to do." One Christmas in Cleveland Grandma Jill became so annoyed by whiny five-year-old Mae that she yanked the hood of her snowsuit, *hard,* shocking my toddler into stunned silence, then tears.

Now that I knew what I was looking at, it was as though I was having a reenactment of my own childhood played out in front of me every time Grandma came to visit. I could hardly believe my eyes. Even if my kids didn't notice it, I did, and it filled me with rage toward my mother.

I had but one guiding principle as a young mother: not to be my mother. But in those early years, when I was most closely bound to my helpless young, experiencing the necessary restraints of motherhood, I found myself wanting to be my mother more than anything. I wanted to slam doors, rage at the innocent, retreat into writing as a mental escape from the endless penguin march that was stay-at-home motherhood. Just as my own mother had done with me.

There were moments when I allowed myself to succumb to the temptation. I let go on my kids and I felt that delicious, immediate satisfaction of serving my ego, of allowing myself to be the victim rather than the person who held all the power. The stunned silence when I yelled, turned on my heel, or slammed the door behind me was my reward. Then, in the still moments that followed, where all I could hear was the blood pounding in my ears and the sound of them crying in the next room, I would tumble into a chasm of remorse. How dare I reenact my hurt with my children? What the hell was I doing?

In order to compensate for feeling like a bad mother, I did an inhuman amount of volunteer work at the kids' elementary school. I directed plays, started a school newspaper, served on the PTA, ran talent shows, and taught Girl Scout troops how to knit. Mother-hood provided the perfect excuse to never sit still and feel anything too deeply while racking up character points.

I also compensated by smoking weed. In the late afternoon,

when most moms were getting into the Chardonnay, I was blowing a big cloud of skunk out by the compost pile. It helped me reframe the remaining hours of the day, energizing me for the final slog: dinner, tubby, bedtime. I felt bad that I was such a habitual user, but I was one of many stoners in my world, and nobody ever judged me for it. Not my abstinent husband, certainly not my pothead friends. I kept myself fogged so that I could keep going without feeling too much.

When my youngest, Mae, was seven, she was cast as Tinker Bell in the school production of *Peter Pan*. It was pure typecasting: my girl was a sparkly, sassy little foot-stomper with silky blond hair. I picked her up from an early rehearsal and the entire cast was assembled in the multipurpose room of our public school with the lights out, watching the 1974 Broadway production that starred a cringe-provoking Cathy Rigby as Pan. I had been taken to this show in its original run, and even at the tender age of ten I knew it was crap.

I checked my watch. How much more time was left? Should I go pick up Grace from her playdate and come back for Mae later? But no, it was already the final nursery scene. And right on cue here came Rigby zipping in through the window, legs splayed like she had them in celestial stirrups, super-jaunty and macking hard for Wendy. Pan sees Wendy asleep in her bed and goes to wake her when a gentle voice stops him.

"Peter, I'm here." He turns to see a mature woman sitting in a rocking chair. Her hair was up in an old-lady chignon, and she wore a shoulderette over a high-necked nightdress. She had needle-work in her lap. It was Wendy, of course, all grown-up and keeping gentle, maternal watch over her sleeping daughter, Jane.

Peter didn't believe it at first, but then he recognized his old friend. "Wendy!" he gasped. "You got old!" It was such a sad revelation, so sudden and undeserved, for this actress looked to be perhaps thirty-five at most.

But in the dark of the multipurpose room of Canfield Avenue

Elementary, the pathos of that line, "You got old," snagged my heart. Suddenly I felt my chest yawn open as the hopeless intractability of time smacked me flat. My own little girl was in this same dark room, dreaming of Neverland. Soon the lights would come up and Mae and her sister would fly out the window and I would be the forgotten crone sitting in the corner.

I always assumed Neverland stood for childhood, the place where we lose ourselves in play and dreams. But of course Neverland is puberty, a time where we are neither children nor adults, but we are certainly beyond the reach of our parents. We can fight pirates and crush on Pan and it's safe. The only real danger is a crocodile with a ticking clock in its belly, reminding us this glory will end.

I was suddenly overwhelmed by a feeling of pure loss. I sank to the dirty linoleum floor and pushed my face into the itchy yarn of my sweater, muffling sobs, grateful for the dark of the room. I never flew out the nursery window; I was pushed.

I thought of my mother sitting alone in her apartment in Manhattan, illuminated by the flicker of the television, a cigarette in her hand, thinking about John le Carré and ballroom dancing, and about how she did what she had to do to survive.

The fluorescent lights in the multipurpose room flickered on and I tried to gather myself. Here was Tinker Bell, with her backpack and excited smile. She came to me, me, me, I was her mother, and she was drawn to me like a girl who hasn't yet figured out that she and I are not the same person. She is still a flower orienting herself to my sun. I pulled her into a hug and she was too full of news to notice I had been crying.

"I am singing a solo!"

"That's so great, Mae!"

"And I'm going to wear a fairy costume!"

"Well, sure, you're Tinker Bell!"

"And I need you to help me learn my lines, even though I really don't have any, because Tinker Bell doesn't talk, she has a bell."

"I will help you ring your bell," I told her.

Los Angeles, Winter 2009

I celebrated my forty-fifth birthday with my closest friends and family in a small wine bar in Hollywood. My sister flew out from Cleveland, Netter and his wife were there, my father, the kids and Paul, and of course Jack and Diana. It was a perfect evening, hosted by my friend Marlon, who owned the bar and had prepared a special menu for our party. I felt blessed and happy.

Then Spade walked in.

He looked like he was dressed for a pheasant hunt. He wore a wool sweater that had a big quilted suede patch on the front shoulder where the butt of the rifle might go. He had paired the sweater with a plaid wool newsboy cap. He went to the bar and ordered an espresso. I kept talking with my friends and waiting to feel his eyes on me, but every time I stole a glance at him, he was staring in the direction of my party, but not at me.

Spade's presence was noted and briefly discussed among my guests. All agreed that he was an odd fish. Most people disliked him, and it seemed everyone at the table could name a different woman Spade had once dated and burned.

I feigned disinterest, but I wanted to hear everything. I wanted to get near him. After a few minutes, I excused myself to go to the ladies' room. I would have to walk past him in order to get there. Then he would surely see me, he would stop me, and we would talk. I drew closer, but he never moved his eyes toward me and shyness overcame me. I swept past him, timing my inhale so that I might catch a whiff of him. He came across in tones of salt and fur.

I locked my flustered self into the ladies' room. This was ridiculous, I thought as I peed and washed up. I had spent a year avoiding him, feeling that he was on the lookout for me but now, here on my forty-fifth birthday, the moment of our collision had arrived and he hadn't even seen me.

I looked in the mirror and was confronted with a newly middle-aged woman, delusional with perimenopause, acting like a stupid teenager. *Straighten up, Schickel. Just simply say hello to him on the way out like a reasonable grown-up human.* I put on some fresh lipstick and fluffed my hair. When I emerged from the restroom, he was gone.

I rejoined my party. "You okay?" Diana asked. "You look weird." "I'm fine."

The cake arrived and everyone raised their glasses and toasted me. It was the last time this group of my dearest beloveds would all be together before I drove them all away.

PART II

THE FAMILY OF MAN

New York, 1950–1978

In 1950, Richard Schickel, a cheese-fed, Prairie Liberal, fresh off the *Daily Cardinal* at the University of Wisconsin, arrived in New York with a few clips, a couple of references, and a childhood spent at the movies.

He was hired as a fact-checker at a new magazine called *Sports Illustrated*. His section, "Events and Discoveries," was the magazine's version of *The New Yorker*'s "Talk of the Town"—little, anonymous snapshots of sports happenings. Before long he was writing the pieces himself.

Dick was lured away from *Sports Illustrated* by *Look* magazine. He snaffled an apartment on Bleecker Street from a colleague who was giving it up to get married. It was a top-floor walk-up with a skylight that the ladies just loved.

Dick's timing was impeccable. He was just in time for a revolution in film and film criticism. The French New Wave swept into American cinemas and film criticism went from being the redheaded stepchild of theatre criticism to becoming an art in itself. My father was an elegant, instinctive, and erudite writer with a deep regard for and knowledge of film and film history, even as it was being made. He and other critics Andrew Sarris, Molly Haskell, and Pauline Kael were the new kids on the block, turning movie directors into *auteurs* and making film criticism an art in its own right.

My parents met on a blind date in 1960. Dad was at *Look* magazine by that time, and a colleague had written a feature on the women of Sarah Lawrence College, one of whom was my mother, Jill Whedon.

When they met, Jill had just finished a graduate program in psychology at Harvard and had moved back to Manhattan. She was working in midtown, editing a glossy magazine that CBS was publishing at the time. Her mother had connections there and had gotten her the job.

After work at his magazine, Dick would cross midtown to the CBS offices to pick Jill up at hers. She would be the last one there, all the lights would be off except for the one over her desk, the radio tuned to WQXR. Jill would be sitting there, glumly editing copy, pregnant with a hurt that Dick could never name because, frankly, he was only interested in it up to a point.

Dick was drawn to my mother's beauty, of course. He liked her tallness, her figure, her pretty red hair. He liked her wit and intelligence. But maybe most of all, he liked Jill's culturally elite family.

By coincidence, Dad had met my uncle Tom at a dinner party months before he met my mother. Tom, a big, funny redhead, was writing for *Captain Kangaroo* and he and Dad had hit it off that night.

Of all the Whedon men, my father admired my grandfather, John Whedon, the most. He was a successful Hollywood radio and television writer who lived in a stylish glass house in the hills of Los Angeles. Cultural pedigree was a big part of Dick's attraction to Jill, and the Whedons had it in spades. My grandaddy had written a Broadway musical and edited *The New Yorker*. To a Wisconsin boy who had grown up reading *The New Yorker* and the *New York Times*, it must have felt like marrying into royalty.

★   ★   ★

The century had been built by and for guys like Dick: white, liberal, antsy to hijack popular culture from the stuffy old guard and blow it open. Everybody was reading Betty Friedan and doing the Mashed Potato, but feminism hadn't fully percolated down into everyday life yet. Bright, talented women like my mother were still caught in the brambles of the 1950s, navigating the whiz-bang sexual revolution with the factory settings of a more conservative time.

My father was certainly no virgin when he met my mother, but I believe she was his first serious romantic relationship. The same could not be said of Jill. She was coming off of a big heartbreak with some asshole at Harvard, but that wasn't much concern to Dick. Julia Whedon was beautiful, trained in the liberal arts, well versed in Rombauer and Becker, and calibrated by her own with-holding father to expect little in the way of affection from men. She seemed the perfect mate for Richard Schickel.

Jill needed to find a safe landing and Dick was a perfectly reasonable bet. He was talented and ambitious, a hard worker and a steady earner. They were a good intellectual match. Jill was well read and opinionated and had a writing talent equal to Dick's. Neither of them were particularly in love, but that wasn't the point. They were just going for the okey-doke.

My parents married on March 11, 1961, at the Unitarian Church of All Souls on Lexington. My father was still in his crew-cut years, and in the wedding photos his face has a Play-Doh softness to it that strikes me as not unpleasant but also not particularly hand-some. My mother was a chic, beautiful bride in a gown of white damask, silk, and organza, made with a fitted bodice with a scoop neckline and a bouffant skirt. She carried a bouquet of carnations and lilies of the valley. A chapel-length veil framed her sad, lovely face. I have a photograph of them in front of their wedding cake, a frilly, three-tiered confection. My mother vamps for the camera, eyebrows up, a *whoo-hoo* look on her face, a cake knife in her right hand, her left is palm out, her new wedding band barely warm on her finger, and her hand is in a gesture of pushing something away.

My father, in contrast, stands next to her, looking at something off-camera, his hands cupped, as if ready to receive it all: cake, wife, life.

I don't know whether the early years of my parents' marriage were happy ones—it was hard to get either of them to admit to any warm memories, even decades after the divorce. But I do know they were both writing, and in that sense the union was fruitful. My father, whose first book, *The World of Carnegie Hall,* put him on the publishing map, followed up with *The Stars,* and he was neatly catapulted into his career. My mother freelanced for "the slicks," publishing regular book reviews and short stories in *Seventeen, McCall's, Harper's,* and the *New York Times.* Dad was her first editor on everything she wrote, and together they shared a few years of symbiotic success. They were a couple to watch: two talented young writers paddling their surfboards out to catch the big wave of the cultural zeitgeist. They threw fondue parties, worked on their issues in group therapy, and dined with Didion and Dunne.

1964 forced my parents onto divergent paths. Dad was awarded a Guggenheim, and Mom was awarded—me.

The night I was born my parents were hosting a dinner party. It was almost midnight when I made my intentions clear, and everyone said a quick good night. They hustled into a cab headed for Mount Sinai Hospital. I was born early on the morning of February 4, an Aquarius, just like my dad.

In 1955, nine years before I was born, the Museum of Modern Art presented a show called *The Family of Man,* a collection of 503 photographs from sixty-eight countries, curated by Edward Steichen. A catalog was published, with all the photographs accompanied by quotes, and an introduction written by Carl Sandburg. My parents, like many New York couples in those days, had seen the show and bought the catalog, and I grew up with it. *The Family of Man* helped form my worldview.

The first picture was of the cosmos—an infinite, mysterious, gaseous space, a bilious cloud of potentiality. The next picture, an aerial photo, showed a bird's-eye view of Earth, with rivers running like mercury between mountains. The pictures felt like flying, then landing on solid ground.

My piece of solid ground was the tony corner of Eighty-Eighth and Madison, on the Upper East Side of Manhattan. Right around the corner from the Guggenheim Museum, whose spiral ramp struck me as the greatest missed roller-skating opportunity in the history of kids. My playground was "The Garden"—the locked garden behind the Carnegie Mansion, which in those days featured swings, a sandbox, and a rabbit-hole slide that looked like a log on the outside, but was shiny on the inside. The nannies all had keys, and my nanny, Jeanette, a warm Haitian woman whom I adored, would wait for me at the bottom of the slide with her arms held wide.

In the winter my mother wore a big rabbit fur hat with fat pom-poms at the ends of the ties that dangled and swung when she walked. She wore round sunglasses that covered half her face, and my dad wore a thick sheepskin coat that curled out at the bottom hem corners like the toes of genie shoes. My mother had a long, red metal claw that hooked to the handlebars of my tricycle so she could drag me down Fifth Avenue, the hexagonal pavers making my voice vibrato as I sang songs that she had taught me, like "Mairzy Doats," or "Hey, Ho, Nobody's Home." My mom made New York feel magical. She would take me to visit "the mailbox tree" that grew in Central Park beside the reservoir. It had a big hole in its trunk just my height that I could drop rocks into, pretending I was mailing letters. After that, we would head over to Madison Avenue to check in on the naked lady. There was a second-floor art gallery that had a small, delicate sculpture of a seated nude in the window, which the gallery owner turned every day so that one day you could see her front side, and the next, her back. Mommy liked the rear view better and so did I. She was a good noticer of things and she told me I was too.

The Family of Man showed me a world that was wildly diverse, and yet united in the human urge toward one another. Mating, marriage, motherhood, friendship, conflict, and religious ritual looked different, but existed everywhere. All around the world people celebrated and worshipped some form of God together, but not us Schickels. My sister and I were raised by orthodox atheists. The only mention of God in our house came when my father took His name in vain: "*Goddammit*, who took my god-damn scissors?"

My parents disdained any kind of programmatic thinking, but Christianity, Catholicism in particular, drove my father batshit fucking-A crazy. Anytime it came up at the dinner table it was dismissed as "utter twaddle." The only thing that merited any clear reverence in my childhood were books and all the lively arts: film, music, theatre, musical theatre, photography, and of course, all forms of dance: Fred Astaire, Pilobolus, Baryshnikov, Torvill and Dean. My father was art's critic and my mother its breathless admirer. Because they were both writers, my sister and I grew up with the percussion of people typing. My father hammered out lines of copy, always on a deadline, and my mother wrote curled up in sunny corners, filling spiral notebooks with her swooping scrawl. She wrote and published three novels, then later, a history of ice skating.

I learned to walk at the Metropolitan Museum of Art. My mother would set me loose to toddle in the museum's huge galleries, which were open and safe. I came to understand the world through exhibits. The dried mummy in the Egyptian wing showed me death, and the Tiepolos gave me an image of heaven, which looked like a visit to the Serendipity ice-cream parlor, all whipped-cream clouds on soft scoops of pale bosom topped with maraschino nipples.

Despite our atheism, at the holidays we celebrated a quintessen-tially WASP Christmas, with all the nondenominational trimmings and just a splash of caroling. The nativity story was treated as narrative, not as truth. Christian rituals were fine as long as they were served in the cooling aspic of culture and family tradition.

There was no praying or saying grace before we tucked into our roast beast. But we had our own humanist stations of the cross: the Christmas windows on Fifth Avenue, the Rockefeller Center ice rink, chestnuts straight from the street vendor's smoking pan.

I played an angel in the school Christmas pageant because theatrics were always encouraged, and nothing is more adorable than blond pigtails under a tinfoil halo. My sister and I put all our faith in Santa Claus, who never failed to crowd the tree with a mountain of presents.

When Grandma Schickel came to town it was its own holiday. She would stay at the Stanhope Hotel across from the Met, and let me and Jessie go through her suitcase, put on her kimono, and trot around in her silky slippers. Then she would take us for crustless tuna fish sandwiches at the museum's Garden Court. After I had eaten she would fish pennies out of her silky little Chinese coin purse to toss into the wishing fountain, a large shallow pool with sculptures of people dancing in the water. I believed in the power of that place, and I would close my eyes and whisper my wish into the penny, *Please God, penny, fountain, give me boobs, give me two daughters when I'm a mom, make Santa bring me a Chrissy doll, make my parents stop fighting.* I would toss the penny and watch it land atop the heap of coins at the bottom of the fountain, lost among all the other wishes.

My favorite part of *The Family of Man* was the series of pages that illustrated sex, motherhood, and childbirth. There was a picture of a couple kissing in the grass. I understood that all over the world men and women were twining up together. I saw them on blankets in the Sheep Meadow, or kissing in the horse-drawn carriages that clopped past. There was a quote on that page by someone called James Joyce:

> *. . . And then I asked him with my eyes to ask again yes*
> *And then he asked me would I yes . . .*
> *And first I put my arms around him yes*

And drew him down to me so he could feel my breasts all perfume yes
And his heart was going like mad
And yes I said yes I will Yes.

These lines made me feel warm and confused. It raised troubling questions such as why would breasts be perfumed? Did ladies put perfume on their breasts? I wondered if my mother perfumed her breasts. I loved my mother's breasts. I called her bosom "my shelf" and would lie across it like an adoring Hummel figurine. She showed me how to dab her Chanel No. 5 on my pulse points, but she didn't say put it on your bosom. I wondered how it would ever be possible for me to ever love some man more than I loved my mother.

But sex... I sat in the window seat of our eleventh-floor apartment with *The Family of Man* in my lap, staring out over the city and understanding that every building I was looking at probably had at least one couple naked and *having sex* inside. It seemed incredible. Then I realized that one day I would be one of those grown-ups with perfumed breasts having sex in the grass or in an apartment, and it gave me a nice, stretchy feeling.

The Family of Man also filled in many of the blanks I had around childbirth and I pored over those images in my window seat. The photos were unsparing and a little scary. A woman writhed in labor, the back of her hand pressed to her forehead, her teeth gnashing. I tried to imagine my mom looking like that, without her coral lipstick, and I just couldn't. Once, when I asked her what it felt like to birth a baby she told me, "It feels like you're having the world's biggest BM." She also told me that when she was in college she had some kind of job interviewing kids for something and had to write their stories, and she had met a girl who didn't know she was pregnant and had had her baby on the toilet. For years, these two pieces of information dominated my thoughts while in the bathroom.

I knew the next picture before I turned the page, because it was the best page in the whole book. It was a picture of a doctor delivering a baby boy. He held the baby upside down by one leg. The baby's eyes were still closed. The umbilical cord spiraled off his belly like a weird sea noodle, and up between his legs was something that I knew was called a penis but also something else that looked like the giblets Mom pulled out of the Thanksgiving turkey.

In 1967, my mother became a pregnant lady, and I watched her tummy balloon under her Marimekko shift until her shelf met her belly and then there was no more lying down there for me and then she went back to Mount Sinai Hospital to have my sister, Jessica.

I barely remember the introduction of my sister into my life, but luckily my father bought a Pentax and began to document his own family of man. The first official picture he took of his two daughters shows me holding my sister. I am four and a half years old—all bangs and knee socks. Jessie is dressed in my baby doll's crinoline dress and she sags awkwardly in my arms, her neck crooked at a weird angle, rolling a stink-eye up at me. I stare, jaw set and unsmiling, directly into the camera's lens. Sibling rivalry *on*.

My sister was a bright, funny, high-octane girl who delighted my parents. I was the darker, moodier, more existential daughter, and *The Family of Man* only served to aggravate my quandary. My sister's birth, combined with all those pictures of other people living their human lives in other countries and other costumes, made me wonder about how people's souls got apportioned into bodies and homes. I could have been born in Java or Germany. I could have been a boy herding sheep. How did I end up here, in New York City, in this family? Why did I have this sister? These parents? Why was I even born a girl?

I felt sure there had to be some kind of an organizing pattern, but that I was just too young to see it. I looked for clues as I grew up, picking up scraps of paper on the street, waiting for the day when I would have enough information to diagram them into a sentence that would mean something.

★   ★   ★

I still have that same copy of *The Family of Man* and I have since learned that the book was roundly criticized for being modernist propaganda framing the world within distinctly American values. But I was too young to know that; I just liked looking at the pictures, and like all important childhood books, *The Family of Man* helped me understand the larger world and my relative place in it. It was a big, wide, spinning world, and a baby could get born anywhere in it. I knew I had landed on a lucky number.

Now, when I look at the childbirth pictures, I see things I hadn't noticed as a kid. I am less transfixed by the glistening baby and his giblets, and I am more aware of how the mother has moved out of the frame. Only her hands can be seen, reaching for her child. She is no longer the sole subject of the camera's eye but a detail, cast off like a useless booster rocket. The baby is the center of the picture now. This is the transformation of birth—new lives for everyone.

I think of my mother, only twenty-seven years old and asked to please step aside, here is Erika, the sacred child, and on some level, she wasn't having any of it. She hadn't been in the frame long enough herself. She wasn't ready to stop being the protagonist of her story.

The following pages in *The Family of Man* are devoted to photographs of nursing mothers, and those pictures feel dew-lit and cliché. A tiny knee presses up against a nipple; dimpled fingers reach. In one picture the buttery baby head is obscured and the woman is back in the picture, but she has been transformed into a Madonna, a perfect being of milk and light, gazing down at her babe in complete, blissful symbiosis.

When I was six months old my parents sailed off to the Cannes Film Festival on the SS *France*, leaving me in the care of a German nanny they found through the Baby Sitters' Guild, a name that to this day still causes a shiver of dread in me. The Baby Sitters' Guild, which is very chic and expensive now, back then was ladies with PBS tote bags and nubby cardigans with tissues tucked up their sleeves. I was too young to remember that first babysitter, but I remember the later ones. They came to our house to read *Reader's Digest* while my sister and I ate fish sticks in front of *Nanny and the Professor* and then were sent straight to bed. Nowhere in *The Family of Man* is there an unattended baby, or a child watching TV alone in a living room, or curled around a Snoopy doll in the dark, struggling to stay awake so she could kiss her mother good night.

New York, Winter 1974

Dad and I were in the back of a Checker cab heading down-town. My sister and I sat on the jump seats, resting our feet on the brown cardboard box of books we were schlepping down to the Strand Book Store. I had on brand-new Mary Janes because today was my tenth birthday and we were having a party. My father had just scored lines in the smooth soles of my new shoes with his pocket knife so I wouldn't slip.

After the Strand we would go up to Cake Masters to pick up my birthday cake and go home to set up the projector in the living room. We would be screening a 16mm rental print of *Seven Brides for Seven Brothers* for my party guests. But we had to do this boring errand first.

As usual, Dad was pissed about the traffic: "Oh for *chrissakes*, let's get *off* of Madison already! Jesus!" I felt myself clench on the jump seat. The cabdriver didn't say anything. My father was often rude to people he didn't know. This created an ongoing tension in my childhood. I wanted to say something to the cabdriver to make it right, but I didn't know how to mediate my father's anger, so I just sat quietly and read the passing ads on the buses for Cutty Sark, *Oh! Calcutta!*, and *Equus*. It was an endless ride down to Thirteenth Street.

The Strand Book Store's slogan was "18 Miles of Books," but it was just a largish bookstore inside. I thought there might be an eighteen-mile-wide basement that ran under all of Manhattan that was filled with the Strand's books. There was a giant, creaking maze of parquet floors between towering bookcases. The smell of all those books always made me have to BM, so I clenched my butt until the urge subsided, shuffling behind my father and sister through the huge store.

I was in the fifth grade at the Dalton School and an avid reader. Dalton was a highly prestigious school; even back in the 1960s, when the world was cheaper and less competitive, there was a long line of anxious parents trying to get their exceptional children admitted.

I was not an exceptional child. My parents tried to get me into a fancy preschool but when I was given crayons and paper by the nice admissions lady who asked me to draw something, I drew a stick figure with a line coming down between its legs, then I drew a circle around the figure and put down my crayon. The lady asked me what I had drawn and I replied, "This is a man, and this is his penis, and he is going pee-pee *allll* over the place."

My dad dodged the whole problem of his ordinary child by writing a glowing piece about the school for the *New York Times*. "Dalton Is an Example of Why There Is a Traffic Jam in the Private Schools," read the headline on Sunday, March 12, 1967, just one month past my third birthday. It was time for me to begin my formal education, and my parents needed me out of the house so they could work.

Dad's piece was a glowing portrait of the progressive school and its "miraculous" hiring of headmaster Donald Barr, whom he described as "a young Orson Welles plunked down in a principal's office." Donald Barr (whose son, future attorney general Bill Barr, was, at that time, being educated uptown at Horace Mann) believed in a child-led curriculum and was known for making unconventional hires (like sex predator Jeffrey Epstein to teach algebra). Clearly the article worked its magic. I was admitted to Little Dalton the following fall.

My well-meaning teachers tried to teach me to read using

phonetics, but I was almost through kindergarten and still sound-ing out words, and still learning to read, not reading to learn. I sat with my parents in the living room one night, my early reader in my lap, sounding out words, "*hoooooowwww nooooooooowwwww browwwwn c-c-coooooowwww*," and my father lost it. "Jesus Christ, Jill, this is like listening to a mental deficient!"

He sat me in a chair next to him with my book. "That's not how reading works, Erika. Look, here is a picture of a cow, here is the word 'Cow'!" By the end of the night I could read. My father always claimed it as one of his great pedagogical triumphs.

The Strand book-buying desk was presided over by a man named Burt Britton, who looked a little like Sean Connery in *The Man Who Would Be King.* He had long dark mutton chops that grew into a salty beard. A row of pens was clipped into his shirt pocket. His shirtsleeves were rolled back to reveal hairy forearms.

"Hey there, Burt," Dad said, hoisting his box of books onto the counter. His tone was warm and cheery. He was so nice with the people he already knew. "These are my girls, Erika and Jessica."

"It's my sister's birthday today," Jessie said, embarrassing me.

"Happy birthday, little lady," Burt said, smiling at me. Then he looked at Dad's box. "What do you have for me today, Richard?"

"Some author copies of the Harold Lloyd book."

"Let's take a look." He counted the volumes. "Could I get you to sign a few?"

"Burt, I'll sign 'em all for you." The two men chatted about their business as Burt handed him his books opened to the title page and my father inked his jittery John Hancock on each one. I wandered off into the stacks to browse. "Watch your sister!" Dad called after me. My sister was six and followed me obediently into adult fiction.

I remember vividly the day I decided I was ready to take the plunge away from picture books and into chapter books. I was six, and it was a Sunday morning and my parents were sleeping in. Somebody had given me *Rutgers and the Water-Snouts* for my birthday, and I just picked it up, got into an armchair, and read it straight through to the end, which took about three hours. Everyone was proud of me, and I felt as though I had found the keys to the kingdom.

Both my parents wrote and reviewed chapter books, and our house was full of all the latest bestsellers. Nothing on my parents' shelves was off-limits to me, so I read anything from David Niven's memoir *The Moon's a Balloon,* which was completely hilarious, to a copy of *Bury My Heart at Wounded Knee* that I found on my father's nightstand. That book, which I only skimmed, gave me nightmares and a vague but functional understanding of man's cruelty to man.

I wandered deeper into the eighteen miles of books, fingering the dust jackets with tempting titles like *Go Ask Alice* and *The Winds of War.* I was thumbing a copy of *The Exorcist,* a movie I'd heard being discussed in the cafeteria line at school, when I heard my father call my name. I grabbed my sister and headed back to Burt's desk, where I found Dad pocketing some cash.

Just as we were about to finally leave, Burt stopped us. "Richard, I'm wondering if I might ask a favor? I have this little side project going, a book…a kind of album, you might say. I'm asking our more famous friends to draw a self-portrait. Would you be so kind as to contribute one?"

"Why, I'd love to, Burt."

Dad was famous? I knew he reviewed movies for *Time* magazine and that that was a hard job that kept him at his typewriter all the time, but I didn't know he was *famous*! It seemed incredible, impossible. I looked at my father in his chinos and desert boots, his sheepskin coat draped over his arm, his shirtsleeves rolled up as always, a pack of Trues outlined in his chest pocket. He just looked like Dad.

We followed Burt down some employee stairs into the basement, which turned out to be another floor of books and office stuff, not in any way eighteen miles long. Burt had a couple of folding chairs and a small table set up in a corner.

"What's a self-portrait?" Jessie asked me.

"It's a picture you draw of yourself." We had tried to do self-portraits in art class at school, and mine always came out looking flat and stupid. Most of my friends could draw a decent pony or superhero. All I could draw were cubes and little houses with a tree in the front yard and some dopey-looking flowers, and I drew those over and over again, afraid to branch out and disappoint myself.

Dad took the sketchbook Burt handed him and sat in the chair. Jessie and I stood behind him, looking over his shoulder as he leafed through the book.

Dad stopped on one picture and chuckled. "Oh, I see you got Woody to do one." Woody Allen was a friend of Dad's. I had met him once at a premiere at the Ziegfeld Theater. His self-portrait was just a tiny head shaped like a triangle, with a scribble of hair, big ears, and round glasses with no eyes. Was it possible that Woody Allen couldn't draw any better than me?

My father found a clean page and smoothed it out on his lap.

He clawed a cigarette out of his shirt pocket, lit it with the sweet *clack-chunk* of his Zippo, and exhaled with a sound that held both relief and anxiety. Sometimes it seemed Dad couldn't really breathe unless it was through a ciggy.

Dad took the pen in his left hand and drew a horizontal rectangle. He started out all wrong; heads weren't square! Then he drew a tripod of legs on the bottom edge of the box. He was drawing a movie screen! It looked just like the one we would set up in our living room for my party later that afternoon, if we ever got home. Within the rectangle Dad drew two dots for eyes and a mouth that was just a straight line.

"What do you think, girls?"

Jessie said, "He needs ears!" Dad handed her the pen and she drew two crescents on either side of the screen.

"And a nose," I said.

"I can't draw noses; you do it," and Jessie handed me the pen. I drew a rudimentary nose that somehow, strangely, reminded me of his, which was a little flat on one side from an old college football injury.

"And a mustache!" Jessie took the pen back and squiggled a jagged mustache over the mouth line. I grabbed the pen and drew two lines for angry eyebrows and then a half-circle for his stubborn chin and there he was, our father, Richard Schickel, the famous movie reviewer.

Dad wrote under the picture, "For Burt," followed by his signature. Then, in parentheses, he wrote, "with a little help from: Erika + Jessica," and he let us write our own names. That was the first publication of anything I had ever written in my own hand.

I had always thought writing was just something boring my parents did. My friends had parents with important jobs where they put on suits and had meetings. My parents did their jobs unglamorously at home in their bathrobes. But that day at the Strand I saw there was specialness in being a writer.

We got a cab uptown to Cake Masters, where Dad paid for my birthday cake with the cash Burt had given him for his books. Books into cake was practically a magic trick. Maybe writing books was really something worth doing.

I started taking notes.

New York, 1976–1978

In fourth grade, when we were still living on Eighty-Eighth Street, I made friends with a new girl at school named Emily Vale. I came home and told Mom about her. "Why, you two used to play together when you were babies!" David Vale and Dad had been colleagues at *Sports Illustrated* and then the Vales moved to Cambridge when Emily and I were toddlers. But they were back in New York and living in a brownstone on Ninety-Fifth Street between Park and Lexington. So that was it, Emily and I immediately became best friends.

Emily was, to me, perfect in every way. She had deep brown eyes and skin that tanned easily. She had a beautiful singing voice, a wicked sense of humor, and a trio of glamorous older siblings.

I introduced her to all my Dalton friends and our parents joyfully reunited. When a brownstone came up for sale next door to the Vales', my parents bought it.

We moved out of our apartment on Eighty-Eighth and Madison, and into the brownstone on Ninety-Fifth between Park and Lexington, and it was as though all my deepest, most girlish Frances Hodgson Burnett dreams had come true. Overnight I went from sharing a small room with my sister to having my own room on the top floor of a cool old house, with a dumbwaiter, a garden, and my best friend living next door.

Ninety-Fifth Street was its own privileged social microclimate. It was the last street before Harlem, and lined with hundred-year-old brownstones, as was Ninety-Fourth Street. Each house had its own small garden in the back, and these gardens were separated by a network of walls and fences that a tribe of us neighborhood kids prowled and played on all the livelong day, running along the tops of walls like gibbons. If we weren't out back swinging off the fences, then we were out front, shooting the incline of Ninety-Fifth Street on our skateboards, dropping water balloons on each other from upstairs windows, or just hanging out on our front stoops, cracking wise. Emily and I had twinned houses that shared a stoop right in the middle of the block, and so we felt we were the queens of Ninety-Fifth Street, holding court until we were called in to dinner. It was as close to an idyllic, classic American childhood as I ever got.

My parents had given the top floor of the brownstone to me and my sister. We were allowed to pick what color of carpet was installed in our rooms. Jessie picked pink and I picked green.

There was a large bathroom between our rooms that had a huge, empty closet that Emily and I claimed as a clubhouse. We dubbed our secret club "The Creture [sic] Club," named for the dozens of little pom-pom creatures with googly eyes and magnets that were the momentary rage. We bought them at our local stationery store, and brought them home to name them and catalogue them in our club journal.

We played a lot of sexy games, reenacting scenes we liked from movies we loved, like *The Three Musketeers* when Michael York withdraws a document hidden in Raquel Welch's cleavage. We did a thing where one of us would breathe in and out deep and fast, then the other would squeeze her around the chest until we passed out. The visions I had while blacked out were epic. I recorded my visions in our club journal. We discussed our crushes and playacted make-out scenes with them. We smoked cigarettes purloined from my mother's purse. We were horribly mean to my little sister. Ours was a potent alliance.

Emily's house was the heart of that neighborhood for me. The Vales were my surrogate, fantasy family. Emily's mom, Kitty, baked crusty bread and Emily's dad, David, a patient, funny man, taught me how to diagram a sentence when no one else could. Emily was the youngest of four dazzling, hilarious siblings whom I worshipped and crushed on. Her big sister Andrea was a concert pianist who gave me weekly lessons in their front parlor. Her brothers Josiah and Zander were both strapping, goofy, and wildly crush-worthy. Emily and I were in the same grade at Dalton, so we could walk to and from school together.

Dalton was a rough ride for me in middle school. Suddenly my friends sprouted into puberty and new social lines were drawn. A couple of girls I knew turned mean; another began to disappear herself with anorexia. Most of the Dalton girls were rich and flossy, wearing the latest styles, hanging out in the trendiest spots. My family was upper middle class, not rich, and I couldn't compete. But I didn't need to. I had Emily. Dear, funny, faithful Emily. One time some boys followed us home from school and cracked eggs on our heads. It was scary, but Emily laughed it off, saying it would make our hair shiny. After that we started cracking eggs on our own heads.

Early one Sunday morning, Emily and I awoke in my Kelly-green bedroom and padded downstairs for massive bowls of Cap'N Crunch with Crunch Berries. We watched a couple of cartoons, then we went upstairs to our closet clubhouse. We played with our creatures, organized our Wacky Packages in order of grossest, hyperventilated each other a few times, and then we were bored, bored, bored. We went out front to see if anyone was up.

It was still early, and Ninety-Fifth Street was quiet. We sat on our joint stoop and waited for our friends to wake up and come outside. Our block happened to be the home of several illustrious New Yorkers. Across the street were the Sardis, of restaurant fame; two doors up from us was Al and Dolly Hirschfeld's pink house. They were a nice, quiet couple with good Halloween candy. A few doors south of Emily's house were the Roiphes, where I occasionally helped my friend Amy babysit little Katie Roiphe when her parents, Anne and Herman, went out for the evening. The Roiphes had a giant Irish setter named Nathan, who humped my leg. This was my first experience with nonconsensual sexual contact.

The brownstone immediately west of mine belonged to the Shannons, a couple of shrinks, and their thirteen-year-old son, Philip, who was in the grade above us at Dalton. One time a burglar broke into their house and Mr. Shannon chased him out and my father caught him as he hit the street. It was so exciting.

As Emily and I lolled on my stoop we heard the second-floor window of the Shannon house clatter open, and Philip Shannon's greasy head leaned out. Philip had cystic acne and some kind of a pigmentation problem that made his arms and neck look both raw and burnt.

"Hey, girls, what's up?" he wheedled at us from his window.

"Nothing." We feigned an air of disinterest.

"Come over here, I want to talk to you." We walked down my steps and up his. At the top of the stoop we were two feet away from his open window. I could see a little into the room behind him and saw a couch and bookcases. "Hey, I dare you to climb from there into this window."

I looked down at the single-story drop from the first floor to the basement-level kitchen entrance to the house. It was definitely a leg-breaker, but Emily and I had been walking on top of fences the past two years; this was nothing. We swung over and into the Shannons' study.

It was a hodgepodge of antiques and '70s chrome-and-glass furniture. Emily sidled in next to Philip on the tuck-and-roll leather couch. Sensing danger, I hung by the door.

Nobody seemed to be awake in this house, either, so we proceeded to amuse ourselves in the manner of unsupervised tweenagers everywhere: telling dirty jokes and making prank phone calls. Then Philip said, "I'll show you something cool." He told Emily and me to put our hands together prayer-style, then slot our hands together.

When you spread the heels of your hands apart and peered into the dark finger-mesh it looked, according to Philip, like a vagina.

The conversation seemed to get riskier with each passing minute, culminating with Philip saying, "I dare you guys to do a striptease."

"No way!" I said.

"Oh, c'mon, don't be chickenshits."

"Fuck you!" Emily said.

"Yeah, go fuck a duck, Philip," I added.

"You guys are pussies," Philip said.

"Oh, is that what you think?" Emily said.

"That's what I *know.*"

"Okay, *fine.*" In a trice Emily was up and doing a bump and grind on the Shannons' shag carpet, accompanying herself with a loose approximation of a burlesque song: "*Da, da, da, DA, DA, dadadada . . .*"

Philip and I watched in stunned awe as she worked her clothes off like a pro, unzipping her hoodie slooooowly. She kicked her feet, sending each of her brown clogs pinwheeling through the air. Then she shimmied out of her dungarees and I thought for sure she would stop there, but she lifted her T-shirt over her head, revealing her breast buds, and flung it to the side. Finally, she slipped out of her underpants, twirling them over her head before she sent them flying, where they landed on a lampshade. She stood before us, completely and magnificently naked. Though I had seen Emily nude many times, in this context her body held a sophistication and ease that I had never noticed before.

Philip clapped and whooped and I joined in, legitimately impressed by my friend. She gave us a quick bow, then calmly went around the room, picking up her clothes and putting them back on.

Philip looked at me. "Okay, Schickel, it's your turn."

"Nah, I don't want to."

"Oh, come on, Er—there's nothing to it."

"No. No way." I was for sure not going to do this. I was deeply ashamed of my body. It was painfully underdeveloped and rigged like a Rube Goldberg machine—I was all clanking joints and angles and mismatched, pointy parts.

"I did it," Emily said, accusal in her voice.

"Yeah," said Philip, "you have to."

"No, I don't." I rooted myself to my chair, trying to become one with the Naugahyde. There was a long moment where the two of them just stared at me with utter disdain, and I realized they were right—I had to. My desire to be as cool as Emily outweighed any scrap of modesty or judgment I had in that moment.

I got up and took my place on the shag and they whooped their approval.

I began with my beloved purple sweatshirt, a garment I had worn almost every day for two years. It was my ally, hiding my developing body from what seemed to be an overly interested world, which included my mother's prying eyes. Slowly, stiffly, I lifted the soft, frayed collar over my head and I flung it to the side with a flourish. Philip and Emily went wild, hooting their approval, egging me on. Emboldened, I fumbled with the top button on my brown corduroy pants. I got them undone and down around my knees before I realized I had forgotten to take my Tretorns and tube socks off. I had to sit down and yank them off before I could get free of my pants. Philip laughed at me. I flushed hot.

I finally got down to my empty training bra and the underpants I had slept in, gray and stretched out around the legs. I could feel my nipples harden with the cold. "Okay, you guys, that's it."

"Keep going!!" they shouted in unison.

"Take it *all off*!" Philip shouted like he was at the OTB, egging his horse over the finish line.

So I took it all off. When all my clothes were finally lying in a little heap at my feet and I was standing stark-naked, pasty-white, and knock-kneed in the middle of Philip Shannon's living room, the door flew open

"Philip? What's going on in here?"

I looked up and saw Philip's mother standing, stunned, in the doorway. Her arms were full of tubes of wrapping paper. Philip leaped to his feet and tried to slam the door. She lost her grip and the tubes tumbled to the floor, like mammoth pickup sticks, jamming the door open.

I jumped up and sought cover behind a table. I tried to hide my great white, goose-pimply self behind a slender French Provincial leg. Mrs. Shannon looked at me sternly. "Erika Schickel, get dressed and go home."

I grabbed my still-warm clothes and crawled over to the foyer on my hands and knees, trying to become invisible, to somehow disappear into the carpet. I stood up in the chilly front hallway, untangling my pant legs, putting on my T-shirt inside-out. Emily brought me my shoes and socks. We stumbled down the Shannons' front steps, shoelaces flapping, and we flew up the steps and through my front door, then up two more flights of stairs to the clubhouse, slamming the door behind us, panting like Labradors.

Neither of us knew what to say to each other, so I pulled out the clubhouse journal and turned to a clean page. I needed to write something down about this thing that had just happened. This horrific accident that had suddenly cleaved my life in half, ending my childhood with a single, tawdry stroke.

I needed to find words for this crossing. A boy had seen me naked. On the top line of the page I block-lettered the word "SEX" with the intention of writing a little controlled essay about it. What might I say about a boy having seen me naked? Not just a boy, a boy and his mother. I didn't let my own mother see me naked, and now Mrs. Shannon had. I saw myself crouching behind that table and my heart convulsed, my brain spasmed, and my hand, which had been lying inert on the blank page, sprang to life and spontaneously slashed across the page in big, ragged letters the word "SICK!"

The next night, my family was walking home from dinner out, and there, hanging off the Shannons' front doorknob, was my purple sweatshirt. The sight made my heart bounce. I prayed we might pass it by unnoticed, but my sister, who was skipping ahead of us, turned and said, "Hey Erika, isn't that your purple sweat-shirt?" My parents stopped and looked where she was pointing.

"Oh," I said casually, "I must have left it on their steps when I was playing." I ran up the stairs and grabbed it, wondering who might be watching from behind their curtains. I imagined Mrs. Shannon holding my beloved garment between two lacquered fingernails, hanging it on the doorknob with disgust.

Emily and I never spoke of that day. I staggered, exposed and abashed, through the end of fourth grade and into fifth grade, my secret growing inside of me like a malignancy, destroying every good feeling I might try to have, undermining my already shaky preadolescent confidence. But Philip never let me forget it. Every time he passed me in the hall he would sing the strip-tease song under his breath, just loud enough for me to hear. Sometimes he muttered "slut" as he passed me at my locker. It dragged all through fifth grade and into sixth. I would never be free of this shame.

Meanwhile, Emily blossomed, becoming accomplished, popular, beloved by our classmates. I, on the other hand, became mute, awkward, swallowed up by shame as I wandered down Dalton's corridors between classes, ever on the lookout for Philip.

Gradually, I noticed boys in the grade above me snickering as I approached. One day I found myself standing in the lunch line next to Mark Cohen, football player and popular dude extraordinaire, and I heard him under his breath sing, "*Da, da, da, da, DA, DUNH! Da, da, da, da...*" and I knew that Philip had told him. The secret I had hoped to take to my grave was now common knowledge. And thus, with little more than the crude tools of the jeer and the sneer, Philip Shannon single-handedly kindled into being my bad reputation. Before I had even made it into high school, ERIKA IS A HOAR was scrawled on the stall door in the girls' bathroom.

One day, Philip saw me on the back fences and called to me from his window, "Hey, Erika, why don't you come over and strip for me?"

I finally snapped, unleashing a stream of invective on Philip so loud and foul that his mother intervened. "Erika Schickel, I am calling your mother," she said, shutting the window.

Ten minutes later Mom called me into her room. "Erika, Joyce Shannon just called and told me that you and Philip have been fighting. Is this true?"

"Yes."

"She also tells me that some time ago you removed your clothes in front of Philip. Is that true?"

"Yes." I waited for her fury. Instead she held out her arms to me. I fell into them, sobbing.

She held me while I cried myself out and then she said, "Erika, sweetheart, all kids do this. It's a perfectly normal part of growing up. In fact, when I was your age I did the same thing."

"You did?"

"Of course. I was a little younger than you, and me and my best friend Charlie took our clothes off together and his mother caught us and was furious. She told Charlie that if he ever looked at another girl naked again his penis would fall off."

"That's awful!"

"It was terrible, but those were the 1940s. It was a different time. But it is very natural for children to be curious. Poor Charlie grew up to be a homosexual." It was an odd parable, as I look back on it now, but...those were the 1970s. The story served its purpose by relieving me of a good measure of shame. With my mother beside me, I felt safer inside of that shame. In fact, I began to consider the protective power of embracing its opposite: shamelessness.

Not very long after my fateful striptease, my parents sat me and my sister down and told us they were separating. Dad would be moving out. But not to worry, we would see him every weekend, and we mustn't ever blame ourselves for the divorce.

My sister cried and I got up from our family meeting, walked out into the garden, and climbed the wall over into Emily's yard. I found my friend in her bedroom, eating Pringles and doing homework. I collapsed on her bed and sobbed out the news. She stroked my hair and assured me that she and her whole family were behind me, which almost made me feel worse, the unity of her big, happy family as compared to my ruined one. Emily looked at me with her soft, serious brown eyes and reassured me I was going to be all right, and our friendship would see me through all this. We would be best friends all our lives until we were old ladies in rocking chairs on our porches.

Dad moved out of our house and into a leathery man pad on the upper floor of a high-rise building that looked like a cell block. He bought a new Mr. Coffee, a new answering machine, a big Sony Trinitron, and an Eames chair. Everything smelled of the plastic wrapping it came in.

Dad was more inconvenienced than he was heartbroken by the end of his marriage. Fully cut loose from the restraints of monogamy, Dick, whose salad days had been wilted by his marriage, was let loose in a postsexual revolutionized world. He slipped on his Bali loafers, combed his stache, adjusted his Aviator frames, grabbed his "fag bag," and went out and *swung*. From 1976 to 1981 Dick Schickel was Mr. Goodbar, mowing down newly liberated ladies like a John Deere in deep wheat. "I once had sex with three different women in one day," my father bragged to me decades later, not that he wouldn't have bragged about it to me at the time. He made no secret of his many conquests.

I got my first period at thirteen, and it was like taking a blindfold off. Suddenly I could see that sex was everywhere and had been all along. Everyone was getting it on: my parents, my friends' parents, my friends, people on TV. Alone and confused in my broken, atheist home, I had nowhere to turn for answers to my pubescent questions about sex, but to literature. I made a fierce study of my parents' neglected copy of *The Joy of Sex*—in which hairy hippies carnally cavorted in anatomically correct pen-and-ink illustrations.

I was fascinated by the mechanics of sex, but I wasn't aroused by the book. It all looked too floppy and heartfelt. Meanwhile, I had stuffed my parents' copy of *Fear of Flying* under my purple sweatshirt and sneaked it up to my room. The cover was incredibly sexy. It showed a woman's breasts exploding from a tight shirt as her zipper was being slowly run southward by an anonymous male hand. Alone, sprawled out on my shag carpeting, I discovered the "Zipless Fuck" in breathless surprise. It embodied all the sophistication, mystery, and emotional remove that I presumed adult sex was based upon.

As I grew up and grew progressively cannier, my father took more of an interest in me and made me his sidekick, bringing me with him to screenings and premieres. The screenings were in tiny upstairs rooms in midtown, where we would run into Dad's movie-reviewer friends and Dad would sparkle. He loved to "shoot the shit" with his colleagues. I liked the screenings because the chairs were swiveled and squishy, and if we couldn't get a cab, they held the movie for us.

I remember one movie date, my father took me to see *Walkabout,* not a screening but a revival. This was a pre-video era where if you wanted to see a movie, you had to catch it in first run or revival in a theater. After the movie, we went out to dinner and talked about it.

"What did you think of that picture?" Dad asked, tucking into his steak.

"I dunno, it was weird."

"C'mon, kid, is that all you've got?"

"The girl was pretty."

"Well, sure, Jenny Agutter, *hubba-hubba.*"

There had been a naked swimming scene. The thought of my dad looking at the naked girl and thinking hubba-hubba made me feel weird.

"I thought the ending was sad."

"What did you think was sad?"

"How in the end she was trapped in the city, and she missed the boy. It's like a sad *Wizard of Oz* where the Scarecrow kills himself and Kansas sucks."

Dad laughed, his high, satisfied cackle that he usually reserved for good comedies and his own jokes. "A-plus, kid, A-plus."

A few months after my parents' separation, David and Kitty Vale sat their kids down for a family meeting, and told them that they, too, were divorcing. The news of their failed marriage shook me more than my own parents' split. I mean, everyone knew my parents hated each other. I had once seen my mother break a small side table over my father's head. But the Vales? Impossible.

On the day David Vale moved into his own leathery man pad, Emily came over and collapsed, sobbing, on my bed, and it was my turn to give her the pep talk. Hey, at least we would be divorce orphans together, I told her, and I meant it from the bottom of my heart. I would never leave her.

Emily and I helped each other keep it together the rest of that terrible sixth-grade year, right up until the day my mom and her dad announced that they had been dating and were in love with each other. I knew my mother had gone on a couple of dates with someone, but David Vale of all people?

Something soured in Emily. It was as though my own dirty karma had rubbed off on her perfect family. I knew it, and she knew it. This was my fault.

My mother sold the brownstone and we moved, with David, into a small two-bedroom apartment in a high-rise on East Eighty-Third Street. Emily refused to come to the apartment, even to see her dad. She kept her distance from me at school.

There was a comic-book store next to our building called Major Fun. It was run by a guy named Dale who kept his store full of neighborhood kids by having a pinball machine and a Pong game in the back. I fell in with a little gang of kids that gathered there. There was Paula and her little sister Kissy, a couple of tough blondes who lived in my building; Mack T, a pasty, Stones-obsessed kid from up the street; and José, a Puerto Rican teen dream from the projects. José had Frank Lloyd Wright cheekbones and train-track braces. He looked so damn good in his overlap slacks and Puma sneakers, I could not help but have a melting-hot crush on him.

Dale, the proprietor of Major Fun, was a shlubby guy in his mid-thirties who only wore T-shirts he got for free at comic-book conventions. He gave me free comic books and slugs for the games, not that I didn't pump most of my allowance into his cash register on other stuff. One day, as he was giving me the latest issue of *Howard the Duck,* he asked me out to a movie. I said okay, feeling embarrassed and a little excited. Was this a date? My first date?

When he came to pick me up that night, he was wearing a real shirt and a sports jacket. My mother not only knew about the date, she met Dale at the door and told us to please be home no later than ten.

I cannot remember any details of the date. Not what the film was, not whether we ate dinner, not if he kissed me. I think he may have, but I can't be sure. The entire event other than the pickup has been deleted from my memory.

Even more frustrating is that I cannot begin to account for my mother's willingness to let an adult man take her thirteen-year-old daughter out on a date. It was, however, not the first time my mother had left me alone with a weird older guy. When I had had an unexpected visit from Flash, the guy who ran the equipment hut at Camp Laurel, she let him come upstairs and surprise me in my room. Flash was a bearded, portly hippie in army fatigues and a bandanna headband that pressed his dark, wavy hair against his skull. We sat and talked, then suddenly Flash tried to start a tickle fight with me and I had to push him off.

In both cases I never said a word about it to my mother. I worried she would make a big deal out of it, and it wasn't a big deal to me. It was just how it was in the 1970s.

★   ★   ★

In his *New York Times* article about Dalton, my father quoted a former teacher who described Dalton girls: "They are the most fashionably dressed, worldly-wise high-school girls I've ever seen. They buy their clothes at Paraphernalia and they all feel compelled by their peers to have mature opinions on sex and pot and LSD and God knows what else. Remember, they're mostly the children of parents on the make—not so much for social position but for eminence, for distinction—and they just naturally have to be up on things in a way that girls at Spence or Chapin don't have to be."

This was completely true for me in every regard but for shopping at Paraphernalia, which my family could never afford. But like these girls, at Dalton I grew up fast and loose and was front-loaded with a lot of adult knowledge, much of it under my father's own tutelage. My father didn't have a predatory bone in his body, but he also had no boundaries with me when it came to talking about sex or exposing me to adult culture. One of his classic pieces of parental advice: "There's only one thing you need to know about men, Erika: When their dicks stand up, their brains fall in the mud."

I wasn't flossy like my Dalton classmates; I didn't have designer jeans and a Barbados tan. But I was a Jodie Foster lookalike in the era of *Taxi Driver*: blond, willowy, and macking for attention.

That year Principal Barr allowed a talent scout to come to Dalton and roam the classrooms looking for a young girl to play the lead role in Louis Malle's next film, *Pretty Baby*. My mother got a call that night asking her to bring me in to audition for the role of the 1917 New Orleans child prostitute. I couldn't believe it. I had dreamed of being a star and suddenly here was my big break!

My mother refused the audition. I begged her to please let me go, but she said I would have a normal childhood, even if it meant I hated her.

And so I did hate her with all the bitterness and rancor that only a thirteen-year-old girl can summon for her mother. Brooke Shields got the part, and I shifted into full bore rebellion.

Every night after dinner I would go out for a walk, skulking around my neighborhood, smoking cigarettes I kept hidden in the inner pocket of my peacoat. I scored a nickel bag of pot in front of the Azuma on Eighty-Sixth Street and rolled it into a lumpy joint from which I could get no draw. I drank Pink Champale with Frank and Paula down by the East River, smoking Kools and practicing the angry butt-flick. In the spring I finally got José's attention and we sat through *Rabbit Test* twice, necking like mad. After that I liked to hang out at the paddle ball courts up in the projects to watch José play. This drove my father fucking-A nuts.

Sex loomed large in the late '70s in New York. People were streaking and swinging and swapping partners. I knew that sooner or later I would get in on the game and the only thing standing in the way was my virginity. The idea of saving myself for someone special seemed hilarious. I had no expectation of that. My life was complicated enough without having to sweat my cherry. I was ready to give it to the first taker.

That turned out to be Ezra, a nice Jewish boy from the eighth grade. We lived in the same general direction and one day we found ourselves walking home from school together and he invited me upstairs. I made out with him in his room a couple of times first. Then, one night, I invited him over to where I was babysitting. The baby was asleep in her room and Ezra and I did it on the parents' bed in the dark. He was gone by the time the parents came home. I walked down Second Avenue, stopping for a slice on my way home, and I looked at myself in the pizzeria's mirrored wall. I still had the same long face, pointy chin, green eyes. I looked exactly the same, but I had been transformed.

One Monday morning I decided to cut school. I stowed my Danish school bag behind a dryer in the basement and left by the service entrance. I stopped at a pay phone and did my best Jill Whedon imitation to call in sick at school, and it worked. I had the whole day to myself.

I started walking down Second Avenue, looking in shop windows, watching New York roll up its gates for the day.

I came upon the Beekman Theatre and saw I was just in time

for the first showing of *The Lacemaker*. I bought a ticket, a box of Jujubes, and tried to surrender to the movie but Isabelle Huppert's character annoyed me. She was kind of a ditz and the guy was obviously a jerk. I would tell my dad that when I saw him next. He would probably agree.

After the movie I was starving, so I stopped at Burger Heaven for a burger deluxe and a vanilla shake. I went over to Lexington and stopped in at Fiorucci, which was the Paraphernalia of that time. All the rich Dalton girls shopped there. Everything was so sparse and glittery and expensive and every article of clothing I touched was tiny; even if I could afford it I couldn't fit into it. I was not the girl this store was for, and that made me feel hopeless.

I fled Fiorucci and went to Bloomingdale's. This store, I under-stood. It was my mother's store: perfumed, silky, and engulfing. I wandered up to Juniors, which was doing a whole India thing for spring. The department was draped like a big silky tent, and a light patter of tabla and sitar music was piped in. It put me into a trance of longing.

The racks were full of twirly skirts and embroidered shirts, harem pants in brilliant hues. Even at the prices my mother could afford, I couldn't afford so much as a scarf.

There was a basket of small stone rings on a counter and no one at the register. I picked out a small lapis ring, slipped it over my knuckle, and plunged my hand into the depths of my peacoat pocket, casually walking out of the store. I hit Lexington Avenue with my heart in my mouth, clutching the ring, feeling both scared and powerful.

When I got home I got my diary out and wrote out the whole day so that I wouldn't forget anything about it. It had been an adventure! Emily would have loved it. I had no one to tell but my diary. I would soon come to regret that.

A month later I was in the lunchroom at school when I heard my name over the PA, summoning me to the office. I was told my mother had called and wanted me to come home immediately.

She was waiting for me in the living room, a True Blue cigarette dangling from one hand, and my fat little gilt-edged diary, Exhibit A, in the other.

She directed me to the couch while she remained standing. She was a pillar of indignation, her long spine fully extended, shoulders thrown back, coral lipstick feathering as she pursed her lips in fury. "I read within of truancy and shoplifting, drinking and tawdry afternoon assignations with boys. Is this true?"

I stood before her, frozen and mute.

"I have no idea who you are or what you are capable of, Erika. I honestly don't know. Well, actually, I do know, because you wrote it all down, didn't you?"

I offered her no counterargument. My stubborn silence only infuriated her more.

"If you have lied, then you are a liar," she said. "If you have stolen, then you are a thief. Do you see how this works? How am I supposed to trust you now?"

She shook my diary at me. "This is not my daughter. This is some other person, and I do not like this person. This person is a liar and a thief." With that, she turned on her heel and stalked into her bedroom, where David was tactfully staying out of it, and slammed the door behind her.

London to Los Angeles, 1976 & 1978

Manhattan passed under the wing of the plane like a mirage. The spires of my childhood kingdom reached up to me. I hadn't been home in two months.

My mother was down there somewhere, and the Good Humor truck, the Guggenheim, the mailbox tree, my sister, my school, my cats, José, and Emily. I longed for them all, but even though this flight would touch down at Kennedy, it was just a quick layover; I was on my way to California.

After the hooky episode my parents, in a rare moment of agreement, decided I needed to be elsewhere for the summer. So, they found me a job working as an au pair for the family of my father's British publisher. My assignment was to take care of the Reynoldses' two-year-old daughter, Charlotte, six days a week, while Mrs. Reynolds tended to her new baby. On Saturdays I was paid £5 for the week and let loose in London.

This was not my first trip to London. I had come here with my family just two years before. Dad was doing a show about the movie star Douglas Fairbanks and was here to interview his son, Douglas Fairbanks Jr. My family had arrived in London after a long flight from New York, and Mom and Jessica had gone straight to bed, but Dad and I were restless with jet lag. So we headed down to Piccadilly Circus because my social studies teacher, Mr. Hendershot, had told me to go see the statue of Anteros.

"Dad! There he is!" We jaywalked across the current of traffic to the center of the circle. A pile of steps led up to the statue's base, on top of which stood a winged boy perched mid-skip, his metal toes barely touching the ground. His bow was loaded and drawn; he was poised to wreak love on London. "Why are you supposed to visit this statue of Eros?" Dad asked.

"It's not Eros, Dad, it's Anteros, his brother. And because Mr. Hendershot said to." Mr. Hendershot was an odd duck in suspenders and a bowtie, with an exasperated manner. Most kids hated him, but he was the first teacher I had who knew I was smart. I wanted to impress him.

"Well, they look exactly the same to me," Dad said.

"Actually, Anteros has butterfly wings. That's how you can tell the difference."

My father got out a little pocket camera my mother had given him for Christmas, screwed his face up behind it to accommodate the burning cigarette clenched between his teeth, and snapped a picture.

I had learned about the six kinds of love from Mr. Hendershot: Eros, Philia, Agape, Ludus, Storge, Pragma, and Philautia. "Anteros was given to Eros, so he would have someone to return his love," I said, repeating what Mr. Hendershot had told me, feeling proud to know something my father didn't.

"You might think of that next time you fight with your sister." I felt the moment lurch into lecture and tried to wrest it back. "Love has to have an object, Dad, otherwise it just swooshes around with nowhere to go. It's not real unless it is received and returned."

"Hm." Dad gave my shoulder a squeeze. He took a final drag of his cigarette, then ground it out with his loafer. "C'mon, kid, we gotta get to bed. I've got Fairbanks in the morning." We took one last look at Anteros and headed back to our hotel.

★   ★   ★

What I didn't know that night, standing in front of the statue of Anteros with my father, was that Cupid's arrow was already zipping across London and would strike him the very next day as he stood in front of Douglas Fairbanks's secretary. He began a dalliance with her that would, within the year, end my parents' marriage.

My parents had a spectacularly ugly zeitgeist divorce. They wrote dueling, accusatory novels about each other. Mom wrote *A Good Sport*, the story of a woman who is unhappily married to a philandering sportswriter. He retaliated with *Another I, Another You: A Love Story for the Once-Married,* in which he revealed through thinly veiled characters his affair with Kitty Vale. He had revenge-fucked Emily's mom to get back at my mom for being with David. Everyone was furious about it, and I guessed Emily probably was, too.

Now I was back in England, homesick, broke, and aimless. I spent my Saturdays wandering around London, sitting in parks and galleries. I went down to the King's Road to see the punks and bought a Patti Smith T-shirt at Boy of London. A dude in a kilt and motorcycle boots handed me a flyer: big red lips on a black background. He was papering the house for the King's Road Theater and I got to see *The Rocky Horror Show* for free. My dad had taken me to a lot of Broadway shows, but this was the craziest musical I had ever seen. Emily would have loved it.

The next Saturday I found my way to Oxford Circus and went to Top Shop, which I had seen advertised on *Top of the Pops,* the British music show that was the highlight of my week. There was a long escalator that ran from the street to the store below ground. The Boomtown Rats' song "Like Clockwork" was pulsing all around me, making me feel cool and dangerous. I went into some kind of a consumer trance just like I had at Bloomingdale's. I moved between the tables of cheap merchandise, shoving accessories into my shoulder bag. I took rubber bracelets and checkerboard-printed earrings, lip gloss and keyrings until my Le Sportsac bulged. I got back on that escalator not understanding that even though it looked wide-open to the street, it was, in fact, alarmed.

Top Shop called the Reynoldses, and I was sent packing back to the States, but Mom was too angry to have me back. I was going to Dad's in Los Angeles. If I could have parachuted out of that airplane into midtown I would have. I would have run all the way up to Eighty-Third Street, dragging the parachute silk behind me like a placenta up Lexington Avenue. I would have dragged it all into my mother's apartment, the mess and bulk of me, and lain down on her perfumed bed and wound us all tightly up in it like a silken cocoon.

The air on the curb at LAX felt like cashmere compared to the Brillo-pad atmosphere of London. It was heavy with the scent of jasmine and sea salt, with top notes of burnt rubber and hot pavement. My dad pulled up to the passenger-loading curb in a rented Chevy Impala. He wore a safari jacket, pressed jeans, and Ray-Bans.

"Hey, kid," he said, grabbing me by the scruff of my neck and pulling the top of my head toward him for a kiss. "How was the flight? Was everything tickety-boo?"

"It was okay. The flight was long." I threw my bag in the backseat and got in the car, buckling my seat belt even though Dad never did.

"What was the movie?"

"*Heaven Can Wait.*"

"Warren's not bad in that one." Dad was in L.A. working on a clip show about monster movies. Sometimes Dad hobnobbed with celebrities in his work. He would say things like, "I actually like Clint" (or Tony or Marty or Woody). "He's a good guy," as though he alone could see past the glitter of their celebrity to perceive the true, sterling human beneath.

He hung his cigarette arm out the window. His forearms were tanned from his regular Sunday tennis game.

"Can I bum one of those?" My English Ovals were in the trunk.

"Sure. So, you're smoking?"

"Yeah, I figure, why not?"

"That's my motto!" Dad shook out a True from his pack. The car lighter popped and together we pressed our cigarettes against its glowing bull's-eye.

We drove down La Tijera Boulevard, past the Buggy Whip Bar and Restaurant, past Pann's Restaurant, landmarks that I recalled vividly from our yearly visits to Los Angeles to visit my grandparents.

"Have you talked to Grandaddy?"

"We played some tennis earlier in the summer, but not since then. But he seemed okay. Working on a script, of course."

Grandaddy was always working. He had written a radio show in the 1940s called *The Great Gildersleeve.* Then he wrote for *The Dick Van Dyke Show, The Andy Griffith Show, The Donna Reed Show, Leave It to Beaver,* and others. Grandaddy was handsome, with deep dimples, a strong jaw, and eyebrows that flared. He smoked a pipe and did "the dragon" whenever I asked, where he would take a deep draw and blow the smoke out of his nose and both sides of his mouth as he raised his mighty eyebrows and glared at me. It was impressively scary and I loved it. But other than that, I have few memories of him coming out of his cork-lined office to be with the family.

Grandma Dorothy, his second wife, was an ex-model who lived every day of her life in a tennis dress. She had a froth of white hair that sat atop her head like Cool Whip and thighs that were as tanned and taut as a pair of English brogues. She chattered mindlessly, took hundreds of vitamins, and juiced, juiced, juiced! My mother positively loathed her.

I loved staying at their house, a modern affair my grandaddy designed himself, in the Pacific Palisades. It was all glass and marble floors, with a tree growing in the middle of the living room and a white baby grand. They had a pool with a brazier, a sunken bathtub in the master bath, and a "chatter pit," a sunken den lined with pillowy banquettes like a genie bottle and a TV with a remote control.

I guessed I wouldn't be seeing my grandparents on this trip. I wondered if they had heard about my crime. I wondered if they even knew I had gone to London.

Dad was staying in an apartment in a big old Spanish building in West Hollywood on Fountain Avenue. "I'm subletting this place from Jay," Dad explained as we pulled into the dark underground garage. Jay Cocks was also a critic at *Time*. "There's lots of stuff nearby you can walk to while I'm at work. Tower Records is right down the street."

The apartment was cool and dark on the inside, with arched doorways and built-in drawers in the dining room, and parquet floors that didn't squeak like the wood floors back in New York. There was a big leather couch and a smoked-glass coffee table, but otherwise not much furniture. Dad tossed his keys down on the coffee table and showed me around. The dining-room table was also glass, with some metal and wicker chairs for theoretical dinner parties, but Dad primarily enjoyed foods that came out of cans. The fridge was empty but for a carton of orange juice and some cocktail onions. I opened a cabinet and found a full supply of Campbell's soups (bean and bacon and tomato), and made the happy discovery that Fig Newtons were in good supply.

The toilet seat was up in the ornately tiled bathroom. Manly brown towels hung from the towel bars. I was shown my room, which was really just a mattress in one of the turrets, accessed by a ladder, which was cool. We went back to the living room and Dad directed me to sit on the chilly leather sofa.

"Obviously your mother and I are very disturbed by what happened in London."

"I know, I'm really sorry, Dad."

"Jesus Christ, this is fuckin'-A bad. Rupert is a colleague of mine. I have a reputation to maintain here. You really screwed that one up." He spoke these lines halfheartedly. Respectability had never really been an expressed value in our home. We had no social standards to uphold that I knew of, so all this talk of name ruination was a little bewildering to me.

"I'm sorry," I said again anyway.

"*Jesus.* Why do you have to be such a knucklehead, Erika?" He jabbed his True into the full ashtray.

"I don't know."

"Your sister is much defter than you. She can ootz around things, but you just run right into things. I wish you would take a page from her." He sighed and groped in his shirt pocket for another cigarette. "Your mother and I have discussed this, and we think that it would be a mistake for you to return to Dalton."

"*What?*"

"My friend has a friend whose daughter goes to a really great boarding school in Massachusetts—"

"*Boarding school?*"

"Goddammit, Erika, just listen. This school is very small and artsy. It's in the Berkshires, a truly beautiful spot. Wait a minute, where's the thing?" He dug through a pile of *New Yorkers* and *New York Times* on the coffee table and uncovered a rectangular paperback book. It had a sketch of a potted plant in white against a brown background. He handed it to me, but I wouldn't touch it. That would have signaled acquiescence of some kind, and I was *not* going to boarding school.

"Just take the fucking thing for chrissake."

I took it and flipped it over. In small letters on the back it said *Buxton School 1977.*

This was like no kind of yearbook I'd ever seen. It was thin and floppy and looked pretty much collaged together. It contained candid shots of people goofing around for the camera. There were hippie kids, posed in groups, playing woodwinds in ponchos, practicing tai chi, making granola, kids in bandannas and ripped jeans and shit-kickers, catching Frisbees. There were headings for different activities like "Mountain Day" and "Work Program."

"*Work Program?* Dad." I could feel my life slipping sideways. I had spent all summer working and trying to get home and now it looked like I might not make it after all. I flipped through the book. There was a photograph of a line of kids, snow shovels in hand, shoveling in what appeared to be a blizzard in the woods. "You can't be fucking serious."

"Look, try to be open-minded. You're out of options. You've struck out with your mother. You two just aren't good for each other right now."

"But why can't I live with you?"

"I'm doing more and more television and I need to be bicoastal. It just won't work, kid."

"Please, don't send me away to boarding school. I am begging you, Dad."

"Look, this isn't Dickens, we're not sending you to a workhouse. It's really nice and it's gonna cost me a frigging arm and a leg, so try to keep an open mind. In fact, you're lucky they will even entertain your application, given your Dalton grades and this late date. The fall semester starts in two weeks."

I began to cry. Dad stabbed his cigarette into a glass ashtray on the coffee table.

"Look, you know I love you, and frankly I don't give a shit if you stay at Dalton, I like having you around, but your mother insists on this, and as she is the parent you would be living with, it's her call. It might just end up being a good thing for both of you. Think of it as starting a whole new chapter in your life."

PART III

BUXTON

Application for Buxton Admission: My Autobiography

By Erika Schickel

August 16th, 1978

I was born in N.Y. And so far, I have been raised here all my life. I have one sister Jessica, aged 10, and 3 cats. I lived in an apartment on 88th and Madison until I was about 9 ½, then I moved to a large brownstone on 95th Street.

A lot happened while I lived on 95th street. I made some new friends and strengthened relationships with old friends. I played many street games and games out in the back yards. There were water fights in the summer and snowball fights in the winter.

When I was 12 my parents got separated and my father moved out. My parents had not been getting along for some time but my sister and I never really expected them to get a separation! When my father moved out we had to get used to a totally new lifestyle. We saw my father on weekends and everybody sort of acted differently.

We weren't doing too well financially and my mother couldn't keep up a whole house, so we all moved down a flight and rented out the top floor to two girls. Finally, even that got to be too much so we sold the house and moved to a nice apartment on 82nd and York.

Somebody moved in with us. A man named David and his cat, Diego. David and my mother plan to be married as soon as my parents get a divorce. Jessie and I are pretty much happy with this arrangement because we like David and everybody involved seems contented with their new lifestyles.

I suppose a lot has happened in 14 years and I think there's still some more to come, but whatever it is, I'll give it my best!

Thank you,
Erika Schickel

August 1978

Mr. Benjamin G. C. Fincke
Director
Buxton School
Stone Hill Road
Williamstown, Massachusetts 01267

Dear Mr. Fincke:

Erika? Who knows? Her adolescence continually takes me by surprise. Half the child who grew up in my house, half a woman whose dimensions of gift and spirit are only shadowy outlines to me.

It seems to me—typically—that our divorce was harder on Erika than she perhaps recognized herself at the time, or showed us. She has a tendency to hide feelings and to resent efforts to pry them out of her. You sometimes have to speak in metaphors—discussion of a book or movie will sometimes elicit responses that tell you more about her than direct questioning will. I think she sometimes will pursue a bad course—lackluster school performance, indifference to responsibilities—until she precipitates a crisis which forces her, and those who love her, to deal more dramatically than might be necessary with her problems. Does she relish drama?

Or is she just the sort of dreamer who really doesn't know how serious they are until they have grown to hugely obvious proportions? Or is she so profoundly independent that she simply must resist, or anyway test, conventions, authority, what-have-you? I don't know.

One thing interests me, though—the contrast between Erika and her younger sister, Jessie, who, like most second born kids, has learned to manipulate, to get her way without confrontation, issue-forcing. She smooths sunnily through life in a way that Erika doesn't. Erika by contrast bangs her head against walls, defends her autonomy very openly, stubbornly, sometimes self-destructively. She has, as a result, suffered a number of defeats that have, I think, inflicted some damage to her self-esteem.

I think that's the area that most concerns me at the moment. Her lack of academic success at Dalton, the really frightful year of unending conflict she endured with her mother, seem to me to have placed her in a position where she looks everywhere—but most especially toward dubious peers—for approval. I think she then gives allegiance to people and ideas that are less valuable than she is, that don't really challenge her, bring out the best in her. And yet, as she once said to me, she knows her own potential, resents the academic and social success of less singular kids who have learned the easy, conventional ways to gain approval, good grades, good (surface) behavior, the politesse of "niceness." She needs warmth, support, non-moralistic concern to find her own way, her own individuality expressed in her own terms.

I confess to failures in this realm. I was preoccupied with my own career, too much a psychologically absent father when she was growing up. Now present in that sense, I have been for the last three years physically absent a great deal. I think she knows how much I care for her, can see how hard I try to keep in loving touch, but I'm certain, too, that she wonders about the depth of my feelings. And, frankly, she has the most serious problems with her mother. She is a cold, disapproving, highly moralistic woman, much preoccupied now with her frustrating efforts to reconstitute her own life. She has not, I feel, given Erika much help during this troubled adolescent passage. If you've read *My Mother, Myself* you have found classic definitions of this mother-daughter conflict that fits Erika's case. I am concerned about her female role model, concerned over her developing a womanliness of a warm, giving and truly self-respecting kind, just as I'm concerned that when it comes to me, she may not have the confidence in her own value that a father should give to a girl.

That's a matter I'm still working on. And in all of the things I've been discussing here, I don't know what role, if any, a school can or should play. What I perhaps haven't stressed enough are Erika's strengths. She has a singular way of looking at the world, which has in the past come out in her writing. Also, like so many others who need approval, she is drawn to performance (singing, dancing, acting) and has, in my quite professional view, good stage presence. (She needs more discipline there, as she does in other areas.) She also has humor, and a certain sweet innocence that sometimes juxtaposes oddly with the knowledgeability in all sorts of expected and unexpected areas she also exhibits.

In sum, Erika needs to gain self-respect through solid achievements in a school-peer group environment, and she needs to have her efforts warmly rewarded. To the degree that the school can act as an emotional surrogate—and I must in all candor add that I was in principle opposed to sending Erika away from home and yielded finally to her sense that it was the best solution to her problems with her mother—and it can give a useful function in her psychological development. Of course, I understand the school's prime function is to be educational, and I also have great faith in Erika's ability to sort out most of her problems herself. I'm also convinced that at this stage the people who will have the largest influence on this often highly suggestible child will be peers. I hope that they turn out to be Buxton's best and that the school itself will help guide her into company that is good for a kid who is extremely sensitive and sympathetic (she's always been that way), rather more innocent than she pretends to be, and very dear to me.

Sincerely,
Richard Schickel

Admittedly, not all of our independent schools are of the caliber to qualify as leaders in education. Some of our private schools have had as their *raison d'etre* satisfying mobility needs of socially striving parents. Now, as in the past, private schools are sometimes elected to cope with various kinds of academic and emotional "problem children." What does a greater separation mean for this child? Rejection or punishment? What is the present and future import of all of this for him?

—George Goethals, *The Role of Schools in Mental Health,* 1962

Williamstown, Massachusetts, 1928

Ellen Geer-Sangster was a good mom with a difficult, gifted child. Her sensitive, delicate boy needed more stimulation than her local Short Hills, New Jersey, public school could offer in the nineteen-teens. The young mother knew there was a pedagogic revolution taking place in American education, led by John Dewey, the philosopher and educator—away from curriculum-based, rote learning where kids were made to read and regurgitate material that had no bearing on their real or future lives, and toward a more child-centered, project-based system of learning. Ellen and her husband, Dan Geer, wanted their son to attend one of these new schools, but the nearest progressive schools—the Little Red Schoolhouse, Birch Wathen, City and Country, Walden—were all in New York City—not close enough for the Geer family.

Ellen herself had been educated by Quakers (those early liberals) at the Farmington School, and had emerged with a distinctly humanistic urge that she first channeled into social work, then motherhood, and then the Buxton School, the school she started for her son.

The Geer family lived in a small house at that time, on twelve and a half wooded acres, in Essex County, New Jersey. They decided to build a school from the ground up on their own property. The building of the school was Buxton's initial curriculum and the school was built in stages by the students and faculty themselves.

Project-based learning integrated traditional academic subjects like arithmetic, literature, and history with more hands-on construction applications. The Buxton kids built classrooms, pig pens, and greenhouses, and engineered imaginary cities, all working closely and cooperatively with their peers and their teachers, learning in close community.

The school was enormously successful. Difficult, sensitive children in particular seemed to flourish in Buxton's supportive, creative environment. "I was frequently asked how we achieved what some of the parents called our 'miraculous' results with many of the children," Geer-Sangster recalls in her self-published memoir, *A Grain of Mustard Seed*. "At first I merely replied that it must be because we provided a program fitted to their needs, but this did not seem to satisfy the questioners. One evening I found myself answering, 'Perhaps it is because instead of a negative attitude of suspecting a child of wrong-doing, we succeed in making him feel that we have faith in him, that we believe in his intentions and in his capacity to learn how to cope and to grow.'" Giving a child the benefit of the doubt was fairly radical in those days.

Geer-Sangster explains how she came by her gentle humanism: "I can see now that I was unconsciously expressing my own rebellion against my mother's too often negative treatment of me and again unconsciously, trying to put in to words some of the nurturing sunshine of my father's contrasting attitude."

In short, Ellen Geer-Sangster had a mean mom, and Buxton had been founded, in part, as redress for that mother wound.

Luckily, Ellen's father, Bentley Warren, was a soft touch who doted upon his daughter. A powerful Boston attorney and devoted Williams College alum, he bought 150 acres at the top of Stone Hill in Williamstown, Massachusetts, and built a summer estate/ working farm for his family. The main house was built of lathe and plaster, and the walls were insulated with hay. The barn and the corn crib were situated down at the end of a long path. The family took the long trip on rough roads by carriage to holiday there.

The farm on Stone Hill Road was a sanctuary for Ellen as a child. She spent lazy days in the hay loft of the barn, or hiding under the branches of the weeping willow that grew in front of the Main House. She had a pony named Tam Htab (Bath Mat spelled backwards), which she rode up Stone Hill Road, the oldest north-south road in the region, the same road George Washington himself stopped on in 1791 to admire the view of the Williamstown Valley before traveling on to Vermont to convince them to be the fourteenth state to join the Union.

Having outgrown the property in Short Hills, and under pressure from parents to open a high school, Sangster converted her family home into a boarding school, and in the fall of 1928 Buxton's first class was matriculated. Exactly fifty years later, in the fall of 1978, I arrived on campus for my freshman year. I was a late enrollee and a high-risk student: bright, sensitive, well bred, raised with all the advantages. Alas, modern civilization had robbed my home of many of the educational features formerly offered there: hard work and community chief among them. This had left me troubled, at odds with myself, misdirected, and prone to rebellion. In other words, I was perfect for Buxton.

Buxton, September 1978

"God, look at that color! You just want to spread it on toast like marmalade," my mother declared from the front seat, pointing at a tree ablaze with orange leaves. David drove silently, his sun-browned arm hanging out the window, a smoldering Gitanes in his fingers. I felt for the trees that were only half-turned with color, as if they couldn't make up their minds about autumn either.

The road led into a tiny New England town. A little white-steepled church and stately brick buildings lined a main street that was actually called Main Street. I snorted in the backseat.

"Is something funny?" Mom asked.

"Look at this place. It's . . . Grover's Corners," I said.

Mom exhaled a puff of annoyance and fell silent.

We drove down a wide road, lined with ivy-covered brick dormitories that belonged to Williams College. The dormitories' stately lawns were littered with stereo equipment, bikes, and laundry baskets—it was back to school for them too.

About a mile down from town was a long, low white building. "That's the Clark Art Institute," David said. "They have a lot of important Impressionist paintings there."

"Let's stop on our way out and have a peek, David," Mom said, already making plans for after I was out of the picture.

David turned off the main road onto Stone Hill Road, a small steep driveway. There was a small gabled house and a sign that read THE BUXTON SCHOOL, EST. 1928.

The road had pine trees on either side, and as we crested the hill a big yellow mansion came into view. It was square, with a red-tiled roof and green shutters and a broad front porch. Stone lions flanked the front walkway. It was quite grand, in a slightly ramshackle way. This was not Holden Caulfield's ivied Pencey Prep. This place was scruffy and weird.

Kids in ripped jeans and faded flannel shirts milled about on the flagstone patio in front of the mansion. A girl with tiny feathers woven into her curls and bells on her ankles spun like a barefoot Dervish, Indian-print skirt parachuting over her legs. A boy in an army jacket noodled on a guitar. It was like the '70s had never happened here and they were just stuck forever in the 1960s.

Already I could see that everything my mother had packed in my silver trunk was wrong. Brand-new dungarees and crisp, white T-shirts were *not* the thing. Old, faded, ripped, patched, cut-off, frayed jeans were. I felt toxic sweat seeping under my ribbed turtleneck.

"Oh God, Erika," my mother said, standing on the porch and looking out at the rolling mountains across from us. "What a view! You're such a lucky duck to be able to live in a place this beautiful." I did not turn to look.

A table was set up on the porch and behind it was a girl with a HELLO MY NAME IS sticker on her flannel shirt that I couldn't make out, it was so spidery and vinelike. She smiled at me. "Hi, I'm Sophie."

She had glossy, jet-black curls and a friendly lilt in her voice. "What's your name?"

"Erika Schickel. S-C-H . . . I-C-K . . . E-L." I repeated it with the same cadence my mother used when she made a dinner reservation, breaking up the Germanic surname into three parts. Sophie ran her hand down a mimeographed sheet. "Oh, wait . . . Erika Schickel! We're roommates! Our room is 'Attic.' Top floor. Follow the signs. So great to meet you! See you later!"

We entered the wide front hallway of the Main House. To the left was the dining hall, formerly a ballroom. The parlor to the right was a student lounge. The vast kitchen was perfect for feeding a hundred hungry teenagers at every meal. The Billiard Room, the place where gentlemen once retired for brandy and cigars after dinner, was now the faculty lounge.

We walked up the front-hall steps up to the second floor, which had once been the Geer family's living quarters. The master bedroom and children's rooms, large and graceful with French doors and fireplaces, now had Indian tapestries tacked up over antique hand-painted wallpapers, twin beds and bunk beds occupying every wall and corner.

We found another set of stairs behind a door in the hallway. These originally came up from the kitchen and were cramped and dark. We emerged into a narrow corridor with a series of doors. The third floor had been used for the servants' quarters, which now served as tight doubles. The rooms all had odd names: Mucket, Tucket, Peacock (named for the room's original hand-painted peacock wallpaper), and Fuckit for the room next to the constantly ringing dormitory pay phone. The largest of the dorm rooms was the attic—it was called Attic.

Attic was a long, low room that had once stored the family's steamer trunks and household overflow. It had four beds. Three were placed in alcoves created by the dormer windows. Those beds were cozy and sunlit. One bed was left unclaimed, the one shoved under the hard slant of the roof. I tried to sit on it, but had to curl over so as not to knock my head on the ceiling.

"You'll be snug as a bug in a rug here," Mom said.

She helped me get my bedding out of my trunk and we made up my bed with my brand-new sheets and the Hudson Bay blanket. When we were done it looked like a catalogue bed. I propped my ancient, crook-necked Snoopy doll on it and he listed sideways, then collapsed in a gray heap.

We toured the rest of the small campus. There was a long path that led from the Main House down to a long clapboard building called the Barn, which had once been an actual barn but now served as the boys' dormitory. Beside it was an old corn crib that had a proscenium stage built in it, with donated church pews for seating. It would be on that tiny stage that I would have some of my most meaningful experiences at Buxton, but peeking in the door with Mom, it just looked dark and musty.

We walked back up to the path toward the Main House, stopping to look at a modern classroom building. There wasn't much to this place. When we got back, David was sitting on the wall with two Styrofoam cups of coffee. They were going to be leaving soon.

Mom draped her arm around my shoulder, and I felt a familiar, instinctive recoil. Her touch felt possessory. A whiff of Estée Lauder rose from her cleavage, the smell of home. Then they were off. I watched their rental car drive down the hill until the brake lights brightened at the bottom of the driveway. Then they dimmed and disappeared into a turn, and just like that my mother was gone.

PART IV

THÉRÈSE

Buxton, Fall 1978

I unpacked my trunk, putting my things into my designated dresser. There was a welcome party for new students at the library, so I changed into the Patti Smith T-shirt I bought in London, thinking I might as well make a statement. I threw on a bunch of rubber bangles to be fancy. I asked some kids for directions to the library and one of them asked, "Are you Melodie Logan's little sister?"

"Who?"

"Melodie. You could be her doppelgänger."

"No."

"Cool. Library's that way."

The library was a two-story, red wood house on stilts with a big wraparound porch. The downstairs floor had an art studio on one side and a tiny library on the other. The upstairs was the private apartment of the headmaster, Benjamin C. Fincke, and his wife Magda.

The library itself was not exactly a "library," but a large living room with catalogued bookshelves. I went back out to the deck, pulled a soda out of a trash can filled with ice, and stood at the railing feeling awkward. There were knots of kids talking and hugging and acting like they were already best friends.

The crowd shifted and parted, and a tall, lithe girl emerged from its center. She was the living embodiment of the 1978 beauty ideal:

halter top, shimmery lips, silky blond hair swirling over tawny shoulders—a Venus in Olof Daughters clogs. She made a beeline for me and said, "It must be you!"

I stared at her in mute wonder.

"Everyone was telling me there was a freshburger here who looked like she could be my little sister, and it has to be you because holy shit I feel like I'm looking in a mirror. I'm Melodie."

Other than the fact that we both had longish, dirty-blond hair, we were not cut from the same bolt of cloth. She was silk to my sisal. "I'm Erika."

"You are adorable! Where are you from?"

"New York."

"City?"

"Yeah."

"Me too! What room are you in?"

"Attic."

"That was my first room too! I'm in Mucket. I'm a senior, so I know this place inside and out, and I'm going to keep an eye on you, little sister." She put her arm around me and proceeded to introduce me to everyone at the party.

Melodie made good on her promise and mentored me my freshman year. Her sophistication paired perfectly with my need to turn my exile at Buxton into a romantic adventure. She let me bum her English Ovals and she dispensed pearls of womanly wisdom like, "The perfect breast fits into a Champagne glass," which made me feel better about my modest bosom. She taught me to spray a cloud of perfume and pause a moment before walking through it. She confided in me that she and Tony Hanlon, my cynical, slightly scary freshman English teacher, were deeply in love.

Everyone knew that Tony and Melodie were a thing. Their romance was widely discussed and speculated upon, at least in the girls' dorm. Tony Hanlon looked like Lucifer, with fiery eyes and a dark, pointed beard. He took no shit from students but gave it in abundance. He called me "Schickelgruber," which I loved, not understanding the Hitler reference. Melodie had told me they were being honorable and waiting until she graduated in the spring, and then they would consummate their love.

None of this seemed particularly odd to me. I would sit in Tony's class and fantasize about him and Melodie up in his coffee-stained bachelor apartment in the Barn, reading poetry to each other as Tony's fluffy, green-eyed cat, Meowzer, looked on. I found, in the back of a dorm closet, a black-and-white photograph of Melodie at a beach, in a bikini, a towel in one hand and a pop bottle in the other. She was so beautiful and sophisticated, no wonder Tony would risk everything for her; her specialness was undeniable. I kept the photograph and have it to this day.

Buxton's faculty was largely composed of Williams graduates who had been hired straight out of college. Most of the teachers were in their early thirties to mid-forties and all lived on campus. Married faculty with children had modest houses on campus, but all the young, single, or childless teachers were dorm parents and lived with us in the Main House, Barn, and Gatehouse dormitories.

The only one who didn't live on campus was Patricia. Patricia was a generation older than most of the faculty, but twice as vigorous. She single-handedly ran the school's ambitious theatre program and college admissions office, did regular bed-checks, and taught us laggards to touch type. Patricia was all business, all the time, motoring around campus in her polyester pantsuits and blond coif, a pen lassoed around her neck, *tsk-tsking* lazy kids, yanking apart necking couples, laying down her own version of the law wherever she went. She had a house just over the Vermont border, and a Jeep that she drove like a getaway car down Stone Hill Road at the end of every day.

All told there were roughly one hundred souls housed on the small campus, day and night. I had never lived in a community before. The closest I had come was sleepaway camp, which I had hated for its compulsory bonding rituals that only made me feel more homesick. But Buxton was something else. This wasn't a month of hiking and sailing, this was long-haul living together. One hundred souls, most of whom were consumed with hormonal chaos, housed together on a drafty old summer estate, in the middle of pretty much nowhere with no television.

The setup was one in which students, cut loose from the context of their families, were free to reinvent themselves. Characters flourished, differences were accepted, oddities celebrated. At Dalton I had felt my worth was measured by my family's wealth, or the size of my Gloria Vanderbilt jeans. But at Buxton social worth appeared to be measured in terms of what a student could contribute to the antic culture of the school. Honesty, wit, gamesmanship, and hard work were all valued here, and suddenly I found I had some capital.

Whatever fun we had we made ourselves. On Friday nights we had Rec Committee, where the whole school would play a game together. There was "Mountain Day," where classes were canceled and the whole school went for a hike. In between there were skits and pranks, sing-alongs and sledding on lunch trays. In the girls' dorm we hung out on one another's beds, swapped records and clothes, did homework, told secrets, stole tampons.

I quickly saw that it was the smoking shed where the cool kids were, so I kicked my cigarette habit into high gear and spent most of my free time out there. Because the Main House was insulated with hay and would burn in under ten minutes, two smoking sheds were built, one behind the Main House and the other down by the Barn. Boys and girls mingled in those little plywood lean-tos, bumming smokes, telling jokes, ribbing one another, and sitting in each other's laps, weeping, fighting, and trying to stay warm through the long winter months. It was in the smoking shed that I truly learned to bullshit—that double-dutch where you jump in and out of conversational flow, drop a joke, or a startling fact, or a bon mot, then hand it off to the next bullshitter.

We lived on top of one another at Buxton, red-hot with unexplored sexuality, full of gossip and liner notes and misinformation about the world. Students dated each other like they were square dancing, and teacher crushes were just a natural part of the reel. We wanted it all: freedom, adulthood, connection, sex, our absent mommies and daddies.

We didn't get grades at Buxton. Grades were noted in our student files and kept secret until it was time to apply to college. Instead we got "progress reports"—long, written commentaries from each of our teachers at the end of each term that could cover anything from our grasp of algebra to our role in the Buxton community.

Though Ben Fincke was, for official purposes, Buxton's titular headmaster, the school was in fact run by an "Administrative Committee," comprised of the ten or so most senior faculty. This group shared executive power, worked with trustees, and decided who got warned, suspended, or expelled from the school, and for what. There didn't appear to be any guardrails at Buxton other than a set of "customs," which weren't written out in any student handbook that I ever saw. The three big customs were pretty standard: no drugs or alcohol, no plagiarism, and no smoking in nondesignated areas.

Fucking was frowned upon, but anybody who really wanted to, could. Kids sneaked out in the middle of the night, parkas and snow boots on over pajamas, getting it on in empty classroom buildings, on the stage with the curtains drawn tight, or in the surrounding woods and fields when the weather permitted. My dorm mother wisely took me to get fitted for a diaphragm my first semester at school, and I made good use of it at Buxton.

Buxton, Early Fall 1978

"Oh man, I gotta pee," Sophie said, drunk as shit, grabbing her crotch, teetering on the edge of the deep rut that ran along the side of the road. Even when wasted Sophie was ridiculously beautiful. She had pale skin and a tangle of dark, glossy curls that never, ever fell wrong. Sophie handed me the bottle, dropped her jeans, and squatted in the ditch, a stream of urine pounding into the gravel between her feet, sending up a fine mist in the chilly autumn air. A panel truck passed by, but the driver didn't seem to notice the girl on the side of the road with her butt hanging out.

"Soph, hurry up. Someone will see you."

"Nature, doll, it's *nature!*" She flung her arms wide toward the trees and almost fell out of her squat.

I had been at Buxton a little over two months and the school had already fully absorbed me. I had traded all my new clothes for everyone else's worn-out hand-me-downs. Now I had a pair of tai chi slippers and a peasant dress that I wore over a red union suit. My roommate had double-pierced my ears using a sewing needle and a wedge of apple, and I had feather earrings dangling from the new holes. My transformation from Dalton School city girl to Buxton bohemian was complete.

On Tuesdays we had morning classes, lunch, and work program, then we were free to go into town and wander, unsupervised, until dinnertime. Sophie and I had spent most of the afternoon on the golf course across the road from Buxton, drinking a fifth of vodka on the seventh green.

This was my first time drinking hard liquor. I had never been really, truly drunk, and I wasn't sure I liked it. It felt like being on a Tilt-A-Whirl—fast, barfy, and out of control.

Sophie did a fanny shake and yanked up her jeans. "I'm fucking freezing. Let's go to the Clark."

The Clark Art Institute was Buxton's closest neighbor. It sat at the bottom of Stone Hill Road. We used the field behind the Clark for girls' soccer practice. Even though I passed by it nearly every day and remembered my mother pointing at it when we first arrived, I had never gone inside. I was either late for practice or too tired, muddy, and hungry to go in and check it out.

We crossed the road and cut through a clutch of trees and paused to finish the bottle. I looked at the museum through the trees. It made no sense, that building. One half was a small, squat, white, Greco-Roman affair, with stuffy Doric columns and slippery marble front steps. It was attached by a covered bridge, a kind of glass-enclosed umbilical cord to the Mother Ship—its later addition, a modern, granite building, slung long and low into the wet Berkshire landscape.

"The Clark is cool," Sophie said, tying her shoe. She did it the kindergarten way: two loops tied together. "Did you know it is a bomb shelter?"

"Says who?"

"Says my dad." Sophie's father was a modern artist who lived in London and was very busy influencing British pop art with his defiantly figurative paintings. She had shown me a monograph of his work in the Buxton library and the paintings looked just like her: blooms of bright color, blocky and fierce, layered, saturated, and exciting.

"You're fucking with me."

"I am not. The Clark was built to survive an apocalypse.

Haven't you wondered why such an important museum is out here in bumfuck Williamstown, not located in New York or Boston, someplace where people can get to it and *see* the fucking art?" I hadn't actually wondered about that at all. "There's all this crazy major art in there, Winslow Homers, Renoirs, and Monets. It's a world-class collection. The Clark is really a vault that's made to look like a museum. If New York or Boston got nuked, the Clark would survive." I tried to imagine a postnuclear world filled with masterpieces. I supposed I would probably really appreciate some water lilies then. Sophie passed me the bottle. I tipped it to my lips and drank. "Listen, Schickel, you gotta pay attention, everything is connected."

I had no idea what she meant. "Totally," I said, handing her the bottle. "It's kind of creepy, don't you think? Warehousing art against the apocalypse?"

"Well, not *openly*. It's just meant to look modernist. I find the clean lines comforting after all that dishevelment at Buxton." Sophie drained the bottle and pitched it into the trees. "Let's go in. We'll be safe there."

I had heard rumors about Sophie. Her mother was dead or something. I thought in time, as our friendship deepened, I would draw her out about her mom, but I never got the chance. Sophie would be busted for drugs and sent back to London before Christmas. The last I heard of her was a rumor that she had painted her bedroom black.

A lot of us Buxtonites came from families like that: brilliant, troubled parents with big careers, big egos, old grudges, lots of press. They were the blue bloods and the nouveau riche, the scene-makers, and the scene-stealers. They were writing think pieces and reviewing one another, intermarrying, creating Escher-esque stepfamilies and winning Fulbrights. We had all been sent here to be trained for similar lives, and to be out of the way while our parents did their very important work.

Sophie and I emerged from the trees and strode over the tightly clipped front lawn. The late-afternoon sun glinted off the low front doors. Inside, the museum was not bunkerlike at all. It was warm, modern, and comforting. I had been in drafty, antique rooms for weeks at Buxton and this was like being at MoMA or someplace back home. I shrugged off my jean jacket and tied it around my waist, relaxing into the climate-controlled environment.

I got a little tin button from the admissions desk and squeezed it onto the neck of my dress and we headed down a long, carpeted corridor toward the first gallery. Large, tinted windows looked out onto the waning New England afternoon. Buxton felt far away.

We turned left into a large gallery. It was full of Impressionist paintings. Monets and Renoirs dappled the walls. Fetching skiffs bobbed in coastal waters, ladies danced under straw hats, water lilies bloomed.

The Clark owned all the greatest hits of Impressionism. The Sisleys and Pissarros were the originals of the posters that hung all over the girls' dorm. The Winslow Homers churned and roiled, and the Whistlers were soft as dew. I paused before each one, aware that reverence must be paid, while Sophie glanced quickly at them and moved on ahead of me. I raked my eyes over the surfaces, trying to pry meaning out of them, wanting to feel something in response. Then I saw something that made me stop.

On the north wall of the gallery hung a portrait of a girl. She was my age. She had long straight brown hair tied back into what my mom used to call a "some-up-and-some-down" hairdo. She wore a simple white dress with an oversized blue bow at the neck that was wider than her narrow, somber face. She looked like she was thinking about some pretty sad stuff. The whole world was in her eyes.

Something in me recognized her, yearned toward her calm innocence. The card below the painting told me it was a portrait of Thérèse Bernard, painted by Renoir in 1876.

What difference was there between me and her, other than time and place? I could have been Thérèse if only the last hundred years hadn't happened in the world and the last two years hadn't happened to me. I might have had her clean conscience, her smooth brow, and the protection of my parents had I not fallen into ruination, deceit, and delinquency. Had I been born not in Manhattan in the 1960s but in Toulouse in the mid–1860s—I might have been sweet and calm and yet lingering in the bosom of my family. Instead I had been called upon by my cultural moment to jump turnstiles, give blowjobs, shoplift bangles, and roll joints. I wasn't born a bad girl so much as I had had badness thrust upon me.

I longed to be walking in the picturesque French countryside, my eyes brimming with tears, faith, and hope, but instead I was sullen, brackish with self-loathing, resentful, and disobedient, wandering around on golf courses with flasks full of Smirnoff and eyes dimmed by Sinsemilla.

I don't know how long I stood there, but eventually I realized I had no idea where Sophie was. I found her in front of Manet's *Moss Roses in a Vase.* She leaned in to examine the brushwork and nudged the painting with her nose, which set off an alarm. We were marched out of the Clark by a security guard and trudged back up Stone Hill Road to school, the night closing around us like a vault. It had gone from chilly to cold.

The mansard roof of the Main House came into view. In the brightly lit windows we could see kids in the student lounge, goofing around as that week's student waiters set up the dining room for dinner. From that angle, it looked actually kind of warm and nice. Sophie and I stumbled into the dining hall just as the dinner bell was rung. I sat at Pilar's table.

Pilar was the head of the girls' dorm and taught Spanish. Her husband, Lou, taught math and music and they lived in the faculty apartment in the Main House. Pilar was Basque and had a long, thin face, baleful blue eyes, and one of the most spectacular noses I had ever seen. She seemed very old to me, though she could not have been more than thirty-five at the time. She possessed an ancient nobility, a calm benevolence that flowed from her small frame. I wanted badly to be close to Pilar and to know her better, so I was surprised when she asked me to come see her after dinner.

Pilar opened her door, holding a mug of tea. I could see behind her that the apartment she shared with her husband and daughter was in homey disarray. A big beaten couch was strewn with books and toys. There were coffee cups on the coffee table and music on the stereo.

"Let's have a seat out here." Pilar closed the door and led me to the stair landing, where we sat. "How are you feeling, Erika?" The way she said my name sounded like "Edikah." She had the kind of accent that added syllables.

"Fine, I guess." My guts tensed, something was up.

"Good. I will get right to the point. Perhaps you have noticed I have a rather large nose?"

I nodded, wondering if it was insulting to agree with her on this fairly obvious point.

"This nose of mine is a very sensitive instrument. It could not help but detect the smell of alcohol on your breath at dinner this evening."

I jolted with panic and surprise. I hadn't had a sip in hours. How could it still smell when I couldn't even taste it and I was no longer drunk?

"Erika, I also enjoy a drink from time to time. It is very relaxing, and there are many beautiful wines and cocktails to enjoy when you are an adult. But here at Buxton, unfortunately, we have customs. We must all agree to live by these customs so that we can all be safe. And one of them is that students are *not permitted* to drink alcohol. So even though, I know, it would be so lovely to have a drink, I must ask you please not to."

It was the most cordial busting I had experienced in a year of bustings. I had screwed up, and yet this woman wasn't angry. I wasn't being grounded, lectured, or sent away. Pilar was just looking at me kindly, setting me straight and giving me another chance. I looked into her eyes and saw love.

Maybe Sophie was right, maybe I would be safe here in Williamstown, far away from the blast zone of my nuclear family.

Buxton, Late Fall 1978

Because the dorm rooms in the old summer estate were so un-equal in size and amenities—some were tiny servants' quarters, others were the family's more luxuriously appointed bed-rooms and sitting rooms—there were no fewer than four room changes each year, so that nobody would get permanently stuck with one of the shittier rooms or a roommate they didn't like. Room change was a huge deal at Buxton. We would all sign up with our friends in the combinations we hoped for, and then Pilar and the other dorm parents would shuffle us into rooms in varying combinations. There was doubtless a certain amount of social engi-neering that went into the room assignments.

Amy Greenwell and I had signed up for a double room, but we got shafted into Mucket with Ali Rubinstein and Jacki Armstrong. It was a diabolically adept move on the part of Pilar and the other dorm parents, who knew that if left to our own devices, Amy and I would be likely to burn down the Main House within a week. We needed the sobering influence of these two naïfs to temper us.

Amy was a frizzed blonde with a chainsaw smile who seemed to wake up with her eyeliner already on. She was the lone punk in a sea of hippies and we spent quality time in the smoking shed discussing bands and celebrities. I traded her my Boy of London sweater for her Norma Kamali dress.

Jacki Armstrong was a sweet girl with a deviated septum that made her snore like a Zamboni at night, but otherwise, she was cool. But Ali Rubinstein was, to me, the 1970s in horrific detail, from her shiny sausage-curled hair to her Jane Fonda leotard and tights. She was the only child of a modern divorce, and over-indulged in every possible way. Her dad, Arthur Rubinstein (not *that* Arthur Rubenstein), composed movie scores, mostly for John Badham popcorners, which gave Ali reflected Hollywood cachet. Ali's mom, Carol, was a theatrical lighting designer. Arthur and Carol had met right down the road at the Williamstown Theatre Festival when they were kids doing summer stock, and it was from this overloaded cultural alliance that my new roommate had been spawned.

Ali hung an enormous New York City Ballet beach towel on the wall over her bed. When I countered with a sepia poster of Virginia Woolf's sad, pinched little face over my bed, Ali unfurled a poster of Roy Scheider in a shiny shirt playing Bob Fosse, Fosse hands and all. My silkscreen of Che Guevara was no match.

Ali's glamorous mother sent her extravagant care packages, big boxes exploding with magazines and Oreos, tank tops from Camp Beverly Hills, and Triscuits and wine cheese. My mother sent me wryly observed slices of her life scrawled on ironically tacky postcards.

Ali nursed from the nipple of a school-bus-yellow can of squeeze cheese and read about the celebrities her father had met at Oscar parties in the latest issue of *People*. I read a postcard my mother had sent from Tanglewood. She and David had gone to a concert there last weekend. She described sitting on the grass next to a young couple with a baby and the mother had a roach dangling from her lip. I had never heard the term "roach" and thought she meant this woman had an actual cockroach on her face. I was confused.

"Hey, Ali."

"Yeah?" she said, mid-cheese-squirt.

"How far is Tanglewood from here?"

"I dunno, not far. Like maybe half an hour, forty-five minutes?"

Mom and David had been half an hour away and hadn't come to see me? Even more confused, I tossed the postcard into the trash and went out for a smoke.

New York, Late Fall 1978

We got three "free weekends" each year, in addition to winter and spring break. That fall home weekend I stayed with Amy at her parents' apartment in the Dakota, the famous double-spired Central Park West apartment building where *Rosemary's Baby* had been filmed, home to many cultural icons, from Lillian Gish to Joe Namath.

The apartment was cavernous, with wide hallways, dark servants' quarters, dumbwaiters. Amy's room lay in utter disarray beneath vaulted ceilings. Sex Pistols, Clash, and Elvis Costello posters obscured dark scrollwork; a window seat was piled with laundry. Walk-in closets burst with Norma Kamali dresses and Betsy Johnson separates. Amy's mother had married the famous theatre producer Arthur Cantor, and Amy's room was a glorious illustration of the kind of gorgeous excess that parental guilt could yield.

Amy and I were sprawled on her bed with magazines when there was a knock on the door.

"Identify!" Amy called out.

"Max Cantor," said a low voice.

"You may enter," Amy commanded without looking up from her *Vogue*.

Max was Amy's stepbrother. He had graduated from Buxton the year before I got there. He was a brilliant, charismatic kid with the kind of energy that would probably get him an ADHD diagnosis. Max was tall, with alabaster skin under wiry dark hair. Max was innocently unkempt, as though he had not been taught the habit of bathing regularly. Nevertheless, he was stupidly handsome. He had a Nerf football in his long-fingered hands that he tossed and spun idly. He looked around the room, seeming to see nothing of much interest. Then he looked at us.

"Wanna smoke a joint on the roof?" Amy and I jumped up, stuck our feet in our shoes, and followed him out the door.

Max was obsessed with the Dakota and its history and gave us a guided tour. "Construction on the building began October twenty-fifth, 1880." Max punched the elevator button. "It was finished four years later, almost to the day on October twenty-seventh, 1884. It was designed by the same architectural firm that did the Plaza Hotel."

The elevator arrived, operated by a wizened black man who had the look of a burnished newel post.

"Clive, my man," Max said, high-fiving the guy, acting all Mr. Cool.

"Max-a-Million," the elevator guy said.

"Take us to the top, Clive."

"Straight up. All aboard!" We got on and Clive closed the outer door, then the inner gate. He gyrated an ornate brass handle that sent the elevator smoothly skyward. Amy and I reposed on a velvet bench beneath a smoked mirror, watching the floors of the Dakota shutter past the elevator's gate. Clive slowed the car expertly, so we didn't even feel the slightest jerk to a stop.

"Penthouse, Mr. Cantor."

The penthouse apartment had enormous double doors and deep carpeting in the hallway. Max led us over to a small service door and up a flight of stairs. Above the penthouse floor of the Dakota was a separate maze of narrow, whitewashed hallways, like you'd find on a ship. "These passageways were for the servants so they could circulate through the building without bothering the residents," Max explained, leading us down the winding corridors and finally choosing a door. He pushed it open and we stepped out into the brisk October night.

I had been on a lot of roofs in my time. I had danced on sizzling hot tarpaper from the Bowery to Park Avenue. I had seen pigeon coops and swimming pools, laundry lines, and Zen gardens, but I had never seen, or imagined, a roof like this one.

It was a city unto itself—a riot of vents and spires, flights of iron steps leading to different levels. The famous pointed dormers, which were fetching accents from the street, stood like small witch huts, arched and spandreled. Max led us over to a filigreed balustrade that lay like widow's lace against the rising moon.

Central Park spread before us like dirty burlap, its lights winking up at us through naked trees. We could see all of it, from Harlem to Fifty-Ninth Street.

"They named it the Dakota because it was as remote as the Dakotas; nothing else was here when it was built." Max led us into the windbreak of a turret and pulled a Sucrets tin out of his pocket. It held a number of pre-rolled joints. He lit one and took a deep drag, speaking as he held his hit. "The building was commissioned by Edward Clark, head of the Singer Sewing Machine Company. And where have we heard the name Clark, ladies?"

Amy rolled her eyes, too annoyed with her stepbrother to play his game.

"The Clark Art?" I offered, quietly, so afraid to be wrong.

"Bingo! You get a hit." He passed me the joint.

"So this building was built by the Clark Art guy?" Amy asked.

"No, the Clark Art was built by Edward's son, Sterling Clark, a dilettante who traveled around Europe with his wife, Francine, buying up art. In fact, the museum was originally supposed to be located on a property the family owned down the street from here, but at the last minute, it was moved to Williamstown."

"So it wouldn't get nuked," I said, remembering what Sophie had told me that day outside the Clark.

Max's eyes snapped on me. "Exactly."

"What the fuck, Max? Now you've got my friend on board with your paranoid shit?"

I almost couldn't bear how attractive I found Max. He was exactly the kind of boy I liked. I was drawn to teenage Dungeon Masters and conspiracy theorists with keen, encyclopedic intelligences, low GPAs, and deep brown eyes—boys so burdened by their own brilliant complexity that they dedicated their days to killing as many brain cells as possible in a misguided attempt to suffer less. I alone understood their pain and shared their interests. I could meet them on the field of their dreams, and I felt called to enact their fantasies with them.

Max sensed he had my attention and couldn't stop. "They say the penthouse apartment that Big Daddy Clark lived in had floors inset with sterling silver in honor of his son, Sterling. I am still waiting to get confirmation on that from my sources, however."

"Max, I'm freezing my ass off," Amy said, hopping in place, flicking her cigarette butt over the edge of the railing.

"The joint was just mood enhancement, ladies. It's not what we came for. Follow me." Max led us around a long, winding path that described the U of the building. He turned his lecture to all the famous people who had lived at the Dakota, from Leonard Bernstein to Rudolf Nureyev, as we went up and down tiny staircases, through passageways, over to the western arm of the building and to the inner balustrade that had a gut-churning view down to the courtyard below.

All of the apartments in the Dakota were laid out so the living rooms were given the park and city views, and the service rooms looked over the courtyard. It was just after eight and we could see the shapes of people moving around in their kitchens, getting dinner ready or cleaning it up. Lives stacked into a grid, each with its own flickering blue light, everyone caught up in the mundane cycle of daily life. I wondered what could possibly be of interest here, but it didn't matter because Max had come up right behind me.

"See where that gutter runs?" Max pointed to a vertical pipe running down the inside of the building. I felt the heat of him down my back, and every inch of my skin burst into goose bumps. "One window down from the roof and three windows left from the gutter." He put his head close to mine and pointed over my shoulder.

I could smell him, a bouquet of Sinsemilla and Camel straights, Shetland sweater and boy funk. I tried to keep my heavy breathing from becoming audible. I focused my eyes and counted over and down to a kitchen window, where a female figure stood at the sink, looking down. I couldn't see her hands or face, as her long, dark hair was in the way, but clearly, she was rinsing dishes and couldn't push it back. A shadowy figure moved around in the room next to her, but the lights weren't as bright in that room; I couldn't make out who it was.

"Max," Amy moaned, "this is stupid, you're already in trouble with the building for this shit."

Max handed me a small pair of binoculars. "Here, get a really good gander."

I pressed the cold oculars to my eyes and dialed in the focus. The person in the dining room had shoulder-length hair, but I couldn't tell if it was a man or a woman, until he walked into the kitchen, carrying some dishes.

"Do you see?" It was a man. He put down the dishes on the counter beside the sink, reached over, and pushed the woman's hair out of her face. It was a tender gesture and I could feel its warmth even at that distance. The man stood behind the woman and put his arms around her, stepping into the light over the sink, and I saw that he was tall and narrow-framed, with shoulder-length, shaggy hair and round glasses. The details rearranged themselves suddenly into iconography, and I understood who I was looking at—it was John Lennon and Yoko Ono. Max was standing behind me, his breath in my ear. This, *this* was the thing I wanted: to be that close with someone that deep, that warm, that brilliant, even if our love was as misunderstood and maligned as John and Yoko's. I would give anything for that.

Buxton, Fall 1978–Spring 1979

I got a boyfriend almost as soon as I got to Buxton. Jonas Dambrowski was a slouchy senior with a curtain of dirty-blond hair. He wasn't a hippie like the other boys. He liked Chick Corea and Jean-Luc Ponti, not the Dead. I liked that he wore oxford-cloth shirts with the sleeves cocked back, like my dad.

I didn't so much fall for Jonas as I let him claim me. A boyfriend was a good social strategy for a new girl.

I had never had a real boyfriend before. I felt lucky. I would sit on Jonas's lap in the student lounge, and it was as Jonas's girlfriend that I got to know the cooler upperclassmen.

The first time I sneaked out of the dorm was scary. The campus looked like a negative in the moonlight and the snow made the silence clog my ears as I crunched down the path toward the Barn. I could see Jonas standing outside the theater, waiting for me.

Jonas took my hand and led me up the steps. He was on Litz, the theatrical lighting crew that all the cool senior boys were on. Patricia didn't let girls on Litz because she said lifting heavy equipment could tilt our uteruses.

We pushed the door open and stepped into the darkness. Jonas called out, "Is anyone in here? Speak now or forever hold your penis!" You never knew what other Buxton couples you would run into in the middle of the night.

We did it on top of the old curtain folded up in a dusty corner of the Green Room.

Sex with Jonas was okay, but he was unsatisfied. According to him I was supposed to be having orgasms, but I had no idea what that was or how to do it. It didn't matter to me, I loved fucking and I just wanted to be close to him.

We would separate before dawn and I would take the lonely path back to the dorm, knowing I would be beat for class in the morning. What I wanted was to spend the whole night with Jonas, wound up safe in his arms. I wanted to wake up and have breakfast with him like adults. As fall semester ground to its conclusion we began to plot how we might spend a night together over winter break.

Jonas's friend Andy Cardiff gave us our chance. His parents were away on a ski vacation and Andy invited us to spend the night in the guest room of his Fifth Avenue apartment. Andy was a curly-headed, pasty junior with a weird, almost slow-motion way to him. His hands were a little too gentle, his fingernails too pointy and translucent, his pale eyes followed me a little too closely. I didn't like him, but this was too good of an opportunity to pass up.

Plus, Andy Cardiff's parents had a doozy of a pad—big windows overlooking Central Park, a refrigerator stuffed with Chanukah left-overs, and a medicine chest full of pharmaceuticals. Andy offered us beer and Valium. I had never tried Valium. Jonas told me it would be better if I took two, so I did.

We sat in the living room, drinking beer, waiting to feel some-thing, when Andy asked if he could talk with Jonas privately. They disappeared into the kitchen for a minute to leave me sitting in the window seat, looking out at Central Park, wondering when I would feel something.

I leaned against the cold windowpane and could see the top of the Metropolitan Museum of Art and the adventure playground next door where my mom took me to play as a kid, and I thought about my family. When I got home from school this time Mom and David had made me a special dinner and even poured me a glass of wine. My sister was off on a sleepover somewhere and it was just the three of us. They were excited to hear all my school news, and David, who had once upon a time gone to the Putney School in Vermont, told some boarding-school stories of his own and we all laughed and had a nice time. Mom had gotten my favorite sand and jelly cookies from Greenberg Bakery for dessert. It felt so good to be home.

Then they broke their news: they would be moving to Santa Fe in the spring.

They explained that they needed to get out of the city, live more cheaply, and be somewhere they could both write. They were taking my sister with them and leaving me on the East Coast with Dad, whom I would stay with on future home weekends and vacations from school.

"You're just going to leave me? Just like that?"

"Erika, you can come stay with us on vacations and in the summer. What's the difference if you're in Santa Fe or New York?"

They had made up their minds.

Jonas came back into the living room and sat beside me. He kissed me deeply. I was surprised by his uncharacteristic emotional intensity. He stopped and looked at me seriously.

"Andy has asked me to ask you a question."

"Okay."

"He would like to join us in bed tonight."

It was such a prim way to put it, I thought, but I knew what he meant. Jonas and I had discussed having a three-way—a topic dear to his heart, but I was not inclined. I was still new enough at sex that dealing with one guy was enough for me. And even if I did ever want a three-way, it would certainly not be with Andy fucking Cardiff.

"I don't think I want to. Is that okay?"

"Are you sure?" Jonas looked at me and rubbed my knee, giving me a chance to think about it a little more.

"Yeah, I just want to be with you."

Looking a bit put out by my avowal of fidelity, Jonas took his hand off my knee. "Okay, if that's what you really want. I'll tell Andrew." He went back to the kitchen and after a minute the two of them came out and everything felt totally cool. I was starting to feel a little swimmy and odd. The pills were coming on.

We drank beer and listened to Chick Corea until I felt too weak to stay upright. Jonas helped me stagger down the long hallway toward the guest room. The Valium made me feel like my body was filled with dense liquid. I had never felt so heavy. I sloshed and lurched and spilled myself onto the bed.

The bed rocked like a boat and I said, "Jonas, anchor me to the world." And he laid himself completely on top of me. The spin slowed, and I felt safely ensconced in my boyfriend's warmth and scent. I closed my eyes and succumbed to the pleasure of him kissing and stroking me. It felt like his hands and mouth were everywhere at once; in my hair, on my neck, on my thighs, he was kissing me and sucking on my toes at the same time.

Wait. My eyes blinked open and there was Andy Cardiff, completely naked, leering up from the foot of the bed, pale and moist. He was sucking on my toes, moving his hands up and down my legs, softly, then firmly pushing them apart.

"Hey!" I said, but Jonas shushed me.

"Wait!" I said louder, but my voice sounded like it was coming from the next room. Jonas shushed me again, softly, told me it was okay, I should just relax, he loved me, he loved me. Andy crawled slowly up my body and stuffed his long pink cock into me. Jonas held my hands over my head. Somebody was saying, "No, no, no, no." It sounded like me.

Buxton, January 1979

My mother sent me a tacky postcard from Santa Fe. It was a picture of a cowboy riding a Jackalope: half jackrabbit, half antelope. Mom and David had arrived safely in their new house, an adobe on Garcia Street. My sister was enrolled in a local middle school.

My mother has jack-eloped, I thought as I filed the postcard with the others in the cigar box in my silver trunk.

I fought off waves of homesickness. I missed the weirdest things about her: the deep, crunchy sound as she searched for her keys at the bottom of her purse, the smell of the exhaust from her Electrolux, her lipstick print on napkins. I would never have any of that again.

At least I have Jonas, I thought.

Then Jonas dumped me.

Pittsfield, February 1979

The nurse said I had a call. I got out of bed and shuffled down the hospital hallway toward the pay phone, clutching my gown closed behind me.

The receiver dangled and spun slowly, like a snake hanging from a tree. I was afraid to pick it up and hear a hiss on the other end. Instead, my mother's voice was warm. "Tell me what happened, sweetheart." She was calling from New Mexico, but she sounded like she was still in Manhattan.

"I don't know, Mom."

Jonas said that because he was heading into his final semester, he owed it to himself to try to date some hotter girls whom he felt he really had a shot at now.

Everything that I didn't know how to feel about the loss of my mother, I transferred to this feckless, toxic boy. It opened up a chasm of grief inside of me that scared me so much, I ended up wedging myself between the toilet and the tub in the dormitory bathroom. Pilar gathered me up and took me to the safety of her apartment. She made me a mug of tea.

"What's going on, Erika?"

"I don't know. I just feel so fucking hopeless." I started crying again.

"Would it help you to get you the hell out of this place for a night?"

"Sure, but where would I go?"

"We can take you to the hospital in Pittsfield just for the night, just to get some rest. How does that sound?" The idea of a good sleep on cool sheets without three other girls farting in the dark beside me sounded like heaven. Pilar drove me to the hospital and checked me in. I hadn't really expected my mother to call.

"Tell me, Erika, are you suicidal?"

To hear that word, "suicide," said out loud by my mother gave my actions a weight I'd never intended. The thought of killing myself hadn't really crossed my mind. I may have mentioned wanting to die when I was scrunched up next to the toilet plunger, but it was only in order to accurately describe the level of pain I was feeling. But I didn't have a *plan*. How would I kill myself at Buxton in the middle of winter anyway? Drill a hole in Ben's Pond and jump in? Throw myself in front of a snowplow? Overdose on Midol and No Doz? Even I knew my breakdown fell solidly in the "cry for help" category, but as usual my mother assigned me a destructive power that felt disproportionate to the situation.

"Talk to me, Erika, tell me what's going on." Mom's voice was creamy with concern.

"I don't know, everything is just . . . hard." It wasn't that I loved Jonas so much. I knew he was a dick. But the loss of his regard was physically unbearable to me. It inflamed my insides, made me feel like I was being tossed off a cliff. He had loved me, then he stopped. Why? What could I do to bring him back? What was wrong with me? I had given him everything. Why did this hurt so much?

"Hard in what way, honey?" Mom was trying, I wanted to give her something to work with, but I knew I would never in a million years tell her what had happened at Andy Cardiff's house.

"Just, Jonas dumped me and winter sucks, and I miss home."

"Oh, sweetheart, I wish I could be there, so I could put my arms around you." My mother's words curdled in my ear.

"Well, you're not."

A long silence.

"Has anyone reached your father?" Mom's voice had cooled and I knew exactly why; she was miffed I wasn't allowing her to perform the Kabuki of caring for me, and now she was pissed. Just like that, we had shifted away from each other, back to our usual distance.

"I don't know. I think Dad's in L.A."

"Yes, well, I'm sure Dick is taking care of Dick. He'll show up when he can find the time."

I knew Dad would pick up his messages in the morning when he got home from whatever date he was on. I would hear from him soon enough.

The hospital hallway was chilly, and I didn't have socks on. I had stuck my bare feet into my Sorel boots. I could feel grit from Buxton embedded in the felt liners. I needed to get back to school as soon as possible. When I'd said yes to the hospital, I thought it would be all chocolate pudding and magazines; instead it was my ass hanging out of a gown in a drafty hallway and having my temperature taken every hour. Pilar was coming back in the morning. I was just here to "rest." I had had my vitals checked but I received no medical treatment, not that I needed any. I was just a very sad girl. I hated the outside world. I wanted to go back to Buxton.

"The school has a referral for a therapist in Williamstown, who you will be expected to see," Mom said.

"Oh, great."

"It is a condition of you remaining at Buxton. These are not my rules, but I do happen to agree with them."

"Fine."

"Are you fine? Are you going to be all right, Erika?"

"Sure. I am just really tired is all."

"Things will look better in the morning." She shifted into her Mommy voice.

I felt my nose sting with tears. "I know."

"Get some rest. You can call me anytime. Do you know that, Erika? I am always here for you."

"Okay," I said. "Bye."

In all my life my mother has never said "I love you" as a sign-off, so I didn't wait for it. I just hung up the phone.

February 3, 1979

Dear Jill,

I was too shocked by the news contained in our phone conversation of the other night to comment on anything but the immediate crisis. About that, I have done what I can—spoken to Erika, her teacher and her doctor and made arrangement to spend next week-end with her at school. She seems as well as can be expected, if still shaken. Like you, I am encouraged by the school's warm and ready response, and by our daughter's sense that she is loved and cared for by friends there.

But in conversation with Erika herself and the others, I have begun to formulate some thoughts about our responsibilities in this sad and really awful business. Until I have spent some time with Erika and with Pilar and the doctor I do not wish to make any definitive statements, but I cannot forbear to say that your failure to communicate with me as early as possible after the events of last week is both unspeakable and unforgivable. Practically you have known since last spring where I was working. Even if, in panic, you might momentarily have forgotten my whereabouts, surely there was time to remember, or to call my office at *Time* which always knows my whereabouts. Given all this I don't for a moment buy the notion that I was too difficult to reach to make it worth your while. My belief is that you deliberately and maliciously kept me in the dark in order to present a picture to Erika of a father that was not only absent but entirely uncaring. Now you have no obligations to me, and if, somehow, it serves your needs to keep your long-standing anger with me at the boil, it is of no concern to me. But you are doing damage to our children—Jessica as well as Erika—and that I cannot in conscience tolerate.

To wit: on the phone you somehow seemed to indicate that it is the lack of final divorce papers that is upsetting the kids. That may be a factor and, indeed, I've been surprised that you did not move last fall to complete them. I'm as eager as you to cross that final T. But that is not what is most deeply the matter at the moment. The trouble is that relations between you and Erika have deteriorated to such a point that she literally cannot bear the thought of living in your home with you. I say this not out of malice, and with a full understanding that in the best of circumstances relations between mothers and teen-age daughters tend to be difficult. I say it also with a full understanding that my own long absences of the last three years have contributed to her feelings of abandonment, of being unloved. Nevertheless, there are very intense feelings that can only be described as bewildered anger there, and they are not directed at me. But yet these feelings do, obviously, color relationships between Erika and me, rob me of her presence in my life. They also, and more importantly, do her terrible damage, damage which I feel may already be irreparable.

Very simply, we must do something. I do not know what it should be specifically, but surely it must begin with a cessation of obvious hostilities between you and me. If ours was without question a bad marriage, ours is surely among the worst divorces and I cannot see why that should be so at this late date. But no matter. We are both strong people and, I should think, entirely capable of bearing grudges on to the grave. Which would be all right, even perversely amusing I suppose, if this habit did not do harm to innocent persons whom both of us love very much.

We must find some way of not merely working together in crises, but of creating for the children a feeling that they were at least born of affection between us and nurtured through their early years in a similar spirit. Surely where they are concerned we can, for their consumption, fake some feeling of mutual respect, not use them (however unconsciously) to lay off the bad feeling we appear to still harbor for one another. I have my private and none-too-flattering judgments of your mode of life at the moment (which, by the way, have nothing to do with your living arrangements; indeed, by all reports David has conducted himself as I would hope I would in similar circumstances, as an affectionate, concerned and thoroughly decent stepfather, for which he has, if he does not know it, my respect and gratitude). No, my judgments center around an attitude toward life that is communicated to the kids on your part, an attitude that finally comes to focus on me as an exemplar of values and behavior of which you disapprove. I do, indeed, resent this scapegoating, as I resent the scapegoating of Erika that has gone on in recent years. Jill, if you are unhappy, we are not the authors of your unhappiness, merely the symbols of it. You can no longer hurt me with this, but you are hurting Erika, and you must find some way to refocus your energies, must lift from her the burden of guilt, of disastrous self-imagery, of almost hopeless expectations that she carries.

I write in anguish and confusion. And I do not write to hurt or to judge. There has been too much of that. I urge you to respond in kind. Get rid of whatever bile you still harbor, and then let us be done with it. Forever. Let us cease to judge one another, let us above all cease to lay these judgments implicitly and explicitly on our children. Let us posit good will, whatever our differences in expressing it, toward the children [and] toward one another when it comes to them. Jill, I love them, you love them, let us for god sake come together to help them, to let them grow strong and straight and able to realize all their gifts. I will do anything to bring this about, and after I have spent some time with Erika next week I will, I know, want to spend some time with you. I have the most urgent sense that we must now act to tear down the animosity of the last three years, that the message Erika was sending both of us was, in the final analysis, a plea for just such an act. I am genuinely open to any and all suggestions as to what we should do next, and I hope you understand that anything I put forward will be in the hopes of finding a similar spirit in you. Please, let us stop the pain of our children, and if we can stop the pain between us, then so much the better. The emotion is a waste of what remains of our lives and carries with it a threat to the two lives we hold most dear.

Faithfully,
Dick

Buxton, Spring 1979

The long, gray winter finally yielded to spring, and the air on Stone Hill became fresh and green, threaded through with tantalizing wisps of heat. I felt oddly bestirred and unfettered that day.

It was Saturday and the dorms were empty. Everyone had gone straight down to Spring Street after lunch to buy records at Toonerville Trolley and hang out at Colonial Pizza. The long, dark winter felt like a bad dream and I had awakened into a world that was all mine.

My boots crunched on salt and slush and loosened chunks of gravel on the driveway heading up to the Main House.

I took the access road up to Pine Alley, two rows of majestic trees that bordered the northern end of the scruffy campus.

At the top of the hill, on the edge of the woods, I could look down at campus. The Upper Field was still brown, the long grass matted with melted snow. Soon the fields would sprout their fresh green mattresses and couples would disappear into the deep sedge on warm Saturday afternoons.

I could see some kids on the path to the Barn, but I couldn't make out who. The theater, the New Building, the Music Shed—all were dumpy old lumps in the middle of the muddy, boggy campus.

The day was warm and the walk uphill, so I peeled off my Shetland sweater and tied it around my waist and rolled back the cuffs of my flannel shirt.

The road bent into the woods and I was surrounded by 150-foot-tall trees: pines and maples, eastern hemlocks and spruces. It was like stepping into liquid, to be surrounded by these woods, so damp and pungent, drippy and flickering with light and the silver twitter of birds. I had been there earlier that morning on Work Program, hacking up a fallen tree with the wood crew. I came upon the sawdusted site and it looked like a massacre had taken place.

The school owned these trees and, in the wake of the gas crisis, had converted to wood-burning stoves for the campus's heat. Chad Walker, in addition to coaching girls' soccer and teaching American history, ran Work Program.

Work Program was an ambitious undertaking. The school had but one handyman and a small kitchen staff that took weekends off. All the school's maintenance and the weekend cooking were done by students. We had kitchen crews and cleaning crews, crews for putting plastic wrap over the windows in the fall, and crews to remove it in the spring. We had an apple-butter crew and a granola crew, we had a crew to sew patches on our jeans. We had crews for hauling wood, splitting wood, and stacking wood. Though I loudly complained that it was completely bogus to make our parents pay $8,000 a year so we could basically be used as slave labor, I secretly liked Work Program. I discovered I relished hard, physical labor. The only labor I had performed growing up in Manhattan was jamming trash bags down the narrow throat of our building's garbage chute or chasing my father's errant tennis balls.

I liked the wood crews the best, even though Chad was a total douchebag. I learned that anything was possible with gloves. I loved wrestling fallen logs from the undergrowth, dragging them out where Chad could get at them with his chainsaw, tossing logs down the line of crew members into the back of Chad's truck, trying to dent the bed with the logs, watching the pile mount.

My favorite crew of all was wood splitting. I had always been good at hitting baseballs, and wood splitting was not much different. I would set a round log on its end, locate the fissure, the log's weak spot, and swing the ax over my head, letting the heavy head describe a delicate arc down to the naked face of the wood. There is a moment of grace in wood splitting, when you can feel the crack in the log pulling the tip of your ax in, and when the blade meets the fissure the log just pops apart with a bark.

I paused to peel off my flannel shirt, down to my wife beater, and admired my pale, muscular arms. I was five-foot-ten and 143 pounds of milk-fed, pulping, adolescent fury. I fucking *dominated* wood splitting, but did Chad ever notice? His dickishness toward me was just as bad on Work Program as it was in girls' soccer. In practice he stood with his par-bald head cocked to the side, his porn stache making him look like a little Pekingese dog, yapping encouragement to the girls he liked or wanted to fuck. Chad always played favorites and always had one special girl. I knew I was a giant galoot and lazy on the field, and I guess that's why he hated me. I wasn't as cute or quick as some girls, but I *owned* wood splitting, and yet he ignored me there too.

I followed the path north until it petered out, then I just bush-whacked my way up the hill. Sooner or later I would reach the top of something. I came to a wire fence—three horizontal filaments demarcating the end of Buxton land and the beginning of the rest of the world. I parted the wires and slid between them. The trees seemed to thin in the distance. The woods felt lighter. The breeze called a different note. I walked up and out of the woods.

The trees opened into a verdant pasture. The sun was in full dazzle, burning away the last wispy clouds, and a breeze whipped the air clean. The cow pasture stretched out like an eiderdown, green and lumpy with cow pies. In the distance a few Holsteins grazed.

I unlaced my boots and peeled off my damp socks. My feet emerged, moist and pale as larvae, the weave of my socks imprinted on the tops of my arches. I broke into a run out into the prickly pasture. The wind was swift, the damp, un-mown grass sliced wetly between my toes, the sun embraced me in its warmth. I put my arms out wide and twirled.

At the center of the field stood a cluster of trees and a large rock. I hiked over to it and summited the boulder. I was now at the highest point on Stone Hill, and my whole world lay before me. Where I once used to gaze out of my mother's twenty-fifth-floor apartment window and see tall ships sailing up the East River, now all I could see was the Clark Art, that fine-arts bomb shelter, with the girls' soccer field behind it. The arena for my autumnal athletic humiliations under Chad's disdainful eye looked like a crumpled brown napkin from up here.

I felt another whirl of joy spiraling out of me and this time I couldn't hold it in. I shouted from the top of my rock and the wind scrubbed my voice away.

I wanted this day on my skin, so I pulled off my sweaty undershirt and felt the delicious bite of wind on my nipples. Wanting more, I cast a careful look around just to make sure it was just me and the cows, and I unbuttoned my jeans and stripped out of them and my underwear in one step. I stood naked on the rock and felt the wet Berkshire wind on my skin like a slap. I was skinny-dipping in air.

I jumped down from the rock and streaked across the field, laughing and screaming as loudly as I could. I cartwheeled and belted out show tunes. I was at the center of my own strange, corny, lonely MGM musical. It was *Oklahoma!* meets *Oh! Calcutta!* and *The Sound of Music*. This, this was the life for me: romantic and free and wildly cinematic. I promised myself I would choose only adventure. I would live boldly, I would have many lovers, I would make art, and I would live a life worthy of biography. And why not? I wondered as I spun myself into a panting heap on the grass. I was the critic's magical daughter, the girl who could turn slush into spring and spin the rough straw of abandonment into narrative gold.

PART V

INFINITE ODYSSEY

Santa Fe, Spring 1979

It sure doesn't look like much from the air, I thought as I looked out the airplane window at Albuquerque, New Mexico. It looked smooshed and gray against miles and miles of beige desert. This was the state in which my mother, sister, and stepfather-figure were now living. The line sounded glib and tossed-off. It had just the right amount of *je ne sais fuck-you* with a soupçon of world-weariness thrown in.

I needed to greet my family with a strong opener. They hadn't seen me since Christmas, not since my hospital stay. I wanted to project confidence. I had finished my freshman year and I wanted to show my mother how strong and grown-up I was. I would stride confidently down the jetway and she would think, *Wow, Erika has really matured. She's one sophisticated traveler.* And then I'd hit her with it: *Well, it sure doesn't look like much from the air,* and Mom would get it, because she was always knocking things, like pan pipes, which she said made her sinuses hurt and I totally got it. She'd think it was funny and we'd laugh together, she would put her arm around my shoulders and we would go home for Pinot Noir and cigarettes on the patio.

I was excited for the summer. It had been a long freshman year. Back in the depths of winter, a spokesman from the Infinite Odyssey outdoor adventure program for teens had come to Buxton to give us a slide presentation.

Winter madness had overtaken the school. Snow was piled up in six-foot gray drifts, boots never dried, theft ran rampant in the dorms, couples broke up, and everyone carried a roll of toilet paper to class to soak up the river of phlegm from the sinus infection that we'd all been passing around since November. There was nothing to look forward to except more cold and mud until spring, which, by the look of the barren snowfield outside the windows, might never arrive.

The Infinite Odyssey salesman filled the dining hall with summer. Panoramic views of majestic mountains and burbling streams clicked past, snagging my freezer-burned heart. There were images of teenage Odysseans cavorting in lakes and disporting in fields of bright alpine flowers. They grinned beneath their baseball caps, their arms slung around each other's shoulders in easy camaraderie. The boys were lanky and cute, and the girls' legs looked trim and tanned in their short shorts.

The salesman explained that the centerpiece of every Infinite Odyssey expedition was the solo. Kids were left alone in the woods for three days to practice basic survival skills and journey deep within their own souls, with only a journal to entertain them. I was so sick of being surrounded by people that three days alone in the woods sounded like heaven. I was primed by the Thoreauvian promise of a mystical encounter with a muskrat. I knew that if I went on this trip, I would surely have an epiphany of some kind in which the meaning of it all—all my deep loneliness and chronic yearning, my propensity for making people mad—would be explained and healed and I would emerge from the woods a strong, whole girl at last.

What I really wanted to do that summer was spend it all in Santa Fe with Mom and David, but Mom said that I was much too emotionally dangerous for her to be around for that long. She just wasn't up for it. Dad was preoccupied with his burgeoning Hollywood filmmaking career and was willing to pay any price to have me out of his hair for the summer. He happily wrote the check for Infinite Odyssey. I was to spend a month in Santa Fe with Mom and David, and then push off into infinity.

There they were, at the bottom of the jetway, David in jeans, a crisp Oxford shirt, and a pukka-shell necklace, looking tanned and happy. Mom was 1979-Southwest groovy in an ankle-length, tiered skirt and a soft denim shirt, her waist cinched by a belt with an enormous silver-and-turquoise buckle. I was struck anew by how beautiful my mother was. She seemed to glow as she smiled and waved at me.

I came down the jetway like Lindsay Wagner in a Samsonite commercial, my blond ponytail swinging behind me. Just before I arrived in my family's embrace I launched my line: "Well, it sure doesn't look like much from the air." I followed it up with a dark, knowing chortle. My mother's smile erased; her face snapped shut.

"Lovely to see you too, Erika." She embraced me stiffly. I turned, spooked, to David, who pulled me into a bear hug. "Yeah, the only thing Albuquerque has going for it is a plethora of bad postcards," he said. David and I had a long competition trying to outdo each other with the ugliest postcard in the rack: parking lots, shad bakes, jetliners parked on tarmacs. He took my bag out of my hand. "Wait'll you see Santa Fe, though. It really is the Land of Enchantment."

Mom and David had bought a brand-new yellow Le Car. I was impressed. I didn't think they were new-car people. It had "Le Car" written on the side in chubby black letters.

"I think we should switch the letters," David said, throwing my duffel bag into the tiny hatchback, "so that it says, 'El Car.'" I laughed. Mom stayed silent.

In the car David and I bantered. He promised to teach me how to drive El Car. We did some corny shtick together. I loved David Vale; he was funny and easy to be around. He liked jokes and stories and one-liners. He would do a bit at the dinner table where he would stuff his napkin in his mouth and speak in a shrill British accent like Queen Elizabeth on the wartime wireless.

Mom's posture, always regal, was ramrod, and she stared with pronounced absorption out the window at the desert landscape, silently telegraphing her displeasure. Meanwhile, David gave me the hard sell on their new, improved life. "You are going to love the house, Erika. It's an old adobe and if you walk to the end of our street you can see the Sangre de Cristo Mountains, which are spectacular at sunset."

"It sounds gorgeous. I'm *dying* to see it. It's so beautiful here!" I enthused, hoping to douse the ember that was clearly smoldering up my mother's ass.

We were halfway between Albuquerque and Santa Fe when Mom cranked around in her seat and, over the tops of her big sunglasses, stared me down.

"You really play fast and loose with people, don't you, Erika?"

I felt the autonomic heat and thud rise through my body that I always felt when Mom was about to let me have it.

"Do you not care how you make people feel, or were you just trying to hurt me specifically?"

"Jill..." David said.

"No, David, I have something to say." She turned back to me. "You do know what I'm talking about, don't you, Erika?"

I waited.

"Okay, then I'll quote you: 'This place sure doesn't look like much from the air.' Where did you learn to talk to people like that? Not from *me,* certainly." I felt myself shut down and become placid and inert as a turtle in its shell.

"I'm sorry," I mumbled.

"What's that?"

"I'm *sorry*," I said, a little louder.

"Okay," she said. She gestured to me, palm down, like she was patting the air in front of her, her red nails glinting in the New Mexico sunset. "This is where we live, this is *our* life, not Dick's, and I won't have you crapping all over it. You're on *my* turf now, and you play by *my* rules. If you break my rules, then your ass is grass and I'm the lawn mower. You got it, kid?"

"Got it," I said.

"Good."

Santa Fe, Colorado, and Utah, Summer 1979

It was a long, tense month in Santa Fe. I had tried hard to make up to Mom for that first, horrible gaffe at the airport. I tried to be helpful around the house. I remembered to ask her about herself, and I put my shoes to the side instead of kicking them off into the middle of the room. I marched down to the Social Security office and got a Social Security number, then I marched into town and got a job scooping ice cream at the Swensen's on Water Street. But there was no hiding the fact that I wasn't up to much good in my free time.

I got involved with a couple of cowboys who came in for cones. The first one took me to a secret swimming hole and taught me how to bend a note on a harmonica. The other one, Jeff, put me on the back of his motorcycle, drove me to his trailer, and showed me how to have an orgasm.

Jeff wasn't really a cowboy. He was a guy in a cowboy hat. He was thirty-three years to my fifteen. He told me he was heir to the R. J. Reynolds tobacco fortune, and I believed him. He was so self-conscious about his tiny dick that he wouldn't let me touch it. My first orgasm was even more transformative than the loss of my virginity. I finally understood what all the fuss was about.

My mother didn't know everything I was up to, but she could smell the smoke in my hair and the liquor on my breath. But her issue with me went beyond my naughtiness, it was more about me than my behavior. She hated my teenage solipsism and lack of consideration where she was concerned. My sharp tongue and quick opinions, which worked in the smoking shed, put her at risk.

By the end of July she was ready for me to be off on my Infinite Odyssey, and so was I.

I turned out not to be the only derelict in my Infinite Odyssey group. We were ten snarky, dope-deprived city and suburban kids led by Todd and Geri, a couple of hippies from Antioch College in Ohio.

We met up in Aspen, loaded up on supplies, and launched into the Rockies, hiking about five miles a day, mostly uphill, eventually reaching alpine heights. I found that I was not a fast hiker, but I was steady and I loved it. I learned to rock-climb and discovered my fear of heights. We rappelled down cliff faces and Tyrolian-traversed across rushing streams and ate granola with Tang instead of milk. We camped at 12,800 feet, baked bread on sticks, and had a snowball fight in August. I picked elephant's heads and silvery lupines and pressed them between the pages of my journal.

Our group bonded deeply. We belayed one another and skinny-dipped together. We played tunnel tag and gave one another round-robin backrubs and amazingly, nobody fucked anybody, except, presumably, Todd and Geri.

At the beginning of the second week, it was time for solos. Todd and Geri dropped us at our secret solo spots up and down the banks of a small stream called, forebodingly, Difficult Creek. We were each given modest stores of gorp, dried fruit, cheese, crackers, and a little instant soup and tea, provided I could get a fire going to boil water.

I had been imagining and anticipating this part of my Infinite Odyssey since February. This was the whole reason I had signed up. I pictured myself lean and brown from hiking, with my sun-bleached hair in a loose braid down my back. I'd weave pine boughs together to build my meditation hut and set up a perfect little outdoor kitchen beside a crackling fire. Instead I found myself frantically tying my rain poncho to bendy pine saplings just as it began to rain. By the time I got my stuff stowed away, the rain was coming down sideways and my jeans were soaked and glued to my still-pale, fat thighs. I stripped them off, rolled out my foam mat, and crawled into my sleeping bag.

In my journal I wrote, *I'm not sure how I feel about all this. A little bored, a little lonely, a little apprehensive of the whole situation. I've got my period, the runs, cuts and scratches all over my legs, and these mosquitos are driving me crazy! How I long for home and Dad.*

The rules of solo were that we were to have no contact with other human beings and no diversions other than our journals. I had imagined befriending woodland animals as I wrote epic verse in my composition book, but it turned out I was just a fifteen-year-old city girl alone in the woods and scared of the dark. Luckily, I had brought my harmonica and I had smuggled a paperback copy of *Lady Chatterley's Lover* in the foot of my rolled-up sleeping bag. I tried to banish the darkness with some white-girl blues, bending notes and singing of loneliness. When I stopped, the sounds of the forest came thundering back all around me. I clenched my flashlight between my teeth, burrowed into my sleeping bag, and began to read my book.

The heroine, Constance Chatterley, was married to Sir Clifford, a paraplegic aristocrat who was about as sexy as my damp hiking socks. He was an enraged and embittered intellectual, and Connie, a young, ripe English Rose, was wilting in their dead marriage. I knew enough about the Laurentian worldview from having read *Women in Love* in freshman English to know that Clifford was probably some kind of allegory for England, which was quickly succumbing to the dehumanization of the industrial age. Clifford's empty efforts at literary greatness were the flaccid enterprise of intellectual life and jolted against Connie's animal heart. Mellors, the gamekeeper, was the lusty Adam in the dystopian Eden that was Wragby. In my woodland hole, I read the book purely for the sex, which was perplexing and workmanlike. I was dismayed by the lack of foreplay in their tryst. Mellors and Connie went straight to

THE BIG HURT 145

fucking, bringing a kind of resolute exhaustion to the sex act that I
was too young to fathom. And yet they copulated as though their
lives depended on it, and that was enough for me.

The next leg of our odyssey was a kayak tour of the Green River.
Our group had been in the Rocky Mountains for two weeks, scrab-
bling down over scree, clinging, white-knuckled, to the sides of
boulders and dropping our filthy jeans to projectile-shit undigested
gorp into holes we dug for ourselves in the woods. It was good to
be back in semicivilization, at a reasonable altitude. We stopped at
a Circle K and I drank a blue Icee that made my head throb. As
much as I had loved moments of my Whitmanesque wandering in
the woods, I was an urban creature. The familiar comforts of asphalt
and polymers, plumbing, and top-40 radio were exquisite.

A leathery river rat named Frisbee drove the gear boat for
Utah Rapid Adventures, the outfitter taking us down the Green
River, which was owned and operated by Keith, an early-thirties
dude who did everything in cutoffs and whose hair was bleached
bone white.

Our group sat in kayaks that gently bobbed in the shallows of the
Green River. Keith had walked us through dock boarding and shore
boarding, sculling and rolling, and was prepared to demonstrate a
wet exit.

"When you capsize, and you *will* capsize," Keith said, "the most
important thing is not to panic." We sat strapped in up to our chins
in mildewed Mae Wests, antsy to get paddling.

"Hold your breath, pop yourself out of the cockpit, and float to
the surface."

He flipped his kayak over and disappeared underwater, leaving us
with the sound of wavelets slapping against the hollow fiberglass hull
of his boat. A moment later he rose up out of the water like a prize
trout, his hair plastered at an odd, rakish angle against his skull.

Keith righted his craft and hoisted himself back in. He braced
over the opening and hovered his legs like an Olympian on parallel
bars. A stream of water trickled from the seat of his wet trunks

into the hull of the boat. His arms were ropy and glistening, and the golden hair on his forearms sprang up and dried like duckling down in the arid Utah sunshine. He was almost too handsome to be attractive to me. My taste ran toward skinny, pasty Jews in concert T-shirts. "Slide your legs inside the boat." He inserted his legs into his kayak in one smooth, forceful motion. Seated in the kayak, Keith looked like an amputee.

We all tried it, flipping our boats over. The river, upside down, was still and green like its name. Its sandy bottom was a peaceful parallel universe. I wiggled out of my kayak and floated gently upward, tilting my head back so my hair would be Bo Derek–perfect when I broke the surface.

I righted my boat and swung aboard. Keith looked over at me and my skin pebbled all over.

With twenty minutes of instruction and practice under my belt, I felt ready to take on the Green River. We launched and began a lazy downstream paddle. The river was wide and smooth and the canyon walls on either side swooped upward, a rough millefeuille of time and pressure.

We ran a couple of Class I and Class II rapids, and they were fun, like going down a log flume at Disneyland. But ahead was our first Class III, exponentially more challenging. Keith explained what wrap rocks were—rocks that had current running around them in such a way that they would grab a kayak and put it on like a shawl. He told us to keep our feet up toward the surface of the water if we capsized. That's how people drown: their feet get stuck between the big rocks on the river bottom and the water flows over them.

The rapids looked like a frilly ruffle from a distance, but as we got closer we were engulfed by its noise and mist. It was a smoker. The bow of my boat nosed into the channel and I felt the rapid suck me in and send me hurtling toward the rocks. I tried to bear off from the boulders with my paddle as I was jostled and dragged down the angry flume. I hung on a barely submerged boulder, then was yanked off and shot down another churning chute. The river was more powerful than I had imagined, and my body and mind were joined in perfect focus as I fought to stay afloat. Finally, I was deposited in calm water once more. The river opened up into flat water and the thundering of the rapids receded behind me. The afternoon was wide and soft once more and I felt, in that moment, like I could have eaten the whole world raw.

We lit on a beach just before sunset. As we dragged our boats ashore, I noticed a couple of little moths fluttering around me, and then there was another, then a few more. Suddenly the air was filled with hundreds, then thousands, then millions of tiny, white, fluttering creatures, a snowstorm in August.

"Mayflies," Frisbee said, unloading gear from the boat. Kids dived into tents, or under their ponchos to get free of the fluttery blizzard.

"What are mayflies?" I asked Frisbee as I helped him unload the boat. We had bandannas tied over our faces to keep from eating the insects.

"Mayflies is just little moths. They lay their eggs all up and down the river and they all hatch at the same time."

This was the miracle that I had missed on Difficult Creek; I shivered as it passed through my body. I closed my eyes and let myself be engulfed by wonder.

Keith came over to the boat to get himself a beer out of Frisbee's cooler. "I am glad to see at least one of you kids ain't afraid of a few bugs," he said, popping and swigging his brew, oblivious to the moths that flapped and dove around him.

"How long will this last?" I asked.

"No more'n a day," Frisbee said. "Most of these little guys will mate and die within a few hours."

"Yeah," Keith said, looking straight at me, "it don't take long to get it done." He winked at me and took another swig of his beer.

After dinner I sat down by the water and watched the mayflies die. The blizzard had dwindled to a flurry and it made me sad. I wondered for the umpti-jillionth time how spirit was chosen. Why was I me, so full of this longing for connection? Why was I not a mayfly? Or was I a mayfly and I didn't know it? Did a mayfly have a sense of its own short destiny? Was I just going to flutter about crazily like this for a brief moment, trying desperately to mate before I simply dropped out of the air into a puddle of ketchup? I wanted to believe I was made for more than that, but I could see no evidence to the contrary. What if I were that ordinary? The thought terrified me.

After dinner Keith found me sitting alone. He sat down beside me. He was still in his cutoffs and T-shirt, even though it was nighttime and chilly, and we were far from the campfire.

"You kayaked like a champ today, little sister. I'll bet you're pretty sore." He started to give me a back rub.

In a pivotal scene in *Lady Chatterley's Lover* Constance and Mellors look at pheasant chicks he is raising for game, and she starts crying over the birds because she cannot, as a modern woman, contain the unattainable perfection of the tiny birds. Confronted by the perfection of Lady Chatterley's back, fire leaps in Mellors's loins, and what is that poor bastard to do, with his loins all aflame, but try to give Lady Chatterley a back rub? *He laid his hand on her shoulder, and softly, gently, it began to travel down the curve of her back, blindly, with a blind stroking motion, to the curve of her crouching loins. And there his hand softly, softly stroked the curve of her flank, in the blind instinctive caress.*

Shall you come to the hut? Mellors asks Connie, laying down a rough blanket on the dirt floor for her.

Keith held open the flap of his tent for me. There was a pile of blankets next to a cooler. He directed me to lie down on my stomach. He zipped the tent flap shut and put his silver flashlight, lens down, on top of the cooler. The tent glowed dark red. He kicked off his shoes and straddled me, pinning me facedown into his scratchy blanket.

The sex between Constance and Mellors that first time doesn't seem great. The keeper's hand is described as knowing how to unclothe her; he gets her knickers off in one deft maneuver, which is hot, but then he pushes himself into her without any tenderness or fanfare.

Keith tried to pull my jeans off over my sneakers but gave up. He parted my legs as wide as my denim-bound ankles would permit. *He allowed himself to feel peace on earth inside her soft, quiescent body.*

In the middle of the sex act, Lawrence changes the point of view to that of Mellors and describes Connie as lying still, *in a sort of sleep, in a sort of dream.* I thought it was weird. Did Lawrence do this because this was where his male imagination ground to a halt? Was he incapable of imagining what a woman might feel during sex, or just not interested?

I, myself, could not have explained then why a girl might need to throw herself, over and over again, at the empty spaces in other people. Now I know it was because emptiness felt like home. But sex held the possibility of transformation and redemption. Mellors was hollow at first, but Connie brought him back from that abyss with her naked flesh, with her hunger for immediacy. It was what made her special in this cockamamie, cock-centric love story and I hungered for that kind of centrality, that primacy. The balm of being enough for someone. It was the hope every time I let myself be fucked by men who did not love me. That I might be able to transact that miracle: turn sex into love in the breast of the loveless. I would redeem them with my love, and by so doing, redeem myself.

When he was finished I rolled over to face Keith, and I saw that his naked body was hairless, as smooth and cool as a river rock. I tried to wrap myself around him, but he bore off and away from me and reached for his clothes.

Mellors walks Constance to the gate at the edge of the formal Wragby grounds. He asks her if it was good for her. Men never seem to ask women if they are having a good time until it is too late. She tells him it was. I hadn't had enough sex yet to have had really good sex, but I was pretty sure this wasn't it.

I left Keith in his tent and found my own way through the rapidly thinning cloud of mayflies, back to the group campsite and my sleeping bag.

We awoke in the morning to a carpet of dead mayflies. They

were in our dishes, in our shoes, in our hair and our hash browns. The tiny waves that lapped up on the riverbank carried thousands of corpses, the invasion of Normandy in miniature. The birds swooped and beat their wings against the water, gorging themselves on dead insects.

I helped load the gear boat, but Keith wouldn't look at me. I tried to catch his eye, but he wouldn't allow it. Every time I paddled up to his boat, he paddled away from me. He dodged me all morning.

At lunchtime we pulled into a small inlet. One of my fellow Odysseans spotted a tiny frog on a rock among the reeds near the shore and Keith stroked over to it and scooped it up with the tip of his paddle. The gesture was so deft and tender that I felt certain he had to be a good guy; he just was trying to protect me by setting boundaries. We would find each other later.

We all paddled in close to inspect the frog. Keith held his paddle out to each one of us in turn. He showed it to everyone else first, and then he extended his paddle toward me. He was giving me the last and longest look, and I knew it was because I was special.

The frog was the size of an acorn. It was an exquisitely formed miniature. Its skin was brown, green, and gold, and it glistened in the sunlight like a wet geode. As Keith held the frog out to me, I felt like Constance Chatterley, reaching into the coop to take the pheasant chick in her hands. *It was the most alive little spark of a creature in seven kingdoms at that moment.* I reached my hand out to touch it in ecstasy. *Life, life! Pure, sparky, fearless new life! New life! So tiny and so utterly without fear!*

Keith jerked his paddle back and raised it over his head. With one, long, arcing motion he brought the face of the paddle crashing down against the hard surface of the water. He looked me straight in the eye. The crushed frog floated limply among the dead mayflies.

Buxton, 1979–1980

My sophomore year was mostly unremarkable. I continued to live a problematic life at school: sneaking out of the dorm at night to sleep with upperclassmen, hanging out in the smoking shed, bantering with whoever else was out there, smoking furtive bowls of weed whenever possible.

With Jonas gone I was free to explore Buxton on my own terms. I got a few lucky breaks that year that helped me begin to lay claim to myself.

First, I was recognized by Patricia, our drama director, as a genuine acting talent. I was cast in the lead roles of all three plays that year (*Richard III*, *The Caucasian Chalk Circle*, *Major Barbara*) and it was on Buxton's tiny stage that I began to feel a sense of place and purpose. The realization that I could drop my personality like a pair of bad shoes and become someone else, be it Queen Elizabeth or Lady Britomart, felt like a superpower I had always known I had. My morale and social status at the school increased exponentially with each role. Each play left me with a sense of accomplishment I had never known before.

Another lucky break occurred when my mother came to visit me at school that fall. She hadn't been there since the day she dropped me off, and she took me out to lunch. I had been infatuated with a junior named Sprague, who was an avowed Anarchist. Under his tutelage I began reading Kropotkin and Bakunin and saying things like "Eat the rich."

My mother laughed at my newfound radicalism and told me I took after my great-aunt Frances, an anti-nuclear activist who was currently living in Berkeley. It was the first I had ever heard of this relative. Mom gave me her address and I wrote to her that night, introducing myself. Frannie wrote back immediately, thrilled to hear from her great-niece. We began a pen-palship that year that lasted until she died in 1993.

Frannie was a brilliant woman ahead of her time. At seventy-nine she had lived and done it all, starting out as a clerk at Lord & Taylor, moving to admissions officer at Barnard College, graduate work at UC Berkeley in philosophy and economics, fellowships, a PhD, professorships at Vassar and Oberlin, followed by a career in urban planning and pollution mitigation in Seattle, leading to her current and continuing work in the No Nukes movement with Helen Caldicott. She still traveled the world doing peace and social-justice work well into her eighties.

Frannie was my new heroine. One I could talk to. I typed her long letters on my Olivetti, telling her everything I felt and wished for: revolution, peace, passion. She loved and responded to me immediately. Every letter from Frannie was a burst of encouragement and interest, asking me about what I was studying and reading. Through her I saw that I had an intellectual heritage beyond my parents. I asked to know more and she was full of stories.

She told me about my great-great-grandparents, David and Catherine Blaine, who hailed from Seneca, New York, the site of America's first Women's Rights convention in 1848. Catharine C. Paine signed the Declaration of Sentiments, married David Blaine, and the two sailed off to Seattle as part of a westward Methodist missionary movement in the 1840s and '50s.

Unlike most pioneers, my great-great-grandparents didn't suffer the indignities of the covered wagon. Instead they booked passage out of New York, sailing down to Panama, crossing the Isthmus by mule, then sailing up the West Coast to the Northern

Territory. They used the extra time it took to sail for study and writing.

They arrived in Seattle in 1853, their assignment, to clear some donated land and found a church. Dressed in his Sunday best (and with no discernable field skills, so he had some help), David Blaine built a twenty-by-forty structure, whitewashed it, and dubbed it "The Little White Church." It was Seattle's first house of worship. Catherine started the territory's first school in her own kitchen.

Frannie showed me a rich family history, bits of which I had gleaned from my mother. Mom had told me about her ancestor who, six days after giving birth to her son, had to flee the Indians in a canoe during the Battle of Seattle, taking shelter aboard the battleship *Decatur* parked in Elliott Bay. Frannie brought pieces of my family history together that I didn't know I had. She showed a girl from a shattered family that her family was much bigger than her mother and father.

All of this made me take myself more seriously as a student. I also began to take a genuine interest in my schoolwork, and my academic reports started to improve a bit.

That year I made a real friend, a freshburger named Mia. She was tall and lanky, with a slanted face, and was possessed of a sparkling, dry wit. She had previously gone to Wagner, a notoriously tough school in the city, and at first I didn't like her at all; she seemed so gung-ho about everything. But that winter I discovered she was brilliant and bossy and hilarious. It didn't matter that none of the boys I slept with wanted to be my boyfriend. I had Mia.

Before I knew it, it was spring again, and the problem of what was to be done with me over the summer once again reared its many-horned head. I wanted to live in New York City with my father and hang out with Mia and my other Buxton friends who would all be getting summer jobs. But I would also have been glad to go back to Santa Fe for the summer and try again with my mother, maybe get my job back at Swensen's.

My parents had other ideas.

New York, May 1980

Dear Erika,

I have spent the day thinking about you and talking about you—with your mother twice, with your therapist, with Jessie, with Dana, with John Dowd, the director of the Great Lakes Shakespeare Co., even with Clint Eastwood, of all people, who happened to call when I was in the midst of all this anxious turmoil. The most striking thing about it all was the kindness and concern about you shown by everyone on that list, the willingness of total strangers to take an interest in your well-being. And, of course, of the people who love you, not too much can be said; we all want the best for you. I wonder if you are aware of all this, of the emotion that has been expended on you over the past few years, of time and trouble expended on your behalf? I don't suppose any of that can mean much to someone as young as you—it didn't to me at your age—but I want to stress that here at the top of what is likely to be a long letter. As you get older these gestures of thoughtfulness, these examples of the sweet side of human nature come to be more important, because at a certain age, like say mine and your mom's and Dana's, we have experienced so much of the sour side of that nature. What finally sustains us all, makes life and even achievement worthwhile, are these constant examples of the willingness of people to put themselves out to help one another. Really, the best thing about show business, the thing that has attracted me to it in late years, has been the camaraderie of it, the extraordinary warmth and givingness of the people who have chosen that hard profession. It was something I had hoped you might come to know in Cleveland this summer, if you had chosen that opportunity, which now I feel I cannot in conscience permit you to accept—for reasons I'll go into later.

I think you have now placed you, and me, in a pretty pickle, and frankly, I don't know what to do about it. But I will lay out here as coherently as I can the dimensions of the problem—without undue anger or special pleading. I'll eagerly look forward to your response.

Let's begin with the realities of your parents' situation. Mine first. I have two singular opportunities before me in Los Angeles. The first, and by far the most important, is that I have a chance to live with Dana for three months, a long enough time to see if there is a reasonable hope of us attempting to make a life together. She is the first woman I have really wanted to try such an experiment with, the first woman I have trusted enough, and cared enough about to take this scary step. Beyond that, I have another first, a chance to do a job that will, for once in my life, overpay me. As a result, I will be in a position to make some choices in my life, to escape if I want to from the demands of weekly journalism, to test my talent against my most profound ambitions. At my age, such opportunities do not present themselves any more often than women of Dana's caliber do. Dearly beloved, Erika, I will do nothing to jeopardize either opportunity. I will not be able to take you into my life except for a week or two, in June and/or at the end of the summer.

[W]ould you really want to intrude on Dana and me at this stage of our relationship? Don't you think we (or anyway I) are entitled to a chance to let it grow without the pressure of a young woman, my daughter, trying to live with us? As for you and me taking a place of our own, the same problems present themselves. How do I work and see Dana, and find you a job and get you to and from it each day? I say this all, without for a moment wishing to imply that somehow I am choosing against you. Rather, I am asking something of you, which is time of my own, time to tend to my life at a moment that I sense to be crucial in it, as I will be doing work, and tending to the possibility of a mature love. So...yes, I love and care for you (can you doubt after the years we have gone through of late?) but, no, this summer I cannot be entirely or even largely be ruled by your needs, your demands.

As to your mother, I can be briefer. I gather from her that the two weeks in Santa Fe were not a success. Tales of dope, of irresponsible companionship, of thoughtless human intercourse are told. Doubtless they are exaggerated somewhat in the retelling. But not, I think, totally fabricated. As of today, Jill says that even a week's stay by you in Santa Fe would have to be very carefully considered. Any thought you might have of living and working there for most or all of the summer is not to be seriously entertained. Your history there is troubled and tangled, and this is not the time or place to go over it again and sort it out. But as I said before, you will not restore that relationship quickly or easily. You have a long, patient process to go through before that love that you want and need is free of the past. The fault does not entirely lie with you, though you must take partial responsibility for it. And you must live with the fact that for now, for the foreseeable future, it appears that you and your mother are doomed to repeat destructive patterns that have grown up in recent years, that are conditioned by your histories. I don't despair entirely about that. Given time and good will those patterns can be broken. But you must not expect leaping progress. There will be no miracles. And I will not permit you to go off as you did this spring for a long stay in Santa Fe. It seems my better judgment about that venture was correct. Short stays in N.M. I'll encourage. But for now, no longer ones.

Now, it seems that you have, for the coming summer, no place that you can really call your own. That may seem a harsh fact, hard to face, but it is a temporary reality. It was why I had so hoped that the Great Lakes Shakespeare Festival might be an answer. Its long season seemed to me, just this once, a blessing. It appears that a brochure they sent to you has gone awry in the mail, which is sad because it described what sounds to me a good program. Here is what it is. The company will do Henry IV, Titus Andronicus, Comedy of Errors, Charlie's Aunt and a program of one-acts. Interns will run each show, working backstage, and all will get at least walk-on parts in the course of the summer. A few will get small speaking parts, based on auditions with directors.

All will be understudies and will be expected to be up on their lines, so they can go on if a member of the equity company can't work and will do the shows at tech rehearsals. They will probably do some other light work on the productions but no heavy construction and no striking or erecting of sets. Mostly though, interns will be working along more academic lines, studying acting under professional teachers. Now, Mr. Dowd, who called tonight, does not really want you, or anyone under 17, in his theater. He's the father of four daughters himself and is concerned about young girls being too early exposed to the rough talk and brisk sexuality of the acting game. He also points out that he has a professional company to run, and that although he will naturally try to keep an eye on his young charges, he can't act as resident psychiatrist or nursemaid, and neither can his aides. He is concerned about disruptive behavior, everything from pot smoking to unwanted pregnancies, and certainly including anyone who is going to be rebellious, sullen, a general drag. Now I think you have the talent to derive great benefit from this company. But I frankly don't think you can handle yourself maturely enough to cope with the life away from the structured activities of the company, and that your manner of conducting yourself would soon seep over into the work you would be asked to do. And that sooner rather than later you would be asked to leave. I have to attempt to deal with these self-destructive (and, I must say, self-absorbed) patterns. But Dowd, who would give you this opportunity if I but said the word, is obviously too kind a man, and too serious an artist, to be burdened with all that. I told him I would speak to him next week to give him final word on his offer to take you on. But I am going to turn him down—regretfully. Your last response to the graciousness of my friends while you were in London brought shame to me, frankly. And though I deeply resent giving in to what I see as a threat on your part to repeat that response in the present instance, it seems I have no choice. I'd rather truckle to you than have to apologize for you—especially since no apology can really undo the damage you are capable of when you are on one of your rips.

If you sense anger in that last paragraph, you're right. I do get angry—mostly at the waste of talent and opportunity that you leave in your wake. That anger does not cancel or even diminish my love for you. But it does sadden and frustrate me. When you are with me I see a young woman of beauty, of wit, of developing style. When I see you on a stage or read some of your writing I sense gift. And I don't mind the show-offy qualities inherent in it. All artists have to have a bit of the show-off about them; it goes with the territory. But I despise undisciplined talent, self-indulgent talent. And talent that refuses to understand that those of us who have a gift for expression have also a responsibility. It is our duty, and it's near sacred, to focus the inchoate feeling of our fellow men, to express their longings and ideals and tragedies and wit, so that they can gain a deeper understanding of themselves and get in touch with their fellow beings by gaining a sense of the universality of certain emotions and situations. The applause is nice, and we all need a bit of it. But a sense of getting something absolutely right—a sentence on a page, a gesture on a stage—that's where the deepest thrills are, that's what really pulls us out of ourselves and puts us in touch with something larger and stronger than ourselves. Working toward those moments, busting a gut to find them, that's really what a lot of life is about, for those of us privileged enough even to understand what I'm talking about here. I had thought that being around adults working toward something like the kind of expression I'm talking about here would be a good introduction for you to this great world. Involved—really involved—in it, you wouldn't have had a moment to moon about your parents' "injustices" or your own hurts. But without quite knowing why, you rejected all that, you have rejected it, indeed, from the first moment I mentioned it to you. And rejected it, as it seems to me because it would have interrupted your perfect concentration on yourself. That sort of concentration, by the way, is what gives bad actors their bad reputations as human beings. They seek only the world's adoration, the "love" they always claim they can feel coming at them across the footlights, which, of course, isn't love at all, but merely a shoring up of faltering egos, something like sex without real affection or caring. If that's all you want from theater, or writing, then I hope you get out quick, because it will distort you as a human being, and just simply hollow out your life.

Well, that's probably a digression. But I have this vision. We somehow get you through June as a house guest here and there and then find you a summer school of some sort which takes us to the beginning of August and then you and I join up in New York for six or seven nice hot weeks in the apartment, when it's too late for you to get even a crummy job. You sleep until noon and look for friends to goof off with through the remainder of the day (and night). Occasionally I look up, catch your resentful glance, or, god help me, throw one at you, and I think of how productive the summer might have been, how you might at least have enjoyed the mutual striving, the laughter, the hard-working fun of a good theatrical company, and wonder how you could so cavalierly have rejected that. And don't tell me how you would have cheerfully undertaken it in the more salubrious climes of Santa Fe. The two experiences, at bottom, were the same. It was merely that Santa Fe would have put you in closer touch with the troubled, druggy people you have so quickly found there in past visits. Don't tell me, either, of your need for a vacation. I'm the one who is 47 and needs vacations, but don't get them. You need change, kid, but not rest, that's a hype when you're 16.

Harsh, huh? Well, I hear you tell it around that I'm a soft touch, that I don't impose any discipline on you. I hope no one believed you. Mostly I've not felt the need to on your recent visits. And I guess you've conned me a few times, especially about pot. But I'll keep a closer eye out in the future. I'm not, by nature, a very good jailer—don't like the role—but if you won't exercise self-discipline, a self-discipline out of which you can develop as an artist, or at least as a functioning, caring and decent human being, I'll try to fill the gap. That's never as good. It's always better to discover your own best nature out of a reasonable process of trial and error. But I'll do what I have to do, however painful that is for both of us. My darling Erika, you will become some kind of grown-up, responsible, intact human being. I will not let you be anything else. But I cannot make the best out of you unless you make the best out of yourself—and neither can Buxton or anyone else. I think your best self, which I see glimmers of all the time, could be someone extraordinary. You have sensitivity and sympathy and a natural gift for expression. That's more than most people start with. Are you really going to dissipate those gifts? Are you really going to screw off forever?

How many tests do you feel you must administer to me, to your mother, to all the adults who have rallied round you, before you accept the fact that you are loved and cared for? Would it really satisfy your need for that proof if I gave up my career and my love for Dana and babysat you all summer? I doubt it. I think ultimately I'd have to hurl myself from the Brooklyn Bridge to make the point. But that I won't do. Tag line from an old movie: "Love has to stop short of suicide." That goes for me. What goes for you is, "self-love (absorption) has to stop short of self-destruction."

But enough. It's almost two AM. I've now devoted 12 consecutive hours to you. Is that enough for today? Can I go to bed now? I promise I'll think almost as much of you tomorrow. And the day after. And...

Understand that this letter is written in love as well as in frustration and puzzlement. I hope it clears the air between us. I'm sure we'll finally work something out, though I imagine that now, alas, whatever it is will fall far short of your ideal or mine. As always,

All my love,
Dad

P.S. If you see any hope at all for Cleveland we had better talk about it no later than Monday. As I say, it would take a lot to convince me, but you can always try.

Cleveland, Summer 1980

D ad dropped me off at the Shakespeare Festival that June. Someone at the theater had found me a room in the attic of an old lady's house. My room had a wrought-iron bed and a dead ham radio in the closet. After getting me situated, Dad hotfooted it to the Cleveland Airport to make his connecting flight to the coast, where Dana Wynter, the actress best known for having played the female lead in the original *Invasion of the Body Snatchers*, was waiting for him. She was Dad's ideal: elegant, ladylike, British, and best of all, a little bit famous. I couldn't compete.

Once again, I was alone in an unfamiliar town for the summer, with a full-time job that paid me no money, and with no companions my own age. Because I was only sixteen, by far the youngest member of the company, I couldn't join my colleagues for drinks at the local tavern after work. On Mondays, when the theater was dark, I would get on my bike, go exploring, and see what was out there. Cleveland, Ohio, 1980, was what was out there.

Though Lakewood, the suburb I was living in, was leafy and bucolic, the city of Cleveland was broken and dingy, ranged out along the Cuyahoga River like a bad rash. The river itself was so polluted it had famously caught fire. But the city felt homey to a kid who had grown up in New York City in the dirty old 1970s.

The shuttered storefronts, boomboxes, dog shit, and graffiti were my familiars. Cleveland felt like Harlem but with clapboard houses instead of brownstones.

It was a hot summer and everybody was on their front stoop, smoking Kools, drinking cold beer out of paper bags, keeping an eye on their kids. I knew these people were desperately poor and that I was the privileged one, but what I saw was community. I was homesick for Buxton.

There was one person at the Shakespeare Festival who paid attention to me; he was a handsome, red-headed soap star who was the biggest name on the marquee that summer. The Star drove in from the coast in an orange Karmann Ghia that matched his big red off-season beard. He was ruddy and strapping and had a lead in *Titus Andronicus*.

Titus Andronicus is best known as Shakespeare's bloodiest play. It features assassinations, executions, cannibalism, rape, and dismemberment. By the end of Act 5, fourteen are dead. The most disturbing scene is when Lavinia, Titus's daughter, is revenge-raped, and her attackers cut out her tongue and chop off her hands so she can't reveal their identities.

I had two roles in this production: First, I played Lavinia's handmaiden (which I always thought was hilarious, as she had no hands). I was to stand there mutely and watch the Star spit and sweat impressively as he did his speeches. Then, when the play was finished, it was my job to stay behind after the house had cleared, and scrub all the fake blood off the stage.

One night, I was on my knees, scrubbing the empty stage after most of the cast and crew had left for the pub. The Star entered from stage left, his bag over his shoulder, and came to stand over me. "That looks like a thankless job."

"It's okay," I said, smiling up at him.

"Well, I don't envy you. It's a pretty tough play."

"Yeah, a lot of blood."

"I'm afraid a lot of that is my character's fault. So sorry."

I laughed. "It's cool. You were born to the role."

"You think?" He seemed surprised. "Wait, that wasn't a compliment, was it?"

Now we were both laughing. "No, I mean it, you're very... emperorly." I felt myself blush to my ears. Why did I have to say shit like that? But he beamed me a kilowatt smile.

"Hey, do you have plans this weekend?"

"Um, not really." It was going to be another weekend of riding my bike around Cleveland, then Stouffer's macaroni and cheese up in the attic.

"There's a pool at my condo. Why don't you come by for a swim on Saturday?"

"I'd love it!"

"You can scrub my floors after." He laughed, jingling his car keys.

It was the only social invitation I had gotten that summer, so I rode my bike over that Saturday, my swimsuit on under my shorts.

He was waiting for me down by the pool in his Speedo. His body was fuzzed in red hair. I whipped off my shorts and T-shirt, and jumped right in the pool. The Star dove in after me.

"Do you want to have a tea party?"

"What's that?" he asked, squinting at me through sun and chlorine.

"You act out a tea party underwater. I used to do it with my sister. C'mon, I'll be Mother." We submerged ourselves, and I tried to cross my legs like I was sitting on a chair and pretended to pour him a cup of tea. The Star's long red, Shakespearean hair wavered above him, a corona in the pale-blue pool current. He grabbed at me and my gasp came out in bubbles.

I was fine having sex with the Star. It was a fast, squeaky poke in his steam shower after. No big deal, but of course I wondered what it meant. It was over before I knew it and the next thing he was showing me the door.

There were no further invitations after that. Like Keith the summer before, the Star would not look at me or acknowledge me again the rest of the summer. Surely this was not what my father meant by "the warmth and givingness" of theatre people.

Meanwhile, Dad was in L.A., basking in the warmth and givingness of his own star.

It was a long season. I counted the days until I could get back to Buxton. I dreamed of the dorm, the fields, even the homework. I wanted to be someplace where people knew me—someplace where I wouldn't be so alone.

Buxton, Fall 1980

Two new teachers came to Buxton my junior year: Henry Baker and his wife, Eileen. Henry taught music and I was in Eileen's French II class. They were very different from the other Buxton career faculty, the "lifers" who seemed to have been born wearing Shetland sweaters and holding Bennington Potters coffee mugs. Henry and Eileen were bohemian and iconoclastic; they wore leather jackets. Like the rest of the faculty, they were in their early-to-mid-thirties, but they acted many years cooler.

Eileen and Henry both wore eyeglasses that darkened in the sun. Even indoors their lenses stayed toast-colored, which gave them an air of druggy subversion and mystery. They had identical wedding bands that they had designed themselves that had been wrought from three kinds of interwoven gold. They had two dogs, Duska and Yevka—tall, slender Russian wolfhounds that looked like hanks of silky yarn pressed between two panes of glass. Every evening at twilight Henry let the Borzois streak across the lower field in an unearthly display of speed and grace.

Henry and Eileen were serving as the dorm parents in the Gatehouse, a smaller satellite girls' dorm at the foot of Buxton's driveway where I was living that semester. Mia and I came down the Gatehouse stairs one day to find a long accordion of sheet music hung up in the hallway. It was a composition written by Henry. The scroll was titled "Gatehouse 1" and instead of musical notes, the staff was annotated with words like "door slam" and "pipe clang." Henry had transcribed all the sounds of the girls above him, all the hisses and gurgles, the high notes of laughter, the tympani of our feet on floorboards, and notated them all on his musical staff. To see our lives laid out like that, measure for measure, felt strangely intimate and also thrilling. It was the first time I understood that art didn't have to be out of reach—it wasn't just a precious painting hung in the Clark Art, or a symphony played in Carnegie Hall—art was everywhere all the time. It was merely a matter of perspective and framing.

Henry came out of his apartment as we looked at the scroll. He was narrow-framed, with big eyeglasses and chestnut hair that curled softly around the epaulets of his Members Only jacket.

"Dude, what's up with this?" Mia asked.

Henry's face, normally inscrutable, cracked into a sideways smile, and a rogue dimple appeared beside his mouth. "It's chamber music" was all he said as he headed out the door.

If Henry was a strange, serene tune by Eric Satie, Eileen was a hot rumba. She was loose-limbed and wide-hipped, vivid, earthy, and risible. She tended to burst into rooms and speak with a raised eyebrow. She liked cheap yuks and Baudelaire. She began each class with the French national anthem, which I can still sing in its entirety to this day. Eileen had a magically Continental air about her in the way she wore scarves and spoke in double-entendres. She understood that the only way to teach French to adolescents was to appeal to their native sense of existential futility. Sartre's *L'enfer, c'est les autres* had special resonance for a bunch of teenagers living four to a room through an endless Berkshire winter.

But I had made peace with being stuck at boarding school. My summers had shown me that the larger world was full of loneliness and peril, so I burrowed into Buxton. I was done being a fuckup. Instead I became a full-fledged "Buxtonite." I got my grades up, headed up more Work Program crews, and spearheaded all-school amusements on Recreation Committee. I continued to play leads in every play and I lived from one production to the next, memorizing lines, living inside my characters as I walked to classes or ate Cap'n Crunch in the dining hall.

Early in my junior year I found myself on the Main House cleaning crew with a new kid, Chris, who had transferred into our junior class. I stopped him in the upstairs hallway, where he was vacuuming.

"We haven't officially met. I'm Erika."

"Chris Brady." He smiled widely and reached out to shake my hand. He was a good-looking kid, tall, with an elegant, triangular, Italianate body. He was built like an archer, but with none of the rootedness an archer would need to shoot an arrow and hit a target. His face was a flip-book of emotion. Fear ponged in his eyes, his hands danced, and his pretty mouth was a rictus of nervous laughter.

"What's your story, Chris? Where are you from?"

"Connecticut."

"Where were you in school before?"

"The Indian Mountain School."

"Never heard of it. Why did you leave?"

Chris's eyes darted around the room as he paused, looking for an answer. "It wasn't the right fit for me." He said this with his fingers in air quotes laughing, his whole body tilting sideways into a comma of awkward submission. I assumed "not the right fit" was code for kicked out for drugs and didn't pursue it.

"What do your parents do?"

"My dad is out of the picture. He was a real Irish mongrel who left us right after I was born. I have his last name, which was B-r-a-i-d-a-i-g-h, but it got bastardized to Brady at Ellis Island. My mother raised me, so . . . actually, I'm thinking of changing my name legally to my mother's maiden name, Dallett."

"Dallett is a much cooler name than Brady."

"I know. My mom's family is pretty old and aristocratic. My great-grandfather ran the Red D shipping line out of Venezuela. That side of the family has an old-money pedigree, though not

much of the old money itself is left at this point, just the pedigree."
He laughed and sputtered and rolled his eyes. I had never met
anyone like this kid.

"Still, that's a pretty cool family history. You know," I said,
"maybe you should think about changing your first name too,
while you're at it."

"Really? You think?"

"Well, at least while you're at Buxton. There are, like, six Chrises
at this school already."

"I know. It is kind of depressing." Chris emitted a wet sound
somewhere between a giggle and a gasp. *Is he gay?* I wondered. He
must be gay. He was far too fluttery to be straight. "But what on
earth would I change it to?"

"What's your middle name?"

"John."

"Crap, we've got too many of those here too."

"I *know.*"

I pondered a moment. "What about CJ?"

"CJ?"

"Yeah."

"CJ Dallett," he said, trying it on. "I like it."

He laughed. I beamed. It was done. I had never named a person
before, and I couldn't believe how easy it was, but I didn't know
how badly this boy needed a new identity.

CJ and I were both in Eileen's French II class, and the three of
us hit it off. We read Paul Verlaine and Baudelaire, we ate runny
cheeses and sang French folk songs. I sucked at conjugating French
verbs and found it an irksome detail in the larger pursuit of *je ne
sais quoi*, but I made up for it by learning vocabulary and smoking
Gauloises and exhibiting sheer panache and *joie de vivre*, which
Eileen applauded.

By midautumn we had included Henry in our clique, and by
Christmas the four of us were madly and platonically in love. CJ
and I spent evenings in the teachers' apartment, listening to Philip

Glass and looking at art books. Eileen served us fancy snacks, like kiwi slices and brie on Stoned Wheat Thins, a combination that was delicious and felt wildly sophisticated. I noted the recipe and filed it away for the day when I would be a hostess.

Henry and Eileen's marriage felt like a song: she was the words and he was the music. Everything about their union seemed equitable, collaborative, and modern. When I compared their marriage to that of my parents, the contrast was startling. They were friends and colleagues who genuinely respected each other's views, who relished their time together, yet gave the other room to pursue separate interests, then came together again over their love of art and ideas and each other. To my sixteen-year-old eyes, they were as exotic and romantic as John and Yoko.

After our evenings together, CJ and I would walk up the driveway back to our respective dormitories, sharing a cigarette, talking about poetry or people. Our friendship deepened that fall and took on a dimension of intimacy that was new to me. It was neither sexual nor without attraction. My bond with CJ occupied a new category of relationship I had never had with a boy. It was pure *philia*, brotherly love. I felt for the first time the sweet abandon of enjoying a boy without the expectation of having to sleep with him.

At Buxton, kids didn't go home for Thanksgiving; instead, the school hosted a big dinner, with Lessie, the cook, and her staff churning out a flock of roasted turkeys and all the fixings. Our parents came up from the city, booked rooms at the Treadway Inn in town, and feasted with us and attended the fall play. That season I starred as Lady Britomart in *Major Barbara*. Dad was proud of my performance. He thought I had real talent. He told me I was shaping up and that Buxton was the best thing ever to happen to me, and I knew he was right.

CJ and I introduced our parents to each other that weekend. CJ's mom, Alice, was one of those New England blue bloods who wore L.L.Bean boots with her diamond tennis bracelet. She had the mannerisms of a warm person, but my gut told me to keep my distance. CJ had said that much of his childhood was spent being ignored while she cavorted with various men. He told me that when he was five she had left him alone on a boat docked in a Caribbean port while she went ashore on a date. He said his older sister had once tried to smother him with a pillow. Alice was dismissive of her only son and seemed to take an instant dislike to me, his best friend. She did, however, appear to like my father very much and flirted with him openly at the Thanksgiving dinner table. After dessert they wandered off for a smoke together and disappeared into the night.

The next morning Dad rolled in from the Treadway Inn, the main hotel in Williamstown where all the parents stayed. He wore a big grin under his mustache and I knew that he had screwed CJ's mom. I panicked, assuming that CJ, like Emily, would end our friendship over our parents' indiscretion, but he just said, "Well, you've got to give it to our parents, they are consistent." Neither of us had to excuse or explain a thing to each other; we just laughed long and hard together and it bonded us for life.

Buxton, Spring 1981

D ad published a book called *Singled Out: A Civilized Guide to Sex and Sensibility for the Suddenly Single Man—or Woman*. He mailed a copy to me at school. It was essentially a dating manual, written in my father's high-hatted style, about how to bang the ladies like a real Michael Caine, whom he described as "a nice guy who...holds his strength in reserve." He had written an article in *Esquire* about "starting over" that struck a chord with the divorced crowd, a booming market. The book featured chapter titles like "The Transitional Woman" and "Something Zipless This Way Comes." In a chapter called "What About the Children?" he wrote, "About your own little Oedipuses and Electras, you will have to exercise a certain care and discretion."

Dad dedicated *Singled Out* to Dana, who embodied the book's romantic, emotive, happy ending. But by the time the book published the relationship had tanked and my father was suddenly single once more.

Buxton's Spring Arts Weekend officially began on Saturday morning, but the long-distance parents began arriving on Friday night, spending an extra night at the Treadway Inn. Dad drove up from the city. He was back and forth in those days between his bachelor duplex in New York and his bachelor sublet in L.A. He was making a TV show and flogging his book.

It was dusk, and Dad and I were sitting on the front steps of the Main House, sharing a cigarette and shooting the shit. The lower field was lit up with fireflies. A rental car came up the driveway and parked.

A female figure appeared in the gloaming. A stunning, silver-haired woman dressed in a flowing silk pantsuit. A note of Cacharel trailed in her wake as she swept past us and into the Main House. My father did a full-on Tex Avery double take; his eyeballs practically flew out of his head and ran after her on legs.

"Who's *that*?" he asked. He cocked what I'm sure he thought was a casual thumb in the woman's direction, but I knew he was pointing at trouble. Everything comes in threes: first Emily's mom, then CJ's, now this.

"That's Ali's mom, Carol."

"Who?"

"Ali Rubinstein? My roommate? You met her upstairs?" Ali and I were living together again, but this time it was of our own volition. After our wretched freshman fall semester together in Mucket, Ali and I had kept clear of each other. But by the spring of our junior year we had both matured to a point where we were able to affect a wry fealty that came from knowing exactly where we stood with each other. Knowing we didn't have to love each other released us both from having to try too hard and offered us the personal space we needed to share a very tiny room on the top floor of the Main House.

"Oh, yeah, Ali, sure. Nice kid. Are her parents, perchance, divorced?"

"No, Dad. They live in Los Angeles."

"Hm" was all he said. I knew this information wouldn't do anything to stop him from seducing Ali's mom back at the Treadway Inn that weekend. And sure enough, that is exactly what happened. Though it wasn't his first Treadway conquest, it turned out to be his last. Carol divorced Ali's dad and married mine right after our senior year. Ali has been my sister ever since.

Buxton, March 1982

M y senior year at Buxton was one of triumph. I had finally become the person everyone hoped I might someday be: responsible, hardworking, academically successful, a solid member of the Buxton community. I also had formed an artistic identity. In addition to finding transcendence on the stage, I had become a poet. I kept my portable Olivetti set up next to my bed and composed a poem on it every day, adding pages to a growing stack I kept in a folder. I didn't show them to anyone, I just read them back to myself and allowed myself to feel tenderness for them.

My spring semester student evaluations were all glowing. Ben Fincke wrote, "I am very proud of Erika and delighted with the direction her life is taking. The Spring term of one's Senior year can be one of great depth and meaning. I feel certain that Erika will make this true of her last months with us. Already her contribution has been more than memorable."

Now that the final evaluations were in, and I had been accepted to college at my first choice, Sarah Lawrence, the rest of the year would be focused on the yearbook. The yearbook was designed and produced entirely by the senior class. I had gone from sneering at it, that day in Los Angeles four years earlier, to being thrilled to be a part of something so meaningful. The pressure of schoolwork was off, the days were lengthening, and my free time was very free.

One Saturday afternoon I was in my room when I heard somebody completely rocking out on a guitar downstairs. I went to have a look. There was a lot of guitar-playing at Buxton—guys were forever noodling out "Stairway to Heaven" in the student lounge or softly twangling "Wooden Ships" for smoking shed sing-alongs. Even I could pick up a guitar and grind out the opening chords of "Smoke on the Water." But this guitar-playing was of a different order. It was a loose, wild, twangy slide guitar. I went downstairs and peeked around the corner to see who was playing.

It was Henry Baker, of all people, nerdy behind his big-framed glasses, his leg up on a chair and a Coricidin bottle on his middle finger. He had Jimmy Swan's stupid Ovation guitar and he was playing the ever-living shit out of it while Jimmy looked on in awe. It was some kind of protest folk song about a guy named John Sinclair, wrongly imprisoned for something-something, set him free, whatever. I came closer and perched on a nearby table. Henry smiled at me and sang,

They gave him ten for two
What else can the bastards do?

He was lit up with the song, fiery and handsome, singing about shooting gooks in Vietnam and selling dope, his hand loose on the frets, that pill bottle sliding up and down the neck of the guitar. How had I never noticed this side of Henry? Henry, Eileen's shy, arty, atonal husband—had hidden fire, and was a stone fox to boot.

"*Got to, got to, got to set him freeeeee!*" He finished the last chord with a big, corny pinwheel of his arm à la Elvis. Jimmy Swan and I clapped and hooted. Henry stood, took a maestro's bow, and handed the guitar back to Jimmy

I felt breathless and light, buoyant with lust and interest. "That was amazing, Henry."

"Well, thanks."

"And that song is so righteous," I gushed.

"Yeah, it's such a great protest song."

"Who wrote it?"

Henry laughed. "Who else? John Lennon."

Buxton, April 1982

Henry greeted me at the door of his apartment dressed in a black suit jacket and pants, with a white T-shirt underneath. He had a second job in the Bennington College music department, just over the border in Vermont. He had written a piano concerto for the school's orchestra to perform and he would be conducting his own work. He needed a photo for the program. He had asked me, Camera Girl, to shoot it. Even though he wasn't paying me anything, it felt like my first professional photography gig.

Henry and Eileen had moved from the Gatehouse into Pilar and Ed's old apartment in the Main House. Pilar and her growing family had been given more spacious faculty housing near the Barn. The apartment was transformed. What was once cozy chaos was now spare and painted gallery-white. The wood floors were glossy and bare. The objet d'art, a large, eiderdown-covered bed, was set on the diagonal across the center of the room, and was brazenly unmade.

"I like what you've done with the place."

"Thanks." Henry seemed bemused by the compliment. He offered me a glass of bubbly water.

"I don't know how you want to do this," Henry said, rubbing his hands together. "But I'd like to have some fun. Are you up for that?"

"I have six rolls of film with me. I'm up for anything."

"Great," he said with a clap. He spun on his heel and gestured to the apartment. "I have some lights, I have this bare wall, let's start there."

We began simply, with some portraits of him seated in a chair, looking conductorish and dignified. It was nighttime, and I didn't have any studio lights, so we pointed a gooseneck lamp at him and did the best we could. After half a roll we started playing with the lighting. We put a small table lamp on the floor and had him squat in front of it, so he was backlit. His hair lit up around his shadowed face like a halo. Then we tried several with him holding tympani mallets and playing different things—pots, a stack of books, a pillow. In an ode to Kerouac we put a portable typewriter on the floor and loaded it up with an unspooling roll of industrial paper towel and staged Henry crawling toward it, reaching toward the keyboard, making words unspool from the platen. We put things on his head and laughed; we posed him behind an African mask that had been hanging on the wall.

We looked around his apartment for other props to use and found a length of gray fabric. I wrapped him in it from neck to toe. I shot a couple of frames and stopped.

"Can you take your glasses off?" He couldn't, because he was mummied-up in the fabric, so I took them off his face myself. The act felt so intimate my legs went liquid.

Henry's eyes, without the dwarfing, heavy frames, were startling. They were pretty eyes, like a girl's, and full of naked depth. He looked back into mine and we held the gaze for a shutter-stop, before I self-consciously broke away.

I gathered myself and turned my attention back to my camera. Henry, a person at that moment with very limited physical options, drew himself up regally. His body was lithe and elegant. The tight fabric exaggerated the triangular taper of his shoulders to his hips, the bulge of his crotch. Henry squared himself and stared into the distance heroically. He looked like an allegorical figure, a mast-head on the prow of the SS *Girl Crush*. He was both conquering and conquered. I pressed the button on my camera and the shutter snapped, I cocked it and shot again and again. I could not expose enough film to capture his beauty. *Snap, cock, snap, cock, snap, cock.*

When I was done, I took the tail of that fabric and spun him out of it. I was dizzy with the moment, with the scent of him as it escaped the closeness of the binding, with the way he laughed with me out of nervousness and surprise.

We were out of ideas and took a break, sitting cross-legged on the hardwood floor, listening to a piece by John Cage called *Music of Changes.*

"You know how Cage wrote this piece?" Henry asked. I shook my head. "He used the I Ching to choose its tempo, duration, and dynamics." I listened to the music and sincerely tried to make sense of it, but it sounded random, like something a toddler would bang out on a piano. There was no melody.

"You don't like it?"

"Well, I don't think I could dance to it," I quipped, but he didn't laugh.

"*Homo sapiens* are animals that see patterns. We hunger for them. But Cage turned it around, creating music that defies pattern and asks the question: If we stop looking for patterns, are we still human? What might a random universe unleash in us?"

"Sheer terror, I would think."

"Or absolute freedom and possibility."

I found this idea discomfiting. I was always trying to find patterns, to understand what things meant. Wasn't that the whole idea? Life felt like a jigsaw puzzle—and I meant to gather as many pieces as I could, so I could sort them into like piles and assemble them into a coherent picture.

Henry sat across from me on the floor, his knees bent and ankles crossed, his arms draped over his knees, hands clasped. His bare hands and feet formed an X, a pattern so perfect I picked up my camera and gathered it all into the frame.

I was at the end of the last roll. I wound the film out of

my camera, packed up my stuff, and went back to my room in the girls' dorm, just down the hall. I lay in my narrow bed that night thinking about the possibility of the random, patternless universe that was spinning all around me, flinging people together and tearing them apart without rhyme or reason. I found it unbearable.

We had just read *Howards End* in Ben's English class and the words "only connect" held deep resonance for me. I didn't believe in God, but I believed in the pattern, I believed in human connection. I believed that those connections built a web that supported us all. I had connected with Henry. I wondered what it meant. I wondered if I would get to see him again without his glasses.

The next day in the privacy of the Buxton darkroom I conjured him back. I worked the alchemy of negative to positive with pops of light in the dark. His image floated up to me from the bottom of the developing tray like a gorgeous hallucination. His deep eyes, his soft hair. The curve of his back in his black suit darkened and sharpened as I shook the tray rhythmically, urgently, greedily. Finally, the image was all there, and I slid it into the stop bath, then fixed it. It was the image I wanted most: his hands and feet, naked and beautiful, and there, on his left hand, the focal point, his three-banded wedding ring.

I thumbtacked several of the prints on the wall next to my bed before lights-out. I got under my duvet and quietly touched myself until I wept with longing. Each day my crush grew more acute. I lost interest in my studies and dreamed through my classes of Henry wrapped in fabric, Henry spinning into my arms, Henry kissing me.

Every afternoon I flung myself onto my bike for long, windy rides, laying down miles of mid-April country road, trying to drive out thoughts of the music teacher with breath and sweat and fresh air.

My body became a compass that oriented to his magnetic north, and my sight the quivering silvery arrow that pointed, constantly, toward him. I knew where he was every minute of the day. I tracked him through time and space. I knew when he was in the Main House, or the New Building, or the Music Shed. I knew when he left campus. I watched him eat in the dining hall. I timed my entrances and exits to match his, so I could pass him in a doorway, catch a whiff of him, catch his eye.

Buxton, March 1982

STUDENT EVALUATIONS

English IV

Erika has had a very good term in English this winter. She has been very enthusiastic and conscientious in her work. Her first paper was superb, and her third was very good. They were extremely well written, incisive and perceptive. However, in her second, on Othello, she fell prey to her own wit and allowed some extremely amusing but inappropriate jokes to control the tone and direction of her argument. She writes so well, responds to literature so perceptively and is, basically, so bright that there is too much at stake for her to lose control. Sometimes the better you get, the harder it is to know what to cut out.

Five Revolutions

Erika has had another fine term in this course. She has been energetic, vocal, and enthusiastic and has done quality work. Her initial paper on Moliere was thoughtful and well written and I look forward to reading her more recent effort on Rousseau due later this week.

Erika has learned some of the less attractive aspects of leadership as well this winter and these are not always easy or comfortable. When one takes risks to assert oneself in any group one is vulnerable. There are lessons to be learned. What Erika stands for at Buxton, however, is important and good and I hope that she will continue to grow and to change with energy and compassion. Erika is a wonderful young woman and I enjoy having her in class.

Ben Fincke—Summation

I am very proud of Erika and delighted with the direction her life is taking. The Spring term of one's Senior year can be one of great depth and meaning. I feel certain that Erika will make this true of her last months with us. Already her contribution is more than memorable.

Buxton, April 1982

For a few weeks that spring, I was ascendant. Ellen Sangster's school had transformed me from a sad, shoplifting, slutty fuckup to a model student and a member in good standing of the Buxton community. I knew my intellectual worth, had made life-long friends, and anticipated a brilliant career on the stage. I would be sad to leave Buxton in June, but I was ready to graduate. I bought a graduation dress over spring break in New York. It was a white, old-fashioned Laura Ashley frock that made me look like Renoir's Thérèse.

I had redeemed myself.

Henry was waiting for me in the doorway of the dining hall after lunch.

"I was wondering if you'd like to go for a bike ride after classes."

"I'd love to!" He laughed at my enthusiasm and I blushed.

I met Henry outside the Gatehouse and we pushed off down Water Street on our bikes, past the library and the golf course, toward Highway 2. The day was bright and warm. We rode word-lessly down Green River Road. We had come out this way three weeks earlier with Eileen, before the photo shoot. I didn't ask why she wasn't with us today.

Eileen and I had ridden abreast that day, chatting and laughing, while Henry quietly cycled behind us. The buds were just opening then, but now spring was fully upon us. The trees had leafed out and were full of grackles. The Green River, which was really a stream, meandered sweetly alongside the road, hemmed in by a dilapidated split-rail fence. Wads of chickadees startled up from its banks and darted across the road in front of us.

We rode slowly. I didn't want to do or say anything that might break the spell of this magical afternoon alone with Henry. All too soon we reached the gas station at Five Corners, the halfway point of our ten-mile loop. Luckily, the second half of the ride was the toughest and slowest.

Cold Spring Road had a long, steep uphill grade, and we both stood on our pedals to pump. Spring seemed to turn to summer as we chuffed and sweated, and the roadside scenery, the Queen Anne's lace and buttercups, went slowly, slowly past. When we finally topped the hill, we pulled up alongside a fence to catch our breath. The splintery old rails held back a small herd of Holsteins that chewed, oblivious to the sweeping view of the valley below.

When our breathing finally slowed, Henry broke the silence.

"I am in torment, Erika."

I looked at him and even though his transition lenses had darkened way down, I could read trouble in his eyes. "What's wrong?"

He looked at me beseechingly. "I haven't been able to eat. I can't sleep. I can't do anything but think about you."

I held very still so as not to interrupt him.

"I watch you in the dining hall, I see you on the path between classes, and every time my heart stops."

I gripped the handlebars of my bike to steady myself.

"Am I shocking you? Tell me to shut up."

"No..."

"I am telling you I am in love with you."

This wasn't what I expected. Had I heard him right? I never dreamed that my schoolgirl crush on my teacher would be answered. He was waiting for my next line, and I grappled for it. I had played this scene onstage. I knew my line was "I love you too," but the line caught in my throat. Instead I said, "But what about Eileen?"

"Oh, Eileen is not who you think she is, nor is our relationship."

"What do you mean?"

"Erika, we're not actually married." He pulled off his bike glove and showed me his fancy wedding ring. "We had these made so we could work at Buxton as a couple. This ring is meaningless. Do you understand what I am saying? I am saying I am free to love you. And I am deeply in love with you, Erika."

As a child of divorce, I understood that marriage was simply an outfit people wore until they grew out of it. But I never imagined that people would lie about being married in the first place.

Henry pulled off his glasses and there were his eyes brimming with emotion. "Do you have any feelings for me?"

My crush on him was still new, I had barely mapped its area, and now, suddenly, it was no longer a crush, but a reciprocated...love? Did I love him? I didn't know him. I didn't know myself either, all I understood was that I was being offered something extraordinary; a story. Here was a fork in my road: one way led back to the safety of the dorm, the other toward romantic adventure. If I were to be a heroine in my own life story, then how could I refuse this offer? Besides, I didn't want to hurt his feelings.

"Yes, I love you."

Henry reached across the bikes that were between us and took my hand in his. I thought for a moment he might press it up against his hard-on as boys usually did, but Henry simply brought my hand to his lips and kissed it tenderly, like Omar Sharif, his brown eyes bottomless and lash-weighted. As he bent his head to my hand the sunlight brought out the chestnut in his hair and revealed a bit of thinning at the crown.

"We must speak of this to no one," he said before we got on our bikes and rode back to school.

The next day I received a letter. It was written on thick, cream-colored stationery and was postmarked from Bennington. There was no return address. It was from Henry, speaking of his elation, our twinned souls, of the lovelessness of his union with Eileen, and his conviction that we were meant to be together. *I know the world will judge us, me the 31 year old predator, you the 18 year old victim,* he wrote, *but you and I are beyond time, age or definition. Love is only available to those with the courage to grab it. Would we cave in to those whose bankrupt "morals" would keep two people who love each other from touching each other?*

Another letter arrived the next day: *Our love occupies a space and time beyond my wildest imaginings. Now that this has happened I can never return to what was. Can you?*

CJ asked me to go for a walk. We hit the driveway and lit up a couple of cigarettes. CJ's hands trembled as he held the match out to me.

"This might sound crazy, Erika, and Jesus, please forgive me if I'm just completely out of line here, but..." He laughed nervously, his eyes darting around in fear.

"What, CJ?"

"I am so fucking scared to say this out loud...but...are you by any chance...are you and Henry...having an affair?" I gave him a minute to laugh off his nervousness. He was so rattled.

"Yes. Kind of, I think. We haven't slept together."

CJ sighed. "Christ, Erika, why?"

"We are in love."

CJ looked at me doubtfully. "Seriously? What do we really know about Henry fucking Baker anyway?" His obvious antipathy toward Henry confused me. We were all friends, why wouldn't CJ be happy for me?

"I know he loves me, CJ."

CJ spat out a laugh. "Sure."

"Ceej, this is the real thing."

"What happens when everybody finds out?"

"You can't tell anyone!"

"God no, I never would, but Erika, this is Buxton, you can't cut a fart without the whole school knowing about it."

"Do you think anyone else knows?"

"Not yet, but listen, this isn't Ibsen, this is real life. He could get fired. You could be expelled." That idea struck me as unlikely. It seemed to me that the school tacitly condoned student-teacher couplings. What about Tony Hanlon and Melodie Logan? What about Chad and every student he had courted in front of us? Chad's fixation that year was Betsy Lawler, a junior with waist-length red hair and a mean right leg. He had presented her with a single rose at the school announcements assembly and nobody said a thing about it. Betsy wore Chad's boxer shorts to soccer practice. Everyone just accepted it.

CJ crushed his cigarette into the asphalt with the toe of his loafer. "There's only six weeks until graduation. Can't you just wait it out?"

But it was already too late. I was in too deep to turn back. "I don't think so."

"How do you plan to keep this affair a secret?" CJ asked.

"We can if you help us."

CJ was breathing fast and heavy. I didn't understand why he was so scared. I didn't understand that this trembling boy in the dark beside me loved me a thousand times more than Henry ever would. I didn't understand that my forbidden romance was only a tiny piece of the tragic tale unspooling on that dark driveway, on that long-ago spring night.

It would be thirty years before CJ would tell me the real reason why he had come to Buxton in his junior year: CJ had transferred to Buxton to escape a predator.

Had I known then what I know now I would never have asked him to pigeon letters between me and my teacher. Or so I like to think. But even when presented with empirical evidence of my own abuse decades on, I wasn't able to see myself as a victim of anything. It never works as cleanly as that.

Awareness around sexual predation was not a cultural talking point back in 1982. Sexual predation was just an everyday reality for children: in the Catholic Church, in the Boy Scouts, in East Coast prep schools like Buxton. For girls and boys like me and CJ, who had been left vulnerable by absent parents and self-preserving institutions, being desired by an adult was standard operating procedure.

It would be decades before any of this would come to light. In the meantime, I enlisted my best friend as a middleman in my passion play, setting him up to play a part in the reenactment of his own trauma.

The next day CJ passed me two letters from Henry, one in the morning, the other in the afternoon. *I am born anew. You came to me in a vision. I looked up and there you were! We gazed at each other as we do and I knew, I knew for the first time that you and I truly are!*

My eighteen-year-old self couldn't see how corny and cliché his letters were, how vague, histrionic, and grandiose he was. I thought this was how true love was supposed to be talked about. Anyone who would put me on that kind of a pedestal deserved, at a minimum, a roll in the hay.

I knew what to do next. I met Henry after classes at the bottom of Pine Alley, near the Gatehouse, and we took off into the woods, looking for a safe place to spread out the blanket he had brought.

I wondered if we would be consummating our love on Buxton land or Clark Art land. Henry unfolded the blanket and patted it down for me. It was more than Keith had done on the river, more consideration than Jonas had ever shown me. We disrobed and stood in front of each other. His body was lean, pale, and elegant. His cock, heavy with blood, pointed to four o'clock.

When I was underneath him, I realized, too late, that what I actually wanted was to be with Henry in the white bed in the middle of his and Eileen's apartment. I didn't want another woodland fuck. I wanted to *be* Eileen, to have her relationship, her artistic alliance, and her bohemian life.

It was over quickly. I remember it vaguely as being goose-bumpy, technical sex, but I don't remember much else. All I can remember was his smell, because he doused himself in cologne, and to this day a whiff of Lagerfeld will yank me back to the spring of 1982, when I fucked the music teacher in the woods and signed myself up for my own downfall.

PART VI

FREE AND CLEAR

Los Angeles, Summer 2009

June melted into July and we began to meet at Spade's arctic-chilled pad at the Ravenswood every day. None of this was hard to pull off. My husband was rarely interested in my whereabouts; my kids were busy with camp and friends. The person I had to avoid was Diana, who liked to check in by phone a couple of times a day. For years we would do a morning call and sometimes an afternoon call. We would tell each other our plans for the day, and laugh at the things that needed laughing at. But lately I had been letting her calls pile up. There was just too much I couldn't say to my friend. I was withdrawing from my world as I built a new, secret one with Spade.

Our whirlwind love affair remained staunchly chaste. He said we could not be lovers until we were "free and clear." But everything we did was adultery: the lying, the long afternoons spent touching and talking, the pile of fevered love letters that grew between us.

I was consumed by Spade: his tastes, his interests, his rap sheet, his ex-girlfriends, his books, his history, his friendships with the LAPD, and the ghost of his murdered mother with whom he'd danced constantly. All of it was weird and new and sexy. I had a role to play in this world; I was his femme fatale. I surrendered to it and felt my old life drift away.

Then Lola was murdered.

Lola was the seventeen-year-old daughter of dear friends. She had been out running errands for her mother when she was abducted by a parolee at knifepoint. He drove her around in her own car, trying to get cash out of ATMs with her credit card, which the card wasn't set up to do. At one point, Lola called her parents and asked them how she might get a cash advance to buy some shoes. "Just come home," they said, knowing something was wrong. Her car was found the next morning in a downtown parking garage, Lola's body inside.

Lola's murder was horror on an order I could not digest. I had known Lola's parents for twenty years through the many friends we shared in the L.A. arts and music world. She was the girl in high-tops, dancing in the living room at her family's New Year's Eve party, the cool older girl my daughters loved to hang out with at dinner parties, and the source of our favorite hand-me-downs. Lola was that rare teenager who seemed to genuinely enjoy the company of adults, who would look you in the eye and ask a follow-up question. She was a magical, beloved only child.

I got the news in an email from a mutual friend. When I had scraped myself off the floor and could think clearly enough to breathe and dial a phone, I called Spade. He already knew. Lola's parents had asked him to use his connections with the LAPD to get a missing-persons case opened on Lola after she'd been missing only a few hours.

I wept with shock and grief on the phone and Spade witnessed my horror and understood it. I was being forced to imagine something unspeakable, the murder of this precious girl. Spade had been imagining exactly this all his life. Murdered women were his métier. He alone in my world contained a context for something that otherwise made no sense to me or to anyone else I knew.

Lola's murder convulsed our community. The world went completely dark. Paul wept helplessly and I held my frightened daughters close. When I wasn't in the reach of Spade's voice I felt haunted and guilty. I had crossed the streams of romance and family and now here was a murdered girl who could just as easily have been my own girl. I could taste child endangerment like pennies in my mouth. Spade's dark places had come to shadow my world.

On the weekend of Lola's memorial, Paul took the girls to his parents' house in San Diego, leaving me at home alone. I put on a backless dress, packed a small overnight bag, and walked over to the local Coffee Bean to wait for Spade. After weeks of doing the antler dance, we were finally off to the Four Seasons to consummate our love. It turned out, we couldn't wait until I was free and clear after all.

Spade rolled up in his M5, got out, and opened the door for me. The car enfolded me in its luxury and my familiar, freeway-adjacent neighborhood receded behind polarized glass. Just like that, I was back in Spade's cool, leathery world. He cast a gimlet eye around my local strip mall—my Toys "R" Us, my El Pollo Loco, my beloved Fallas Paredes—and said, "Baby, this is the shits. I'm going to get you north of Pico Boulevard if it's the last thing I do."

I waited in the hotel lobby while Spade checked us in. He was wearing white jeans and a loud Hawaiian shirt. As he leaned over the concierge desk, his jeans sagged on his hipless frame, revealing a long slice of ass crack. I turned to study an elaborate flower arrangement.

Was I really going to do this? Was I going to sleep with this weird man sixteen years my senior? Did I love him enough to break my marriage vows? As it was from the day I first met him, Spade felt like a foregone conclusion. Was this even a choice?

Of course I was going to sleep with him.

It was a small suite on a high floor, all white, like the inside of an igloo, and chilled to a temperature to match. Every inch of my skin pebbled up as Spade pulled my dress over my head. "God, you're beautiful. You're a tigress," he whispered, and snarled into my ear. That tanked my mojo for a minute. He sensed my retreat. "Let's get horizontal," he said.

Everything that was weird or discomfiting about Spade disappeared when he was horizontal. He may have been a jacked-up stooge on the vertical, but get him flush and he was Nureyev: graceful, tender, and powerful. I felt myself loosen as I lay down beside him.

I had read an interview Spade had done in some men's magazine. He was asked what he thought the secret was to being a good lover. His reply: "Take your fucking time." I had never been made love to at that pace. He approached my body with reverence and deep awareness, putting his mouth on me and taking it off when he knew I was over-amped. Then putting it back and keeping it there through one faked orgasm and then a real one.

I had finally found someone whose hunger for intimacy matched my own.

Our fucking brought my period on. I was horrified to stain those snowy-white hotel sheets, but Spade was unbothered. We took a long bath together and ordered room-service cheeseburgers. Over dinner he gave me a gift: a copy of his soon-to-be-published novel.

On the flyleaf he had inscribed, "For Erika Schickel, In blood and to the death. Sam Spade."

Lola's memorial was that Sunday. I arrived at Barnsdall Park scrubbed and buttoned down to properly mourn my friends' child. There were easily two hundred people attending, most of whom I knew from my twenty years in L.A., writer pals and guys who had played in bands with Paul over the years. Everyone was dressed up L.A.-hipster fancy: sharp cowboy shirts, vintage dresses, freshly blacked Doc Martens, shades. I scanned the crowd for Spade—he wasn't hard to spot.

Spade was dressed in his dapper best: chalk stripe suit, silk pocket square, porkpie hat. There was so much natty fabric happening on his six-foot-three frame that I didn't know where to put my eyes, so I simply met his gaze.

We made our way through the crowd toward each other slowly,

casually. I got stopped on the way by friends who asked after Paul and the kids. They weren't due back from San Diego until later that evening. My family. I had a family.

Walking through that crowd felt like walking on a swaying rope bridge over a deep chasm. On one side were the people I knew, friends and colleagues, people who knew me as Paul's wife, a responsible person, a mother, a friend. On the other side of the chasm was Spade, holding his torch, waiting for me to get across so he could use it to burn the bridge behind me.

Fresno, August 2009

I was coasting downhill in my dying Subaru, the heater blasting on high to keep the engine from overheating, hoping I would be able to coast straight into the bay of the nearest mechanic in Fresno. My husband and daughters were in the Civic, following behind. We had been camping with close friends in one of the most remote and beautiful spots in California, and I had barely been there.

I had been out of range for a week, and the only conversation I was interested in having anymore was the ongoing one I was having with Spade. I continued it nonstop in my head, and in a twenty-five-page letter I wrote to him over that long week. I would hand it to him tomorrow.

I rolled into Fresno and we got the Subaru up on a jack at a garage next door to a Rally Burger. We lunched on greasy hamburgers on a grassy median in the parking lot while we waited for our car. I tried to avoid looking at the turd our terrier, Maggie, had just left four feet away. An expensive interim fix would get us back to Los Angeles, but I knew the car, like my marriage, was a total loss.

The kids finished their burgers and we gave them each $5 to spend at their discretion at the Dollar Tree, in comfortable view of our lunch spot. They took off. Paul and I sat on the curb, finishing our drinks.

"So, where do you want to go on vacation next year?" Paul asked.

"Nowhere."

"You don't want to go on vacation?"

"No."

"Okay, then what *do* you want?"

"I want a divorce, Paul."

"I see." He had his elbows up on his knees and was worrying a blade of grass. I squinted out across the parking lot.

"Can I presume this is somehow Spade-related?" His voice was calm.

"Yes."

"Are you in love with him?"

"Yes."

"Okay then." Paul got up, used his wrapper to pick up the dog turd, and threw the whole mess into the trash.

The girls came back with grainy coloring books and toxic Chinese crayons. The car came down off the rack. Paul would drive the limping Subaru home, so I loaded the kids into the Civic and we began our separate journeys: Paul driving my dying car the two hundred miles from Fresno to L.A., contemplating the loss of his life as he knew it, me driving the kids, listening to them chatter happily in the backseat, unaware that a bomb had just exploded in the center of theirs. Grace was soon to start her freshman year of high school, and Mae was about to enter the giant spank-tunnel of middle school. I was going to make an already difficult time in their lives unbearable.

I grappled with the enormity of what I had done. Grace was the same age I had been when my family split apart, on the cusp of her thirteenth birthday and puberty. Mae was still just a happy, free-spirited little girl like my sister had been. I had sworn never to replicate the trauma of my original family, and yet here I was, reenacting it perfectly.

I had planned this life, this beautiful family, as a rebuke to my parents, and I had almost succeeded. I had cooked family dinners, over-volunteered in their school, taught their Girl Scout troop to knit, and canvassed for Obama. I had done everything I could to be a model of motherhood, but now the jig was up. In that moment I attributed it to the magnetic pull of Sam Spade. Now I know that I couldn't resist the dark seduction of reliving the trauma of my adolescence, in its every excruciating beat.

All I knew then was that my life looked an obscene origami, a sheet of paper that folded over and over into itself to create a shape that I could not yet discern. August 2009 folded against the spring of 1982, when I last blew up my life for love, when I became known primarily for fucking and for fucking up. Scandal was my métier, and I was about to excel at it like never before.

Los Angeles, Fall 2009

W e presented a calm, hopeful, united front to the kids when we gave them the bad news, but their reactions were predictably bitter. Mae stormed out of the dining room and slammed her bedroom door. Grace sat with us a while longer, asking us follow-up questions that we barely had answers for. She took off for her boyfriend's house.

There followed a roughly two-week period where the marriage was over, but I continued to live at home and sleep in the bed I shared with Paul, while Paul slept in the trailer. My husband knew how to keep a lid on himself, but sometimes he would boil so hard his lid would rattle. He would isolate himself in his workshop and take it out on inanimate objects. He would smash something, or screw up a fret-job on a guitar neck and curse himself ragged. Things happened in the middle of the night that I could only guess at.

While I was grateful that he didn't take his rage out on his family, none of this did anything to release the tension between us. I had wanted a fight with my husband for a long time. I wanted hot words, tears, counterarguments, slammed doors, makeup sex. But for twenty years we had maintained a cordial, friendly distance that left me feeling lonely and insane.

Because we shared no real intimacy throughout our entire marriage, talking to my husband about my feelings felt oddly inappropriate and embarrassing. He didn't seem interested, so I would save it all up for when I got to Jack and Diana's house.

Most nights, starting when the kids were small, after I had put them to bed, and Paul had done the dishes, I would hop in the car and drive the eight minutes to my friends' house while Paul would go work in the garage. At the Margolins' I would find companionship, warmth, and genuine intimacy.

The three of us spent evenings watching *The Daily Show* telling stories, talking freely about sex, literature, and politics, telling truths about ourselves and making each other laugh. Hard. It was in the Margolin household where I felt most bright and alive, most free to be myself.

Jack and Diana's relationship had all the passion and immediacy mine lacked. They had met in college, and like swans, they had mated for life. I had never witnessed a marriage as solid and road-tested as theirs. They fought and fucked with equal energy and the few times I walked in on one of their battles the feeling of released energy fritzing the room both terrified and thrilled me. Could people fight and then find each other again? In my experience people just gave up and left.

Paul and I had made several good-faith attempts to save our union over our nineteen years together. We scheduled date nights and gave each other thoughtful gifts. I had surprised him with a couple of romantic trips—once to a sexy hotel in the desert, another time to Paris—to try to resuscitate our romance. Both times we were able to find each other again and remember what good company we were for each other. My starved libido would take the reins and I would fuck Paul into exhaustion. We'd hold hands all the way home. But always, inevitably, as we settled back into our home life, the tide of Paul's sadness would rise and I would drift away from him, into my personal life with the kids and my friends.

At one point, we engaged the services of a marriage counselor. Dr. Duchamp was a lithe, elegant, stern woman with a tidy pony-tail and a small, chic office in Beverly Hills. Paul and I aired our marital complaints and Dr. Duchamp became convinced that Paul was fine, and I was the one who needed extensive therapy. I began to see her alone.

The more I told Dr. Duchamp about my family and my past, the more obvious it became that the problem with my marriage was me. She tried to tell me I had trauma, and even did a little EMDR on me, tapping her fingers together, a tiny distraction, powerful enough to unhook my defenses. I was a willing patient, but I really had no idea what she was talking about. What trauma?

The problem, as I saw it, was that I was no longer in love with my husband, not that I got kicked out of boarding school. Spade was yet three years in the future, I wasn't in love with anybody else, I had lost interest in the project of working on the marriage. Even if it could be saved, I wasn't sure I wanted it. That didn't mean I wanted a divorce. I wanted to carry on with the old okey-doke as long as we could, for the kids' sake.

But now that I had committed infidelity, that possibility was closed. Paul and I both knew there were volumes of things to say to each other, but he had no response beyond silent, distant rage. He wasn't going to make an attempt to win me back, and I didn't want or expect him to. Many years later my sister would tell me that Paul had called her during that time and had wept on the phone, telling her he wanted me back. He never said anything like that to me. I thought we were both done.

I did whatever I could to not be at home while simultaneously projecting stability to the kids, which meant waking up in my own bed for the time being. But whenever I could I would escape to Spade's, where I could dive back into the swoon of our love and remember why I had caused all this hurt and ruin.

We hadn't figured out the problem of what to do next. I assumed that Paul would move out, but he gave no indication of what he wanted. So we commenced a strange living limbo where I openly went to the Ravenswood to be with Spade, then came home late at night, reeking of sex and betrayal.

One of those nights I came home to find Paul on the side patio, drinking with a friend. I came out to say hello and he looked at me with withering disgust, excused himself, and went out to the backyard, picked up a shovel, and slammed the back of it against a mound of dirt over and over until he was spent. The friend excused himself and went home and I went quietly to bed.

The next morning Paul told me that since I was the one who had destroyed our marriage I would be the one to move out of the house. I was too ashamed and demoralized to argue with him.

Spade made good on his promise and set me up in an apartment north of Pico by half a block, eight blocks away from my marital home. My apartment was an upper two-bedroom in a 1920s court-yard complex. It was compact, but the living room had a vaulted ceiling and French windows that opened onto treetops, making it feel rather grand and spacious. There was a second bedroom for the girls and a sunny bathroom with a fantastic bathtub. It was close enough to the house for the girls to ride their bikes over whenever they wanted.

Spade cosigned the lease just like my dad had done for me when I lived off-campus in college. Spade paid first and last month's rent and would pay my rent for many months to come. I was officially a kept woman.

That night, before I had even gotten the electricity turned on, we made love on the bare hardwood floor, our aging, grasping flesh lit by a stripe of streetlight from the window. Spade dubbed my apartment "The Fuckpad," which was meant as a joke, but that's exactly what it was.

I moved out in tiny increments, doing a slow dissolve from the family home, hoping Grace and Mae wouldn't notice. I didn't want to disturb anything in their environment, so I took only the essentials: some clothes, my laptop, my trusty cast-iron frying pan, and a blow-up camping mattress. I left everything as though I would be back soon.

Now that Paul and the kids knew, it was time to tell Diana. I asked her to dinner at our favorite neighborhood sushi joint. I poured us each a sake and told her everything, from the Festival of Books to the present. After I finished my story, my best friend looked at me and said, "I'm just afraid you're going to abandon your children."

I nearly gagged on my edamame. I was guilty of many terrible things, but child abandonment was not among them. Diana had watched me parent my children almost every day for a decade. She knew how much I loved my kids. I was the woman who had once saved her own daughter from choking to death. I wanted to prove to her that I was still that person who was steadfast and true, who loved her children and her friends. But it was too late, I had let too many of her calls go to voicemail.

I was furious. I was hurt. This wasn't about her anyway, this was about me and the end of my marriage. Why was she taking it personally? I had been cheating on my husband, not her. Could she not appreciate that these had been extraordinary circumstances? Didn't she know how much I needed her now?

Most best friends, once they heard about the secret love affair and the family in crisis, would let the misunderstanding about radio silence go and rally by their friend. But Diana was wed to the idea that my carelessness was a betrayal. No amount of apology, explanation, or beseeching would bring her back. I had obviously triggered something very deep within my friend that I could only guess at. I had to let her let me go.

With Jack and Diana gone I had lost not just my two dearest friends, but also my literary muse and my professional mentor. I was officially cut off from everyone and everything that mattered to me, that had made me who I once was.

Paul, meanwhile, in his enduring rage, called most of my closest friends and had given them the news of our split and his side of the story before I could. Most people were aghast and sided with Paul. A few remained loyal to me: my sister, Mia, Ali, and Netter were my mainstays, checking in, making me laugh occasionally and remember who I was. My friend Sharon regularly brought me lunch and kept tabs on me.

The news of what was happening in my private life began to leak out to my larger social and professional circles, and most people were perfectly horrified by what I had done. I had committed the worst sin: I had left a good man for a bad man and abandoned my children. Even worse, the bad man was famous in my field, so my choice could only be chalked up to naked ambition, an unforgivable sin in a woman.

My downfall wasn't entirely personal. All of these events were occurring against the backdrop of the economic downturn of 2008. Just about every outlet I wrote for trimmed their staff and tightened their freelance budgets. Local alternative weeklies got bought and sold, the dedicated book section of the *L.A. Times* disappeared, existing as a pale shadow at the back of the Lifestyle section. The days when a writer might support a family off of full-time freelance work were officially over.

Even Richard Schickel couldn't pay his bills from writing anymore. The twenty-first century was no place for a gentleman writer. He had left *Time* a long time ago, and had made most of his living in television, which supported his book writing and his freelancing. But as column inches shrank for film reviews and the noble art of criticism was degraded by thumbs-up/thumbs-down bullet reviewing, my father became less interested in the endeavor and more cranky about the sheer stupidity of contemporary culture. He raged against the blogification of film criticism. A medium in which "any asshole with an opinion can hold forth," he would sputter on film panels whose audience was made up mostly of film bloggers.

It didn't matter that my outlets were narrowing; I didn't have a single article idea to pitch. The only thoughts I had in my brain were about Spade and the kids. Unfortunately, my adolescent children only wanted to be where I wasn't, so that left me with even more time to think about Spade, write him long letters, perfume my breasts, and wait for his next visit.

All of this was so familiar. Even as I lay in bed, legs spread, listening for Spade's key in my lock, I understood that I had once again made myself into a modern-day Hester Prynne, a woman scorned for her romantic choices.

No one could see the man I loved because he only showed that side to me. In the world he was a bully and a show-off, but with me he was soft, sweet, supportive, and tender. But even those worthy adjectives couldn't describe his hold on me. Simply stated: I stayed because of how I felt when my head was on his chest. What he held for me was primal. The only other time I had felt that peaceful was as a kid, when I would suck my thumb and rub my Snoopy's fur with the tips of my fingers. Spade's heartbeat, the rise and fall of his breath, had the effect of making me feel like all my broken parts were being knit back together. I was a love junkie and he was pushing really good shit.

But if I was being honest, I was also beginning to see that there were two sides to the man I loved. The calm, controlled, tender lover had an ugly counterpart: a triggered, paranoid, jealous, tantrumming child. If I ever mentioned another man's virtue—his wit, intelligence, or, God forbid, his looks—Spade went into a rage. His voice pitched upward, his jaw ground in circles, his body became tense and jittery. He yelled epithets and stalked about, stiff-legged, or slammed down the phone. I once mentioned that I admired Dave Chappelle and it nearly ended our relationship. He was particularly triggered by black men, whom he was sure all women secretly wanted to fuck. It was ugly. It was racist. It was a deal-breaker—except it was too late for me to renegotiate the deal. I had put too much on the table; I would not be able to sustain the loss of him. I was too hooked.

During those first months of being free and clear, I swung between shame, loss, anger, and confusion. Desperate to defend myself against what I felt was a chorus of haters I lashed out. I argued for Spade's character in high-minded letters to editors, I unfriended Facebook friends, I wrote passive-aggressive blog posts about other writers. I flailed and fell, trying to stay relevant in my own life, a life I was trying to both salvage and abandon. As I came to understand the depth of Spade's destructive paranoia, I dug in deeper with him. Now I needed him and his resources or I would be lost both emotionally and practically. I shuddered at the thought of life without him. This relationship had to work, and I would do absolutely anything to defend it.

And then, an hour later, the storm would blow over, and he would be back, indescribably dear, contrite, beckoning me back to the horizontal, where everything was sweet and even. All my worry erased. I would topple to the mattress, falling back into his arms, telling myself that my love would fix everything in time.

All of this dovetailed perfectly with Spade's agenda of having me all to himself. He dismissed the Margolins quickly and laid down some strict rules and opinions about my friends: He did not want me to be friends with any man I had ever slept with, which cut out a couple of old pals I had slept with in my early twenties. He didn't like me to talk with friends on the phone when I was with him. He required 100 percent of my attention when I was with him. I was free to spend time with women, as long as it wasn't at a Korean spa where we would see each other naked.

The more isolated I became, the more dependent I was on Spade. I met the few friends he had, and it was a motley assortment. There was his agent, his manager, the Cougar, another writer he tomcatted around with but was currently not speaking to. There was Stu, a Beverly Hills anesthesiologist he liked to have lunch with, a man with no discernable personality.

There was only one person in Spade's world who became a friend to me: his assistant, Lisa Stafford. Spade had exactly three skills: shitting, fucking, and writing—everything else he needed help with. Lisa was a Southern blonde with a disco-ball personality: bright, twinkly, and fun. She was also the single most capable person I had ever met. She ran his life from income taxes to dry cleaning, serving as an invaluable buffer between Spade and the world. More than that, she was a devoutly Christian woman who could meet Spade on the field of their shared faith. They loved each other like brother and sister, and like a sister, Lisa had Spade's number. She held no illusions about him and she knew exactly why I loved him because she loved him too. We all wanted this relationship to work.

Spade had a deluxe, king-size mattress delivered to the Fuckpad, and handed me an envelope with $4,000 in cash and told me to go buy myself some sheets.

When standing in the parking lot of Bed, Bath & Beyond with a stack of twenties as thick as a slice of challah, one either falls into a shame spiral for being now, officially, a kept woman, or one can erase such troubling thoughts and pretend she is Julia Roberts in *Pretty Woman*—a damsel being rescued by her prince—a damsel who likes fine home furnishings. Somewhere Héctor Elizondo was cheering me on.

I was not a gold digger, but I dug Spade's gold. It was both deliverance and damnation. I went overnight from keeping receipts in an envelope for later inspection by my parsimonious husband to being handed an envelope of cash like I was Tony Soprano's *goombah*. I felt like a hot, fucked-up game-show contestant: Behind Curtain Number 1, a complete set of new Egyptian, long-staple cotton towels! Behind Curtain Number 2, the complete loss of self-respect.

Early on in our secret courtship, Spade had presented me with a pair of expensive cowboy boots. They were custom-made, shiny, pointy, with gaudy yellow insets and orange stitching up the shaft. They were hideous, and I couldn't imagine the occasion where I would want to wear them and blow both my fashion and romantic covers at once. But even though I hated the boots, I also wanted to keep them with a desire that gnawed at my guts. I hid them in the trailer and pulled them out to marvel at them when I was alone. They felt like hard evidence of another world I could hardly believe I was living in. A world in which I was no longer myself.

I had to tell somebody, so I called my sister, the only person who knew about Spade.

"That's crazy. He shouldn't be giving you gifts. You're married. You're not his mink-stole girl," she had said.

I slid the boots out of their box and touched them, imagining with pleasure how much they would hurt my feet one day. The fact was, I wanted to be a mink-stole girl. I liked how it felt to be someone's glittery prize. I kept the boots. Months later, when we were safely out in the open, and I had officially assumed the role of Spade's arm candy, I dared to wear the gaudy kicks in public. I felt like Ann Richards. It was the boots' only public outing.

Money has always been complicated for me. I am an equal mix of my father's Protestant work ethic and my mother's magical financial thinking. Dad ground out a solid, upper-middle-class living on his typewriter, and what wasn't spent on tuition and summer camp, my mother spent lavishly at Bloomingdale's and Bergdorf Goodman.

It was my father's curse to be married to two impecunious women. His second wife, Carol, drowned her own big hurt in consumer goods, compulsively buying things she already owned. When she died she left behind a closet full of silk pantsuits in a rainbow of Rubbermaid colors, and drawers full of extension cords.

As much as I judged my mother and stepmother, I, too, was a spendthrift. I have never been a status shopper; I don't sport-shop at outlet malls or go to Beverly Hills for anything other than doctor appointments. I have never longed to be rich in the car-and-mansion sense. My bourgeois dream had always been to live effortlessly off of gigs, make do with my good old Le Creuset pot and a single Henckels chef's knife, and stay out of corporate cubicles.

My game is the Goodwill and Big Lots!, but the compulsion is the same; I have often used thrift shopping as a distraction from life. I could easily have frittered our family's fortune away $20 at a time.

Spade, on the other hand, had known actual hunger, had been raised on a hot-plate diet, had gone to sleep in public parks and woken up in drunk tanks. He had educated himself in public libraries and written his first novel standing up at a dresser in an SRO hotel. Because he knew he could live without money, he gave it away freely. He maintained what he called "a high-roller mentality," driving expensive cars and keeping his pockets tufted with twenties that he would throw at waiters, aestheticians, car-park valets, and homeless people. Every night that he spent in a swank hotel was a personal victory lap for him.

When our first Christmas came around I puzzled over what to get a man who wanted only things I could never afford. I bought him a conductor's baton. I thought he might like to conduct Beethoven's Ninth in the privacy of his own home. He handed me a small, square box. Inside was a gold Rolex.

"Isn't it beautiful?" he asked, taking it off its velvet tuffet and shackling it to my wrist. It was thick and heavy and so . . . shiny, and . . . so gold. In all my life I had never had a moment's desire for a Rolex. Now I owned a Rolex.

The mink-stole girl prowled the aisles of Bed, Bath & Beyond, choosing thick, ivory sheets and a DKNY matelassé bedspread in a pale teal. I bought king-size down pillows and a fluffy white throw to toss over my pretty little pedicured footsies.

As I shopped for bed and bath, what I felt was beyond anything I had ever known before: power, shame, anxiety, guilt, and a deep grind of sexual longing. There was something primal in being kept. At forty-six I could still be someone's sexual prize.

Naturally, there were some explicit conditions that came with being Spade's mink-stole girl, rules to which I was expected to closely hew.

No garish nail polish: The sight of dark, "whorish" colors on my fingernails or toenails sent him into a paroxysm of paranoia and triggered a full-on panic attack. We compromised: I could get manicures and pedicures, but my fingernails had to be clear-polished and my toenails could be painted in only a pale, sparkly color. *Like a surfer-girl color,* he clarified. To veer from this polish palette was considered total betrayal.

No dope-smoking: According to him, I was a drug addict. He claimed there was no way that I could rise to the sanctity of the truth with him if I was stoned. I was permitted to drink at that point. That rule changed later on.

Modesty in dress: He liked me in button-down shirts, cable-knit sweaters, and tweeds, none of which were in my wardrobe. He was turned on by tartans, penny loafers, and shirt-dresses—the drag of aristocracy. Of course, I had none of that in my wardrobe. If I left the house in a camisole he made me go back for a sweater. I differed from most mink-stole girls, in that I wasn't meant for display. If he could have put me in a burka, he absolutely would have.

No spas: unless they were ultra-deluxe private spas, and he was with me, and we both had female masseuses. It was a classic double-standard; he could be trusted to have a woman's hands on his body, but the reverse was out of the question, his premise being that all men were perverts and waiting to hit on me.

No R&B, funk, blues, hip-hop, rock 'n' roll, or rap: No music other than classical could be played when he was near. When I heard his heavy footfall on my front stairs I shut off the music or switched it right over to Sviatoslav Richter.

No dancing: I was not allowed to dance with a man, with friends, with my children, or alone. The prohibition also included any kind of body movement that could be construed as terpsichorean: finger-snapping, head-bobbing, foot-tapping. A random shimmy from me could incite his rage and ruin our whole evening.

Of all his rules, his limits on dancing were the most difficult for me to follow. If there is any kind of bass riff or drum beat, my body will find it and start moving to it without my even being aware of it. I will dance to phone-hold music if it has a groove. I could set Spade off with a single unconscious toe-tap. I had to police myself carefully and constantly. To allow myself any physical pleasure outside of his embrace was considered adultery within the nonnegotiable terms of our affair. He had a panic attack once when I took my shoes off to walk on the beach.

What he really feared most was what he called my "susceptibility." I was a sensualist and I was open-minded and, therefore, always prone to temptation. He wasn't entirely wrong, but what he failed to see was that I had already fully succumbed to my susceptibility by succumbing to him.

I argued that dance was more than sex; it was communion, ritual, religion. I cited dancing babies as proof that dance is just part of being human, but this was not an intellectual discussion. He covered my eyes in the ballroom scenes of *Pride and Prejudice*. He once pulled me out of a wedding reception when people started dancing the Hora. His was a primal terror fused into the very strands of his DNA by the trauma of his mother's murder. The last people who had seen her alive saw her dancing with a swarthy man.

All of this, Spade's world, Spade's rules, Spade's jealous paranoia, was as strange to me as standing in a checkout line at Bed, Bath & Beyond with a mountain of dry goods, fingering a stack of twenties. As my mops, pans, and towels were scanned, I wondered where this would all end. We had yet to begin the sweetest months of our relationship, when we lived free and clear, swaddled in luxury and steeped in love. Yet I already knew that whatever good was coming, it couldn't possibly last. I had seen the beast in him.

I looked over my domestic haul and thought of my mother in New York, to whom I had been tithing $400 a month to keep afloat. My sister, uncle, and father also chipped in the same amount, and thus the family kept Jill from eviction and starvation. She hadn't held a job in years—her age and exacting standards for others combined with the economic downturn made her virtually unemployable. I thought constantly of her, with her chipped saucers, pilling sheets, tar-stained kitchen cabinets, and threadbare furniture, waiting for my next deposit, just as I waited for my donations from the various men in my life. My father was paying my ex-husband a salary, part of which was being meted out to me per the terms of our divorce. Mammon filtered down through the strata of my family, extracted from the air by men at their desks, handed to women who spent it on high-quality, nondurable goods.

I peeled off a thousand dollars, paid the cashier, and trundled my haul out to my car. When I got home I hid the rest of the cash in the toe of one of the cowboy boots. I filled that boot with cash over the next two years, right up to the shaft, until Spade and I finally separated. I was saving against a future in which I would turn out exactly like my mother, sitting in my apartment with my cat and basic cable, beyond the ken or care of the children I had alienated with my own impulsive selfishness, unfuckable and alone. Every mink-stole girl knows that her life is built on a lie, and that money, like love, never lasts.

Los Angeles, 2009

Mornings were the clean slate. We would wake and roll toward each other, curl around each other, and he would growl, *Coffee.* It wasn't a command (though I would obediently rise and start the pot), it was a call to commence the sweetest part of our day.

When the coffee was brewed and served, the great slosh-and-fuck would begin. Cups tilted precariously, flesh moved in cycles of tension and release, and all of it was threaded through with words: shit-talk, stories, fantasies, plans. We laughed and laughed, at the world, at my parents, at our unseemly selves. We titled our story "Dipshits in Love." Our log-line was "A love so strong even they couldn't fuck it up."

Spade was prismatic with stories and gossip and would unspool it all for me—the known material about being a peeper and a former drug addict who had come to epic sobriety in the late '70s, and the stories that only his lovers knew, the minutiae that hadn't made the cut in either of his memoirs. All of it was heavily recycled material, but damn, he could tell it.

Spade was in command of every cliché and personality from every noir film ever made: the Punk, the Thief, the Dipshit, the Sidekick, the Jailbird, the Ne'er Do Well, the Tough Guy, the Patsy, the Doomed Lover. All of these belonged to him, and he could cartwheel through them all in a single conversation. He riffled the card catalog of his encyclopedic memory and retrieved names, dates, titles to support every story he told. I fell mute with awe, and that muteness worried me. I felt so much less than him. Where were my good stories?

Because he was born in 1948, his stories went back to a time and a Los Angeles I had never known. In wandering with him through his memory palace I got to see a lost Los Angeles. Its lavish movie houses, corner markets, the liquor stores he had shoplifted from, and the Hollywood porn shop where he had once worked. One night, on our way to a literary gala at the Beverly Hills Hotel, he pointed to the park across the street, and said, "I slept there once."

Spade's life story had arc and heft, theme and focus. His late twentieth-century rags-to-riches tales bore the imprimatur of Theodore Dreiser, the gonzo antics of Hunter S. Thompson, the macho romance of Hemingway. It was a deeply masculine life and sometimes I felt like I was making love to sixty-one years of American history. He was a master of understanding, constructing, and communicating his own narrative arc.

Meanwhile, I continued to struggle to piece my own complicated story together, made even more perplexing by Spade's presence in my life. It was easier to be his muse than to find my own.

After a couple of hours of the slosh 'n' fuck, we would rouse our-selves from our coffee-stained sheets and embark on the day. Spade would be sated and full of "the tremor of intent," ready to get back to his desk and produce high-income-yielding fiction. He would pull on last night's clothes as I wrapped myself in my robe.

We had a daily goodbye routine. He would lumber down the stairs and I would go to one of the full-length French windows that overlooked the street. We would blow each other a final kiss before he went loping off down the street, back to his desk at the Ravenswood, and I would watch him until he was gone.

Los Angeles/New York, Summer 2009

My father fell hard for Spade. He was impressed by Spade's fame and enjoyed having someone around who was as encyclopedic about old movies as he was. But their connection was deeper than that. They had both grown up bookish, lonely, only children with family roots buried deep in the Wisconsin permafrost. Both men had caught the big midcentury culture swell and ridden it to respectable fame and reasonable fortune. Both wrote in first draft, both were published by Alfred A. Knopf, both had questionable personal hygiene and an abiding love of processed meats. Both of them loved me devoutly. Whenever I brought them together, I could feel something knit together inside of me.

The Wood Fire Grill was a corporate rib restaurant with plastic steer horns on the wall and a menu that pleased these two deeply carnivorous men. I steeled myself for the sight of my father. His grooming had deteriorated, and he had lost a noticeable amount of weight. He hadn't bothered to buy new pants, he just cinched his trousers tighter, and his hair was always skewed up on the side of his head from his afternoon nap. This was the sight that greeted me as we slid into the booth. Dad smiled, and I saw that his two bottom front teeth were missing.

"Dad, what happened to your teeth?"

"Nothing," he shrugged. "I was eating a peach, and I broke my teeth on the pit."

"What?"

"I broke my teeth. Okay? Moving on!" He stared intently at his menu. "Where is that fucking waitress? I want my drinky-poo."

Spade took my hand under the table and squeezed it. A hysterical laugh rose in my throat, and I tried to repress it. My father *bought a peach and ate it?* In my entire life, I had never once witnessed my father eating a piece of fresh fruit. Was it even possible to break two teeth on a peach pit, I wondered, doing speed and density calculations in my mind. The only logical answer was that he had taken another fall and was lying to me about it. Again.

"Richard, you're still a dog. Have a steak. I'm picking up the check." Spade snapped his fingers. Dad, the cheapskate, gave us a quick, gummy grin.

"Seriously, Dad...a peach pit?"

"This subject is *closed*, Erika."

"How's the book coming, Richard?" Spade redirected.

"Rather well, actually. It's really taking shape, in fact." Dad was working on a book called *Keepers*, a collection of essays about his favorite films.

The drinks arrived, martinis for me and Dad, Pellegrino for Spade. I held my breath as I watched my father bring the wobbly, overfull glass to his lips. His top lip reached toward the gin like an eggtooth, hooking over the rim of the glass. He sipped his martini and sighed like a man with a gorgeous thirst, though he was not alcoholic. He never had more than one drink, and his enjoyment of it was always perfect. He wiped his mouth with the spotted back of his hand. "I think this will probably be my last book," he said.

"Oh, I'll bet you've got a couple more in you," Spade said.

"I don't know...I am rather fond of this one, though. I really don't know what else I have to say after this." I had never considered that there might be a point in life where my father had run out of things to say. Who would he be if he weren't working on a book? But this would be his thirty-seventh, and he was almost eighty and tired. "Goodness knows, I don't need the money."

Dad fancied himself a man of substantial means. He had worked hard his whole life and lived modestly. His great wish was to leave his family a small fortune made entirely of freelance and royalty money.

"You're a real high-roller, Richard," Sam said.

"Well, I don't know about *that*, but I've done okay."

"How many books will this be, Richard?"

"Oh, well, I believe it is my thirtieth."

"It's a helluva life's work."

"Oh, now..." my father demurred, but I could tell he was pleased.

Spade was the son-in-law my father had always wanted. Or maybe he was the son he wished he'd had. Spade magnified me in my father's eyes. I had finally found a station in the cultural firmament. We both would have preferred it if I had achieved acclaim through my own creative efforts, but being Sam Spade's muse was a decent second. I had brought glory to the family by making it more culturally interesting.

The pillow talk following a night out with my father was always palliative and sometimes diagnostic. We would rehash the evening, laughing at my old man's foibles, and Spade, who had an uncanny knack for reading people, would say things to me like, "Sweetheart, your father is a rank misogynist." It would be stated so simply and so without rancor that I could hear and accept it, and suddenly my father would make more sense to me.

Spade performed a kind of emotional dialysis with my complicated feelings about my father. I gave my fear and confusion to him, and he fed it back to me, purified with reason, compassion, and humor, referring to my father as "a crusty old cocksucker" in the most loving way.

All of it was a sweet release for the increasing worry and frustration I was feeling around my father. He was quickly becoming more and more enfeebled. His bathroom floor was slick with urine, and he had stopped shaving the right side of his face. Spade and I would laugh about my dad until I cried, then he would hold me close and tell me he would be with me through whatever would come. We would deal with it together.

★   ★   ★

My mother fell for Spade too. We flew to New York so Spade could be interviewed by the *Paris Review* at the Public Library. His interlocutor was Nathaniel Rich, son of Frank Rich, my father's longtime colleague at *Time*. Nathaniel was sixteen years my junior and in the full sway of his own brilliant literary career. I quickly compared my insides to his outsides and came away in tatters.

As for my outsides, I was turned out in my finest Sam Spade arm-candy attire: my hair in a French twist, heels, a modest-yet-sexy off-the-shoulder dress. Spade introduced me to everyone, and even though I was notable for being Richard's daughter and Sam's date, I felt keenly aware that I wasn't very interesting in my own right.

The next night we had my mother up to our suite at the Lowell Hotel. Spade had steaks sent up, and he turned on the charm, asking her questions and follow-up questions, talking me up, displaying chivalric deference to us both. Mom was impressed by a tiny bottle of Johnnie Walker Blue in our honor bar, which he cracked open and poured out for us. At the end of the night, he escorted her to a cab that he'd paid for. The next day he had a full bottle of Blue sent to her apartment.

"He's a real old-school gentleman!" she trilled to me on the phone the next day. Spade was the kind of man Jill understood; hyper-masculine, accomplished, and generous. She gave me her seal of approval: a lifelong damsel in distress, my mother knew a knight in shining armor when she saw one. She was proud of me. Our old alliance around star-crossed love was being revived. I hadn't felt this close to her since the last time I presented her with an inappropriate older lover back in 1982.

PART VII

BUFFALO

October 28, 2009

12:17 a.m.

Darling Spade,

I was going to call you, but it's really late, you're probably asleep, and I've just read your letter, and I'm afraid we'll fight.

Your letter is so full of commandments: God's and yours. Okay, so you are not a humanist. I respect your faith. But if God has indeed sent me to you then consider this: he sent *me* as I am: Mortal, flawed, human—a person who loves to dance and joke, a person who balks at behavioral dictates handed down by paranoid lovers. Maybe God is testing you specifically with me. Maybe He sent me to you because he wants you to move past this crazy bullshit and just relax a little.

Here's what hurts me: I gave you everything I had today. I scraped out my heart and soul and served you every morsel. I loved you and fucked you cross-eyed, I wept out my gratitude in your arms and then I went out to hear some music with my teenaged daughter. I was thinking about you the whole time, about how much I love you and couldn't wait to call you and tell you about the music, and that whole time you were sitting in the dark thinking I was out betraying you by dancing. It's fucking crazy and it undoes all the sweetness that I felt over the last 24 hours.

You say you love me and then you tell me to not be myself. It doesn't help. It makes me withdraw from you. Instead, just let me love you, like I did today. Relax, trust me and watch how it plays out. I am in this because I fucking love you, Spade. Don't you believe me? I love you not by divine commandment, but because you are a man who is divinely worthy of love. *You* inspire me to love you. I love you because you speak to my heart, because you are deep and brilliant, you are brave and handsome, you are unique beyond measure and you give me love of a kind and quality I have never known before. The more you move away from rigidity and paranoia the more I will love you. Don't you get it? When you order me to adhere to rules you alienate me.

Come out of the dark, Spade. Turn on the lights. Come see the world. The 21st century is happening out here and you are lucky enough to have lived long enough to see it. Sure, it's full of noise and bullshit, but it's also full of beauty and magic.

I'm not telling you to stop being yourself. Of course you must brood and write and pray. But don't miss out on the rest of it. This is what I am here for—not to bury myself in the dark with you, but to lead you out into the light, to dance and laugh with you. Come see what there is to love in the world. Let's have a little less "potent destiny" and a little more fun. There's room for both things, honestly my darling.

Have faith in us.
E.

Los Angeles, Spring 2010

I did everything I could to live Spade's edicts simply to keep the peace.

I had long wanted to quit smoking weed and was pretty happy to give it up for him. Now that I wasn't saturated in THC I remembered my dreams, and they were like billboards advertising my anxiety. In one, I came home with my girls to find the mothers of the Canfield Avenue Elementary School assembled in my living room for an intervention. They had been cleaning my kitchen and organizing my closets, and they told me I was doing a shitty job of caring for my children. I shouted, "We're fine! Please leave!" but they wouldn't.

The fact was, we weren't fine. Paul, in his grief and rage, withdrew into himself. My daughters now lived with what I considered an emotionally absent father. Paul was still working full-time for my father's production company. Every day they came home from school to an empty house and larder. My larder was achingly full, and I had set up the second bedroom with twin beds and desks for them, but they didn't want to be at the Fuckpad, they were teenagers who wanted to be in their own rooms.

My children were going through the hard march of puberty. Grace, just fourteen years old, was in her first romantic relationship with a boy four years her elder. Even though he was a good kid and the son of close family friends, the relationship was beyond her maturity level. I did my best to chaperone them from a distance, but I had no way of actually enforcing physical boundaries. Also, the hypocrisy of me setting sexual limits was not lost on my sneering teenage daughter.

Mae seemed fine but was having to process the agony of her parents' separation and middle school largely on her own. She kept up a sunny disposition that made us all think she was mostly all right, but she wasn't. Both my daughters experimented with self-harm in those years, cutting faint tracks into their forearms, signaling their pain. Grace did it first, and I put together a first-aid kit for her to keep in her backpack. I begged her to tend her physical wounds. In the meantime, everyone was in therapy.

I tried to monitor my children the best I could from a distance, but it was a lousy setup. As a child of divorce, I well knew the peril in which I had put my daughters. I imagined them doing the things I had done and it made me frantic with worry. This resulted in an almost compulsive vigilance in me that chafed at the kids, who were also naturally at an age where they needed to pull away from me. I called them constantly, I confronted their behavior, I had meetings with their therapists and their teachers. I did everything I could to protect them from both the harm I had suffered and the harm I had inflicted on them.

I began to show signs of stress. I developed a nervous tic where I scrunched my nose uncontrollably and ground my teeth until my jaw ached. I also developed a strange and savage itch that would pop up all over my body. There was no rash, just an itch that I would scratch until I was raw.

Always a good sleeper, I became an insomniac, sleeping fitfully, then jacking awake for good at four a.m., which, of course, was the perfect, Spade-mandated hour to begin the workday. But unlike him, I didn't brew coffee, shit, and bend to my task. No, on the mornings he wasn't with me I lay in bed tic-ing and fretting until it was time to get ready to drive the carpool.

★   ★   ★

One night I dreamed I moved to Buffalo. It was the dead of winter and I was living in a small gray house in the frozen tundra of upstate New York. The house had neither warmth nor charm. It was cramped and cold and lonely. The linoleum peeled off the kitchen floor, the faucets leaked, and the beds were gritty. I stood in the house's dirty mudroom and looked over the frozen backyard and thought, *This is what I have to do. I have to give up everything I love to live here and write my book.*

I woke up and told Spade the dream and he was delighted. He felt it was a portent of productivity. This was exactly the kind of isolation I needed to write.

This was my writing day: After carpool, I would first attend meticulously to my housekeeping duties, fluffing and buffing, even doing windows, until the apartment sparkled. When I had nothing left to do but work, I would turn to my desk, which I would see also needed tidying. After I windexed its glass top and had blown the dust from between the keys of my keyboard, I would sit and stare at my shiny blank screen until lunch.

Spade would call midday, exercised by a morning of writing peerless prose in first draft and ready for a post-lunch dog nap before he began his second shift. I didn't know how to work like him or like my father, who also called daily to check in. "Come on, kid, get to work!" he would cheer. But writing a memoir was like trying to describe the ocean as I was drowning in it. I knew what was happening with Spade was part of the story. I knew that far from being dead, the story of what happened to me in high school was repeating in midlife. And if history was to be fully repeated, then surely I was headed for another monumental heartbreak. But I didn't know how to write about any of it.

I thought my problem was technical. I had only written short-form essays and articles, never anything over ten thousand words. My first book was an essay collection, I had no idea how to organize a full-length book.

Spade told me to start by doing research. He told me to go

through every year of my life and catalogue its events personally, politically, and culturally. I dutifully went about it and compiled an enormous Word document that included every journal entry and school report. I told my father about the project and asked if he had any of my kid stuff. He had in fact saved every scrap of paper from my life in a file drawer in his office. I was able to source materials I had never seen before: teacher reports, letters I had written to him from school and camp. I, too, had saved all my written ephemera: journals and correspondence, Henry's love letters, which I transcribed faithfully into the enormous document.

By the end of a year of this relentless cataloguing, I could tell you that on the day I was born the United States Government ratified the Twenty-Fourth Amendment, outlawing the poll tax. I could tell you that "Shadow Dancing" by the Bee Gees was the big hit of 1978 and, sure, I had danced to it, but I couldn't tell you what it meant to my story. But it didn't matter. Creating this catalog allowed me to work every day without having to write.

Spade called the feeling of having your teeth into a piece of work "the tremor of intent." He said he felt it every time he sat down to work, where every fiber of his being was taut with the anticipation of making great art, and nothing could keep him from his pages. I had known that feeling a few times, back when I was always on deadline writing stuff that made me laugh out loud and excited to publish. But I hadn't felt so much as a flicker of intent in months. A great sadness had settled on me, extinguishing my wit.

Spade upgraded his elliptical trainer to a fancier model and had his old machine delivered to my apartment. Every day I got on it and did an imitation of Spade; I listened to Emil Gilels play Beethoven, I pumped away on the machine, trying to conjure up my own tremor of intent. The elliptical had an entropic quality that felt, if not good, at least honest. It had a nice "wax on, wax off" feel. Maybe I would run into my book simply by jogging in place.

In April, eight months after I moved out of the house, I was on the elliptical machine, blasting Beethoven's Hammerklavier Sonata, trying to summon that elusive tremor of intent, but all I could feel was the tremor of fear, self-doubt, endless churning, never going forward, growing older, and going in circles. I was trying to conjure my own genius, but all I could think about were my children. I realized with sudden and horrific clarity that I had no idea where they even were at that moment, or what they were doing. I stopped, heart pounding. The pedals sank under my weight and the heaviness of what I had done. Writing wasn't my work, my family was, and it was deeply creative, important work. I had spent years fashioning not complex books but complex human beings, lives that would have greater impact on other lives than anything I could ever possibly write.

I knew how to create something that Spade had no idea how to make—a family. I had spent the best, most creative years of my life building this tender, beautiful thing, this sweet, singular unit that I had fashioned out of blood, sweat, and Bisquick—and then I had thrown a stick of dynamite into it. My children were scattered and broken, my union with my husband destroyed beyond repair, and my friendships and allegiances all in tatters. My career had been subsumed by scandal, and my writing voice, that bright, witty cockatiel, had gone silent. Everything I had was broken and Spade was the bulldozer pushing the wreckage to the side.

I staggered off the elliptical and grabbed a pen and the red diary that I always kept nearby. I turned to the first clean page and wrote, "I HAVE MURDERED MY FAMILY." And there it was, the worst thing that could possibly be said about me, and it was the truth.

Los Angeles, Fall 2010

S pade finished his memoir about his pursuit of women. Lisa sent me the manuscript. It was no longer called *The Big Hurt*. He had retitled it *The Baedeker Curse: My Grand Tour of Women*. My Green Room prediction from 2008 had finally come true. Not only was I in his book, the book was dedicated to me.

The memoir was essentially his greatest hits from a legendary lifetime of pussy-hounding and feverish romantic projection. There were the Hancock Park moms who had fused his libido around wide hips and twisted bra straps. There were the younger girls he peeped, crawling into their houses through pet doors when they weren't at home, stealing panties, raiding refrigerators, stroking himself in their quiet bedrooms. All his exes were in the book, rendered in tender, yearning, respectful prose. I already knew many of the stories from our pillow talk. I had always hung on his romantic tales of conquest and defeat, feeling a giddy mix of both jealousy and arousal. His love life was a tawdry tuxedo twist of romance and perversion that I slurped up.

All along, he told me I was different from the other women. I was his Immortal Beloved. I knew I was being put on a pedestal and I let him do it. But as I read his newest memoir, I saw that in fact everything he had said or done with me he had done with someone else before. It was all there in black and white: the one-liners, the cashmere dress, the Beethoven, the flower deliveries. None of this

THE BIG HURT 231

had been inspired specifically by me. We weren't writing a story together, we were following a script.

All along he had been putting me through the paces of his obsessive-compulsive love ritual. He often joked that his gambit was "seduce, contain, marry, impregnate." He had been married twice, and had tried for a third with the woman before me. She had even gotten pregnant, but she had aborted his child and run.

Children were a thing Spade fantasized about obsessively, particularly daughters. In other words, he wanted what I already had. I told him that even if I could produce a viable child at forty-seven, there was no way I was going back into the sandbox. I was done.

The Baedeker Curse published late in our first year together. It was the clearest warning I could have had that there was something terribly wrong with his ideation of me. He described the pacing and events of our affair accurately, the resistance I put up, the fevered faxing, all the advances and the retreats. He described me as "vexed, unbodied and riddled with ennui," which also rang pretty true. But when my character spoke, what came out was unrecognizable as anything I have ever said.

Spade had me saying things to him like *Your single-mindedness is so furious that it recasts projection and puts you in an entirely different league,* a line I could barely comprehend, much less speak. Or, even more baffling, *Your brutal will moves and horrifies me.* He could have cribbed from any one of my many letters to him, he could have used his steel-trap memory to transcribe any of the many hours of things I had said to him on the phone or in person, but instead he rewrote me to sound like himself. It was like looking at a Michelangelo sculpture of a female nude: beautifully executed by someone who had absolutely no feel for the subject. I was a feminized portrait of the artist as an old man.

I played no part in his mind other than the part I had been cast for: *Her.* What were the necessary qualities of "Her"? Intelligence, probity, mojo. Like most of the broken souls of the world, he wanted his mother, but with a keenness of appetite that would have put Oedipus to shame.

Anything I was outside of what he wanted either threatened him or didn't interest him. So I kept those pieces of myself out of his view, and by so doing, became less and less of myself. No wonder he didn't quote me. It was possible I hadn't said anything memorable or quote-worthy to him. I was a dull blade. A helium balloon. A fondant female without any layers.

I thought of the girl who had hung out in the Buxton smoking shed, flipping shit with her friends, foulmouthed, quick on the uptake, full of political opinions and Shakespeare. Now I was the woman with a Republican boyfriend who hid her Obama fridge magnet when he came over for dinner.

Just as in fairy tales, I had gotten my wish, and it had turned out to be a curse. He had lured me to him with the promise that he wanted to grow and change, but instead he was hammering me on the forge of his fear. In *The Baedeker Curse*, a ten-year-old Sam Spade had wished his mother dead and then she died. But the curse did not die with her, it was exacted upon every woman he had loved ever since. Every woman who had to be, but could never be, *Her.*

Because he used my real name in every scene I was in in *The Baedeker Curse*, my reputation as a mink-stole girl was cemented in the wider public eye and the mixed reviews were pouring in. Joyce Carol Oates referred to me as "an opportunist" in *The New York Review of Books*. Another critic suggested in print that I run for my life. I flip-flopped between shame and self-righteous umbrage as reviewers commented on my broken family and obvious lack of self-awareness in falling for Spade. Elaine Showalter wrote a scathing review, to which I rebutted in the comments, "Sam Spade will always be, at bottom, a boy whose mother was raped and murdered—a boy who received no subsequent counseling, little education, indifferent parenting, and a boy who turned to a dead German composer (Beethoven) as a role model when others failed to emerge. That this boy is even alive today, writing, loving, and searching for his own artistic and emotional truth, is a testament to his bravery and strength of spirit. Spade's strident persona, obsessive nature and compulsive heterosexuality make him seem predatory, but in fact, he is a true and tender champion of women."

That I was arguing for my oppressor's feminism to Elaine Showalter makes me flush hot with embarrassment today. I was so desperate to explain myself, to explain him, it made me expose myself further to the world's incredulity and opprobrium.

And yet, even now, older and wiser, as I hope I am, I can still feel my heart surge for that "boy," that buried child who deserved compassion and rescue, as all children in extremis surely do. I can still hear him, trapped under the rubble of his mother's abysmal life and death, crying out to be rescued. I can still feel that flutter of panic and adrenaline I felt every day back then, as if my own child were pinned under an I-beam; I would have lifted it and thrown it over my shoulder to save him. But it turned out he didn't really want to be saved.

Buxton, Spring 1982

I walked my bike up the steep driveway. Pilar was waiting for me at the top, by the stone lions. "We need to talk."

We found a soft, grassy spot up from the driveway. She wore white sweatpants but didn't hesitate to sit on the ground beside me. She leveled her blue eyes at me. I held my breath.

"Eileen found some love letters between you and Henry. Naturally, she is very upset."

I had no idea what to say, so I stayed silent.

"Erika, I'm not angry." She put her hand on my arm. "How long has this affair been going on?"

I had to think for a minute, the answer seemed too incredible. "A week."

"Ah, me…" Pilar sighed. I saw Mia and her roommate come out of the Main House. She waved to me as they headed down the driveway, but I didn't wave back. Mia raised a "What's-going-on?" eyebrow. I sent her a shrug back. She had no idea about me and Henry. I hadn't told anyone other than CJ.

"You realize this is a very serious situation, don't you?"

I actually didn't, but I nodded anyway.

"Henry has been fired and has already been escorted off-campus."

Escorted. Did they put him in handcuffs? Was he perp-walked to his Le Car? Was he allowed to make a phone call or pack an overnight bag? Where had he gone? Bennington? Or some other place? I think he may have mentioned that he was from New Hampshire, but I realized I actually didn't know anything about him or his people.

"Erika, are you listening? The Administrative Committee has been meeting all afternoon. This is a very, very difficult matter. We have been trying to decide what would be best for both you and the school."

I didn't understand what was so difficult. Weren't teacher-student relationships accepted at Buxton? For four years I had watched Chad Walker fixate upon one female classmate after another, a new one for each of the four years I had been at Buxton. Tony and Melodie had shacked up together the minute she graduated, giving their affair a John-and-Yoko legitimacy that everyone seemed to respect. There was a teacher who I heard liked to take boys to a local quarry for midnight swims. Years later, one of those boys, grown into drunken manhood, confirmed it to me.

Since teacher-student affairs seemed so obviously tolerated by the school, I assumed mine wasn't any big deal. But it appeared I was wrong about all of it. "I fucked up. I'm so sorry, Pilar." I hated to disappoint her.

Pilar squeezed my hand. "Erika, you do not have to apologize. This is not your fault." But of course it was my fault. I could see that she was really struggling, that she was in pain, and I had caused it. I had gone on that bike ride. I had fantasized about Henry. I had gone to the woods with him. My mother was right. All I did was hurt people.

"This is the situation: Eileen would like to stay and finish the teaching year. The Administrative Committee feels you would be an upsetting presence to her and to your classmates. It would disrupt the whole school. However, because you are legally under our care, the school cannot actually expel you."

"What?"

"Buxton cannot legally expel you, but the committee feels it would be best if you left, for the sake of your classmates and the community."

"But what about graduation?"

"Of course you will graduate, and we will mail you your diploma. None of this will go on your transcripts." I had made my plans to attend Sarah Lawrence in the fall, but that wasn't the point. The last two months of senior year at Buxton were the big payoff. Seniors got to design the yearbook and write their graduation speeches. I didn't want to miss it.

"So, what are you saying, that this is my decision?"

"Legally, yes." Pilar said this with deep weariness. Just like that, everything I had been and had become at Buxton over the years was erased, and I was right back to being who I really was: a girl who had to go.

Pilar's eyes were points of deep concern and love; her narrow hand held my wide, white, pasty paw as though it were a beautiful seashell. "I want you to know I absolutely feel that you should be allowed to graduate with your classmates. But alas, I am overruled by the Administrative Committee." I would find out, many years later, that CJ and Ali had gone before the AC that day and ardently pled my case.

"Do my parents know?"

"Yes, we have spoken with them. The plan is that you will go to your mother's house on Cape Cod." Mom and David had left Santa Fe and moved back east last year. This was surprising news to me.

"My dad must have been pretty pissed."

"I spoke with him, and yes he is angry, but only because he loves you and is worried for you." I knew it was probably more complicated than that.

Thirty-three years later I met Pilar for dinner in Orange County. Over a bottle of wine we rehashed those long-ago events and she shared with me a detail I hadn't known. She had spoken with my father on the phone that day and he had said to her, "Couldn't Erika's punishment be that she stays in school and suffers the opprobrium of her peers?" We both laughed at this. I loved him for at least asking.

I wish I had been able to speak to him that day. It made me wonder if events might have turned out differently if either my mother or father had been there to counsel or advocate for me. But they weren't and didn't, and so without so much as even a short conversation with either of my parents, I agreed to leave the school.

I went up to my room and packed my silver trunk. I packed my ripped jeans, my shit-kickers, my flannel shirts, peasant dresses, and my Snoopy. I packed the diaphragm Pilar had taken me to the clinic to get my freshman year. I packed my cloth-covered journal and my Patti Smith T-shirt. I unpinned the postcard of Thérèse Bernard, I rolled up my Virginia Woolf and Eldridge Cleaver posters and packed them away. I threw a bunch of clothes into the Free Box in the hall. Finally, I took down the photograph I had taken of Henry's hands and feet. I stared at them and wondered how I had managed to get so tangled up in them.

CJ found me in the smoking shed and handed me one last letter from Henry, written earlier that afternoon:

Dear Erika,
I am alone, we have been ripped asunder.

Do not let them mislead you, my darling, they want to protect the school so we, and our perfect love, must be sacrificed. Of course they feel this way, don't take it personally.

Do not weep for Eileen. I was loyal to her for many years and was only repaid with scorn. Her betrayal of me was not physical but I am not physical, I am of the air. I have warred my whole life against those who would destroy beauty. My art is my weapon, and you are my pennant.

They tell me that you are an actress, and I am well aware of it; for after all, I am an actor myself. We are both poets and dreamers. Was your performance true? Mine was. We must decide whether we love the characters in this play deeply enough to live with them, to be them, and to commit ourselves to them.

Remember no matter what: there is nothing more beautiful in

life than—TRUE LOVE. And that already belongs to us. I am waiting for you. I believe in you. You must decide whether you believe
in yourself.

Now, as an adult, this letter shocks me in a way it didn't when I first
read it. Now I can see how dissociative it is, him asking us to be
true to characters. It just confused me as a kid. I was feeling pretty
dissociative myself. I did not know if I was in love. I just knew I
was part of something very adult and exciting. I was too young to
notice that nowhere, in any of his letters, does Henry talk about
me specifically.

Also, it seems the school had immediately begun the work of
framing me as duplicitous and at fault for the scandal by saying I
was an actress, as though I was putting one over on everyone.

That Henry asked me to be true to myself when I was eighteen
was like asking me to solve for x. The algebra of my own heart
was an equation that would take me another thirty years to solve.
All I knew then was I had done something inexcusable and I was
supposed to pack up my shit, say my goodbyes, and leave Buxton
forever.

CJ found me before I was driven into town and put on the bus.
He had a camera slung around his neck. "Come on, I am taking
your goddamned yearbook photo," he said, leading me down the
driveway. We walked to the Clark Art without talking. CJ had me
stand in front of its travertine wall and shot a half a roll of film.
Then I took the camera from him and shot the rest of the roll of
him smoking a cigarette in front of the same wall. CJ asked me for
a quote for my page. I was wholly unprepared and drew a blank. I
had a copy of Douglas Adams's *The Hitchhiker's Guide to the Galaxy*
in my knapsack, a book I had started reading before the affair had
even begun, in a time back when I was just myself, not some focus
of scandal. I had underlined the last thing that had made me laugh:
a pithy bit about dolphins being smarter than humans because

they didn't give a shit about anything. I scribbled it down for CJ, thinking it was a good idea to go out cracking wise. Then CJ and I walked up Stone Hill Road together for the last time.

Pilar said goodbye to me at the top of the driveway by the stone lions. She pressed a small inlaid wooden box into my hand. Inside was a ring, just a thin band of gold set with a deep, purple stone. It was her Basque baby ring, the kind of gift a mother would save for her daughter. We lingered in our hug goodbye.

Patricia drove me to the bus. My trunk and I were loaded onto a Peter Pan bus out of Williamstown. My bus had "Wendy" stenciled on the side, and I remember thinking I was like Wendy, except instead of flying out the nursery window in my white Laura Ashley graduation dress in June, I was being shoved out the window in my underwear.

The April day was warm and bright. I pushed my doubts away and put myself back into the safety of my heroine self. I said to myself, *Here I am, the scandalous femme fatale, off on her bold adventure. I have finished not only a gripping chapter in my own epic life but am also the subject of a bona fide sex scandal. Huzzah!*

The bus passed through a tunnel and everything went dark. All I could see was the reflection of my own startled eyeball in the window.

PART VIII

BIG RED

Los Angeles, September 2010

I straddled two radically different worlds with Spade. In one I was a mink stole Cinderella, jetting off to accompany her big-shot author on his sumptuous book tours, and in the other I was back in my own little corner being Mom: delivering forgotten lunches, shopping for teacher appreciation gifts, checking homework.

One night during that strange season, I stood coiffed and smiling beside my big man, throwing a party for him in a private bungalow at the Beverly Hills Hotel, and the next day I was standing in clogs at a school picnic, a sagging paper plate in my hand, making small talk with John and Sally, some parents I had known during my marriage when our kids were friends in preschool.

Our conversation was standard L.A. parent talk: kids, LAUSD lotteries, bullies, gossip. "My gosh, they have grown! Does that mean we're older too? Ha-ha!" It felt good to be back in my familiar milieu. I liked wearing jeans and sensible shoes, comparing notes on our kids, catching up. I loved many of the people I had met parenting in Los Angeles.

The Los Angeles I was raising my children in was a rainbow coalition of unified thought. We were staunchly multicultural and stood against all forms of racism, sexism, homophobia, and any binaries that hindered our beautiful, self-celebrated individuality and the fulsome development of our precious young. I had raised my daughters among kind, conscientious people, and despite their emotional ups and downs, that is what my girls were turning out to be as well.

During a lull in the conversation Sally excused herself to go check on the kids and John turned to me with an odd look and said, "I read the *L.A. Times* interview with Sam Spade. *That* was pretty interesting."

Spade had given an erratic interview to the *L.A. Times* on the publication of *The Baedeker Curse*, in which he ranted about his identification with Beethoven and sex as divine fire in the sacred merging of men and women. He mentioned me by first and last name in almost every paragraph and claimed he and I were divinely deigned. He talked about how all he did every day was write and drive over to my apartment, which was true. But when seen in the flat afternoon light of a school picnic, it seemed weird and unseemly.

"I mean," John tried again, "it seems like a lot."

I stood with a hot dog in my hand, the sun blazing off my coppery-dyed hair, and I laughed nonchalantly, but it came out as a Phyllis Diller bray that abraded my own ears. John looked at me quizzically.

My personal life, my dubious romantic choices, my questionable parenting—all of it was on public view. I felt naked and exposed. I was not telling the story here; a story was being told about me and in it I felt a caricature of a woman run amok.

"Yeah, well, life is crazy." I laughed again.

John's daughter Macy had been to our house to play many times in preschool. Now John looked at me as though he had just found out I had been keeping a loaded gun in the house the whole time. The loaded gun in this metaphor being my hungry cunt.

I knew that what I was modeling for my daughters in my relationship with Spade looked like bad messaging, but it was in fact mixed messaging. Yes, there was a lot of crazy press, but they weren't reading it.

They didn't know about the increasingly bad times. Those were private. What they saw was the best of us: connected, affectionate, happy, especially in that first year. I was getting to model something they had missed at home: two people in love.

Spade was never anything but kind and proper with my kids. He had sworn to me that he would never come between me and my children, and in that regard, he kept his word. His romantic projection of mothers and daughters as another divinely deigned bond kept him on his best behavior most of the time.

He was respectful and easy with them. He played the fool for them, doing his one-liners and animal jokes, and they laughed or groaned. He made it clear he would never presume to be any kind of father figure to them. He called them his "cubs" instead, which worked with his deepest animals-safe-in-their-dens fantasies and created a sweet, respectful familial boundary between us. For all the upheaval and anxiety I went through, in that first tumultuous year, I was happy with Spade in a way they had never seen me be with their father, and that went a long way with them.

There was no way I could explain all that to John, who was just trying to make conversation. My life had become so dichotomized and compartmentalized, so off the tracks that I barely understood it myself. I couldn't tell him that Spade was Jekyll and Hyde, two men trapped inside one six-foot-three roiling meat suit. Nothing about my life was suited for picnic talk.

Winter 2009

S pade's big novel published right after we got together, and then his memoir after that. Our relationship was interrupted by long bouts of book touring.

Spade was one of the last authors who got splashy book tours. Most authors try to book a few readings at local bookstores, maybe a couple of cities where they can crash with friends. Spade had a limo pick him up and drive him to the airport. He flew first class and upgraded himself into the finest luxury hotels in Europe.

Touring for Spade was dangerous business. He tended to crack up on book tours. All of the new people and places made him jittery. He kept himself sane by cosseting himself in luxury and isolation. He checked in, drew heavy shantung blackout drapes against the lights of Paris, the domes of Florence, the ancient streets of Rome. He ordered cheeseburgers and took sleep meds and passed out until it was time to get up and go back to work.

Spade's fear of the world was equaled only by my longing for it. But going on book tours with him was a bizarre bait-and-switch. He would fly me to a beautiful city to be with him, the man of the hour, and because he was who he was, the world was ours for the asking. But Spade didn't want to meet new people. He didn't care about food, he didn't drink wine or festive aperitifs, he didn't want to explore the city or go to museums. He wanted to bring me back to the suite, order cheeseburgers, and "make love like tigers."

Every morning we would wake up to a continental breakfast and then a car would take him to a day of interviews and book signings, and I would head out alone into the streets of beautiful, unfamiliar cities. I would wander for hours, taking in art and architecture, snapping photos, sitting alone at outdoor cafés, puzzling over maps, trying to locate myself in a wholly unfamiliar geography, making notes of my thoughts.

Then, when he was finally free of obligation, he would draw me back into whatever cashmere cave we were inhabiting. He was un-interested in the stories of what I'd done or seen that day. Anything that drew my attention away from him, from us, that was outside of what he called his *perv-view*, was barely tolerated. There weren't any follow-up questions. We hurried right back to the Story of Us.

At night, he did readings. At every one he would take the stage, locate me in the audience, and blow me a kiss. It made me blush to the roots of my hair. At first, I loved it. I thought it was romantic. Then I realized it was his way of signaling to every man in the room that I was *his* woman. *Back off.* In Paris a man kissed my hand and Spade shoved him. I came to hate that blown kiss.

All of this travel only made my hunger for the world more keen. It wasn't scenery I longed for, it was other people. It was the freedom to get to know someone new. The delight of seeing Spade in a fresh context, of hearing him speak to someone other than me or his audience. I wanted to adventure forth with him.

I turned forty-seven in Bologna on a long Italian tour that began in Milan. The cities and towns rolled by, crowds lined up for him, books piled up and diminished, plates of pasta and espressos were consumed in a blur. There were drivers and translators and publicists and fans. It was thrilling and exhausting.

I left him in Rome to continue his tour and flew back to the States to resume my life. I had children in duress, a fractious divorce to attend to, a Goodwill dresser that needed to be spray-painted. Loneliness. My life without Spade was not exactly Champagne wishes and caviar dreams. It was grinding, stressful, thrifty. I went back to the carpool, the late homework assignments, bank fees and credit card debt, the ongoing drama of girl world, and my ever-present writer's block.

After his tour ended, Spade came home superhumanly exhausted and slept for the better part of three days. Obsessed with his insomnia, he began to take sleep meds during the day, so he could nap to make up for the sleep he had lost the night before. Days became an odd scramble. I would call his pad and get his machine. Then, hours later, when he finally woke up, he would call back sounding fine.

But I knew he wasn't fine. He was withdrawing from me and a space had opened up between us, I could feel it: the honeymoon was over.

He was seeing a quack psychiatrist in Beverly Hills, "Dr." Hunter, who worked with a prescribing concierge doctor, and those two guys kept Spade supplied with enough benzodiazepines to keep Shrek zonked. Theirs was a scattershot approach of giving him Lunesta, Xanax, and Ambien by the scoopful, and when that didn't work they tried Provigil—an upper that pilots and shift workers use to stay awake. The idea was to amp him up to the point of exhaustion so that he might finally sleep. But nothing really worked. Every day Spade tallied his hours of sleep, planned long, midday naps, popped pills to sleep, to calm his nerves, or to make his dick hard when it was time to see me. Every time I vacuumed my bedroom floor I could hear his dropped pills rattle up the tube.

Dr. Hunter had Spade's Amex on file, which he whacked for every session, every phone call. Spade was completely dependent on Hunter and it was costing him a fortune. There were endless therapy sessions and a raft of prescriptions.

At one point Hunter suggested he try cannabis for sleep, and so, just like that, Spade declared my weed sobriety was over. He got a med card and went to a dispensary. He came back with a shopping bag full of Kush, weed candy, brownies, and even an eighth of a hybrid strain that had been named after one of his more popular novels.

One day I brought him lunch at the Ravenswood and found him slurred and out of it on the couch. I thought maybe he was baked and suffering from low blood sugar so I made him eat the sandwich I had brought. As we ate lunch I confessed to him that I had taken a puff of a joint at my book-group meeting a few Sundays back, before the cannabis ban had been lifted. Now that we were both regularly getting stoned as begonias together, it seemed like a pretty minor offense to admit to. Spade suddenly jumped to his feet and pointed at me. "You are a drug addict! I cannot be with a woman who uses drugs socially!" He stood before me, slurring and unsteady, his fetid dog breath filling the stuffy room. He was high on something other than cannabis.

If there is one thing in this life I know, it is stoners. We are a loopy, doofy, mellow lot. I had once, in college, seen Ali get high and have a bad reaction. This was not that. Spade was on something else, something much stronger than pot. I went into the kitchen and found Valium scattered on the floor. That was when I understood that I was living in some kind of bizarre geriatric after-school special. My sixty-one-year-old boyfriend was a full-fledged lying, using drug addict.

By June he was a rolling disaster. He couldn't make coffee without grounds exploding all over the kitchen. He would get up in the night in an Ambien haze and raid my peanut butter. One morning I awoke to a Skippy *Helter Skelter* in my bathroom, the wall behind the toilet smeared and sticky where he had leaned against it to piss.

He wasn't interested in Us anymore, or the Task or our sacred union. He talked only about himself, his sleep, his work. He stopped calling me by my name. He called me Tigress or Big Red; gone was "Erika, Erika, Erika, I can't stop saying your name." I could feel him abandoning me and returning to his relationship with the original redhead: his dead mother.

The gallant, attentive man I had fallen in love with less than a year before was gone, replaced by a slurring, paranoid child who couldn't wipe his own ass. He got thrown out of restaurants. He lost his car. He walked out of readings. Lisa and I were constantly on the phone, trying to figure out how to help him, trying to run interference on his self-destruction.

CJ and I were on the phone a lot too. CJ had done a good deal of trauma research on his own behalf and he shared everything he knew with me. We were certain that Spade's drug problem was a trauma response. He used drugs as a way to escape the agony of his own sentience. I had been researching treatment centers that dealt with trauma and had bookmarked one in Arizona that seemed fantastic, if I could ever convince him to go.

In June I brought my mother out to L.A. for her birthday, and Spade wouldn't leave us alone. He kept calling and calling until I stopped answering. Then he turned up on my doorstep, zorched on benzos and wearing two left shoes. Whatever good first impression he had made on my mother in New York was obliterated. "That man can't leave you alone. He's dangerous, Erika."

"Mom, he's just sick."

"Well, be that as it may, I don't care about him. You are who I care about, and I am worried for you."

She didn't understand the extent of my compulsive loyalty. I had developed it in response to her having once thrown me away. I loved Spade more than I loved myself. I would never, ever give up on him and he would never get rid of me.

Beverly Hills, June 2011

We came rolling up to the Beverly Hills Hotel in "The Beast," Spade's brand-new Cadillac CTSV. The carhops took a deferential step backward before reaching out to the freshly detailed door handle. The boys were scrubbed and eager, with Balboa tans under their green polos. They looked like they had their own money and were probably working for connections.

"Welcome to the Beverly Hills Hotel, Mr. Spade!"

Spade slid a twenty out of his billfold and held it out of sight in his cupped palm, the first "slide" of the weekend at the ready. *Keep it close, brother,* he told them, as if we might need to make a quick getaway. It was a movie line he had heard when he was a kid and saved up for the day when he would be a rich, famous writer, the day when he would pull up to the Beverly Hills Hotel in a boss car, with a big, good-looking redhead at his side.

Hotel staff orbited him as we proceeded up the steps and into the lobby—smiling, assisting, crisp in the perfectly choreographed synchronized swim of grease and snap. Bellmen and carhops, housekeepers and room-service people all walked away from an encounter with Spade twenty bucks richer. *Spread the love!* Spade would riff. *Let it ride!* It was joyful and easy, and it hid his real agenda, which was control.

Spade liked the control that a luxury hotel offered. Everyone there was mediated by money and it made Spade feel safe, and when he felt safe he relaxed and was charming. The twenties Spade passed out to carhops and bellboys were pellets in his own operant-conditioning program. We sashayed through the big doors into the stiff, old lobby. We were greeted with a sycophantic chorale of "Dog! Mr. Spade!" Our pleasure was their purpose. Mr. Briggs, the hotel manager, emerged from his office behind the reception desk.

"Dog!"

"Briggsy!" A manly handshake followed. "How's it shaking, brother?"

"Not bad, not bad. We have your bungalow ready. It's one I think you've never had before." This was perhaps our fifth stay at the hotel, one of Spade's favorite places. I dropped my small overnight bag onto a huge brass trolley. Spade hung on to the brief-case that held his shaving kit, his electric toothbrush, and, most important, his pills.

We wound our way through the lobby and out a side door. Tawny paths of decomposed granite threaded between lush fronds, a soft, verdant maze leading to exclusive and historic pleasures. It was a hideaway to the stars, the adulterous, the suspect, and the notorious.

We passed a small bungalow that Briggsy pointed out. "That was Katharine Hepburn and Spencer Tracy's bungalow. They lived here for years, of course, while he was married. The one you'll be staying in is famous for being Marilyn Monroe and Yves Montand's hideaway." The men engaged in their prurient historical gossip while I, Spade's lady-ornament, listened in and cooed notes of appreciation. At the Beverly Hills Hotel, I felt the full weight of the adulterer's mantle. I was not here as myself but as Spade's woman, the squeeze, the twist, the prize of his celebrated status.

I ogled the lush greenery. I had gardened a patch of land down in my old neighborhood, the one Spade had plucked me out of. I knew the kind of manpower it took to keep these grounds free of wilt or decay. Silent Hispanics toiled among the fronds, with-drawing from our path so as not to impede our privileged progress toward our swank pad. I could hear the gentle *snick-snick* of clippers popping discreetly in the distance.

Briggsy led us up a walkway to a big paneled door abutted by lounge chairs. He stuck the heavy, toothless brass key into the magnetic lock and the door softly clicked and swung open.

It was a Bonnaroo bungalow, fit for Marilyn and Yves, fit for Spade and Schickel. It was soft and muted, jungle greens and seashell pinks, gilt and plush. It was the Beverly Hills Hotel's decorative theme: hot, rich grandma. On a long table sat the requisite cellophane-wrapped cheese-and-fruit basket. Spade, already weirdly jumpy, ignored it and headed straight to the TV, which was on and tuned in to the hospitality channel. He snapped it off. He hated television. It could offer up panic-inducing imagery, like couples dancing, or men in swim trunks, at any moment. He ordered a pot of coffee from room service and stretched out on the bed.

The bedroom was off the dining area, with a door that opened to a private patio. The bed was a raft of frilly throw pillows and tropical linens. The bathroom was enormous, caked in pink travertine with a steam shower and a jetted tub. A private toilet room had a phone and toilet paper folded to a point. Every luxury hotel came with a stack of what Spade called *Man, We's Rich!* magazines. These glossies were mostly made of advertisements for luxury goods, with skimpy articles squeezed in between Patek Philippe and Rolex watch ads. Once, in a "10 Must-Haves for Summer" article, we had spotted a $4,000 wood-and-canvas camping cot and we had laughed our heads off. Spade loved money in the way only someone who grew up poor could. He understood its feckless ways and spent it joyfully. It was all a big goof to him and the more he spent the harder he had to work, which was how he liked it.

When we first came to this legendary hotel, I was excited. I wanted to try all the taps, lounge in the plush robes, steal all the soaps. I brought my girls and their friends to swim in the pool, which had speakers underwater, so they could mermaid around to Pachelbel's Canon in D. But this visit marked our second anniversary, two years since I had sent him that first fateful Facebook message, and I had in that time become somewhat inured to hotel luxury. I had other things on my mind, primarily Spade's weird behavior. He had been skittish of late. He no longer focused his eyes on me.

We flopped on the bed. I kicked off my shoes and lay back and "assumed the position," my head on his chest and my left leg thrown over him. I had lain in this position so much in the past two years that I developed a persistent backache, which didn't stop me from doing it. It was our closest mesh short of intercourse.

After a while I felt peckish, so I got up to explore the complimentary gift basket. I popped the Champagne and poured myself a glass. Spade was sober, but that didn't mean I couldn't celebrate. I nibbled at some cheese. I hadn't eaten all day.

"What do you want to do for dinner? Do you want to go out?" I asked, crawling onto the bed beside him with my snack.

"I'm not hungry, but you go ahead."

"Well, what if I ordered us some room-service spaghetti Bolognese?" This was one of his favorite meals.

"Sure, baby, let it ride." He was so agreeable, so ineffably sweet and good-humored. I kissed him deeply and his tongue tasted strangely sour.

"I think you need to drink some water, babe."

He reached over to a bottle of Fiji water that the hotel had sitting in a silver caddy on the nightstand and took a big swig. We kissed again but the weird taste was still there. Something was wrong. It was like licking a battery. "Your mouth tastes so weird. Have you eaten anything at all today?"

"I'll go brush my teeth," he said, getting up.

He was walking past the foot of the bed toward the bathroom when he paused, and wavered.

"Sam?"

He didn't make a sound, just fell in two parts, first to his knees, then down onto his face, and he lay there. It looked like a pratfall.

"Very funny," I said, crawling to the foot of the bed to catch his smile. But instead I watched his face draw back into a grimace and his hand curl up beside him into a claw. I ran to him and shook him, but he didn't respond.

I called the front desk and they called the paramedics, who were ten interminable minutes away. By the time they got there he was upright again. He told them he was fine and sent them away. As soon as they were gone, he collapsed again.

An hour later my prince lay on a gurney parked in the hallway of Cedars Sinai Medical Center grinning up at me, his teeth missing. I yanked his hospital gown down over his ass. We were still waiting for his intake and diagnosis, but I assumed he'd had some kind of stroke.

"Darling, I'm afraid I have not been completely forthcoming with you," he said.

"What do you mean?"

"I have been taking Provigil for the past four days."

I should have known. This was not Spade's first jitterbug with uppers. He had been taking them off prescription and behind my back. He was severely dehydrated and completely wacked out of his gourd.

I ended up spending our anniversary in a chair next to Spade's hospital bed weeping like a human saline drip. Spade was asleep at last. I looked at his face. He had knocked the bridge out of his mouth in his fall, and he looked gummy and frail. I felt all my anger drain away. I loved this man, this drug addict, so much, his vulnerability only amplified his dearness to me.

He had been abusing all of the prescriptions his doctor had been prescribing him for months. He was buying Valium illegally over the Internet, picking up odd packages at a PO box he had set up in Hollywood. Now, finally, everyone could all agree there was a real problem and we would get help for him and everything would be all right.

Spade's quack shrink had connects to the One80 Center, a luxury rehab in Benedict Canyon run by a couple of ex-junkies with a celebrity roster of patients. I begged Spade and Hunter to consider the trauma place in Arizona. But Spade was scheduled to host an awards dinner at the police academy, and the One80 Center was going to allow him to go off-campus for the event. I fought his enablers, begging them to listen to me, but instead they told me I needed psychiatric help as well. I did feel like I was losing my mind. A tiny window had opened in which Spade might finally receive the care he needed, and it was being slammed shut by these opportunists who had their hooks into my big-ticket boyfriend.

Once he was installed in the One80 Center I got on a plane and left to go visit my sister in Ohio.

I spent five glorious days reconnecting with my family and myself. I wore my bathing suit without censure, danced with my niece and nephew, drank beer, and belly laughed in the way I only could with my sister and her husband. I began to remember who I was, apart from Spade—someone who loved mini golf and irony and silliness. Released from the prison of a thrice-daily check-in with my always-suspicious lover, I felt the knot in my stomach loosen.

When I returned home from Ohio I went straight to the One80 Center to visit Spade. I expected to find him zonked, angry, weepy, maybe remorseful. Instead I found him upright in a chair, with his briefcase across his knees. He had a stack of lined binder paper on top and was scribbling away, outlining his next novel. He had taken back his control by starting a new book. Even at his lowest, he still could summon the tremor of intent.

Spade looked up at me as I entered, and smiled. "Red!"

His face was calm, his eyes were bright, and he looked like the Sam Spade I had fallen in love with. I hadn't realized how much I missed him. I began to cry with relief and happiness.

"Red, Red, c'mon, don't cry, let's get horizontal."

We stretched out next to each other on his bed. I put my head on his shoulder and threw my leg over him and felt the peace of reconnection. I had missed him so much. I had sent him a big bouquet of flowers, and I looked up at the opulent arrangement wilting on the dresser and felt that maybe I had done it: I had helped save him and opened a road to sanity for him at last.

But even in that blissful moment I could tell something had shifted. I felt it like a change in cabin pressure.

With the drugs gone, he began to build a new bulwark between us. Instead of disappearing into drugs, he used his sobriety to drive me away. He threw himself into his sober brotherhood, spending most evenings at meetings, or in fellowship with his new friends. He began to monitor my drinking, convinced I was an alcoholic even though I had been temperate around alcohol my entire life. It had nothing to do with drinking. Without the filter of his own addiction in place, he was left unbearably vulnerable to fear, and I, as the woman who loved him, was who he feared most.

Cape Cod, April 1982

My father wouldn't speak to me, as I had once again brought shame to the House of Schickel. So staying with him in New York was out of the question. For a moment, I didn't know where I would go from Buxton. I called my mother, bracing for a lecture and more rejection, but to my astonishment she said, "Darling, come."

Mom and David had made several moves since Santa Fe, eventually ending up in a small house in East Chatham on Cape Cod. David was forever working on his second novel, which, as far as I know, was unfinished when he died in 2004. Moving was their remedy for internal stasis. In the ten years he and my mother were together, they lived at six different addresses.

I was greeted by both of them on the Cape with open arms and a roast chicken. Mom was strangely receptive and sympathetic to me and David was his usual warm, jovial self. After a bottle of wine and a salad made of delicate butter lettuces, Mom sat me down and brought me into a family secret: I was a third-generation teacher-fucker.

The first girl in my family to be seduced by a teacher was my great-aunt Frances, who married her English teacher back in 1918. The other teacher's pet in the family, my mother told me that night, was her. She had slept with her professor at Sarah Lawrence College.

George Goethals was a visiting Harvard psychology professor my mother's freshman year when they began an affair that lasted several years. When Goethals received his tenure and headed back to Harvard, my mother got a Woodrow Wilson scholarship in psychology, and followed him to Cambridge to assist him with his work.

My mother told me she once worked on a psychology study where she had to interview teenagers and write up their stories. There was the girl who had a baby in the toilet. Another was a boy who was awestruck around my beautiful mother. He had thought Miss Whedon was "Miss Sweden," a bona fide beauty pageant queen.

But this part of the story was new to me, how she was the lover of her married teacher all through college and graduate school. She told me she ended their affair when her fellowship concluded, and she left Cambridge for New York, where she soon met and married my father.

My mother represented the whole thing as a mature, if doomed, love. My father's take on it, when I asked him about it later, was more damning: "That asshole really did a number on your mother. He was into some sick scenes. So was the wife. They had a ménage à trois and they fucked your mother to a fare-thee-well." I never believed him, my uptight mother would never have had a three-way back in the 1950s; it seemed too impossible. But it was clear that her teacher had gotten inside her head and altered her somehow.

That night, in Mom and David's guest room on the Cape, my mind whirled through my mother's surprising escapade and my family legacy. I couldn't completely reconcile the idea of my mother in a desperate love tryst. The only memory I had of my parents being physical was the time my mother broke a small table over my father's head during an argument at a summer rental in New Hampshire. Other than that, I could not summon a kiss, a hug, a pat, or a pinch. Mom's relationship with David seemed like affectionate householding. There was no sizzle between them either. She simply never seemed like a sexual person to me.

But this story painted another picture of my mother, one

illustrated by a photograph she had hanging in her hallway. It was her at age eighteen, poolside, in California. She is sitting in a white maillot bathing suit, her legs tucked under her, and she is luminously beautiful. Her shoulders are wide and creamy, her long, wavy, auburn hair pulls down the sun, her spine, even in repose, a plumb line. Her expression, as it was in almost every photograph ever taken of her, is stern and hidden, but it is a younger, less set version of the face I knew. My mother never felt any compunction to smile for a camera; but in this photo, she is a dreamy Aphrodite. She must have driven that old professor to madness.

My mother made me feel proud of my affair with Henry. We were both women who had given everything up for love. It bonded us. She hugged me and told me how happy she was that I was there. None of the problems that existed between us in Santa Fe were evident. We sat on her patio and smoked cigarettes and drank cold Tecate and watched David, up on a ladder, drunkenly dismantle an old carport with a claw hammer. It was heaven.

Her birthday came and I made an angel-food cake, her favorite, beating egg whites by hand until my arm ached. Everything that divided us had disappeared in a sigh of mutual womanly understanding. We were made allies by our passions, by our swooning, romantic narratives and our family legacy of forbidden love, a tradition that I had bravely, if unwittingly, carried forth.

On Monday morning I tracked Henry down at Bennington and we finally got on the phone. He was overjoyed to hear from me. He had been staying with a colleague on a goat farm in Vermont, not far from the college. He told me he would drive down to the Cape on the weekend to get me. We would return to Bennington and look for a place together.

Relieved of worry, I found myself in a near dream state. I let myself relax and enjoy the experience of being in accord with my mother. We shopped at roadside farm stands for dinner and cooked together. She gave me a shorthand course in cooking, and wrote her favorite recipes out for me so that I might cook them for Henry. One day, short on cash at the supermarket, she whispered to me conspiratorially, "I'm going to have to kite a check." I had never heard the expression before and I had yet to open my first checking account, but it felt like we were friends, in adult cahoots together.

Finally, Henry arrived that Friday night on my mother's doorstep. I had gone through so much to get to this moment, the moment when I had my man, and there he was at last . . . a guy in a polo shirt. When I presented him to my welcoming mother, he seemed adult and civilized and I could tell she immediately liked him. I watched him out of the corner of my eye. Now that I wasn't being flattened by the steam press of forbidden love, I began to perceive Henry as human and somewhat ordinary. The four of us had dinner together and we ate the last of the angel-food cake I had made. Some whipped cream lingered at the corners of Henry's mouth for long minutes during which I prayed he would pick up his napkin. After cake and berries Henry and I drove back to his motel room.

Other than our hasty blanket encounter in the woods, Henry and I had never really made love. That night we made sweet, celebratory, official love and fell asleep in each other's arms.

We spent the next afternoon at the beach, just to have one day together on the Cape before we headed back to Vermont and everything that lay ahead of us. It felt strange doing something as normal as going to the beach with Henry.

We stretched out, letting the hot sand leach the stress out of our bodies. I thought about Buxton, so far away. It was Saturday and Work Program would just be ending. Kids would be getting ready to head in to town to hang out at the Colonial Pizza and Toonerville Trolley. There were six weeks left until graduation, but here I was, on my weirdly early summer break.

I don't remember many specifics of what Henry and I talked about that day. All I remember is that as we talked I pushed sand into mounds with my hands and patted them. The feeling of these sand mounds, the soft solidity, calmed the flapping I felt under my breastbone. I felt like I was at the crest of a roller coaster, weightless and terrified. The sand mounds made me feel anchored. I wanted to bring them with me and I told him so. He patted the mounds himself and agreed they were relaxing. We fantasized about packing up the sand and taking it with us as a traveling art/therapy work. We would pour out the sand in various settings and let stressed city folk pat it and relax. Maybe we would rent an entire gallery in TriBeCa and fill it with sand and let Wall Street people come in on their lunch hour to pat and play and be comforted by the sand.

"What should we call our installation?" Henry asked.

"Mother," I said.

Vermont, Summer 1982

Henry and I rented a large, charmless, unfurnished upper unit in a drafty clapboard house in North Bennington. The apartment had several rooms, none of which we could afford to furnish. My father had cut me off financially and we were living on what was left of Henry's Bennington pay. The apartment came with sprung and loaded rat traps, which Henry gallantly removed while I shrieked and hopped in circles. We dubbed the apartment "Rat Land."

We bought a futon and plopped it in the middle of the living room, replicating Henry and Eileen's apartment at Buxton, but we had none of the arty accessories that might have lent it élan. Because the futon was our only piece of furniture, we lived our entire lives on it. We ate and slept and read and worked on it. We dragged a couple of loading skids off the street and stacked them into a kind of table that was more awkward than useful for dining—our forks falling between the slats. I kept a coffee can stuffed with wildflowers, which sounds better than it was. Wildflowers wilt quickly and my rusty can was always rimmed with a gummy brown fringe of dead blooms. We bought a complete set of glass dishes for $10 at a yard sale, but since neither one of us knew how to cook, we had no real need for anything beyond cereal bowls and coffee cups.

I set up my Olivetti on a plastic milk crate next to the futon, wrapped my legs around it, and wrote poems and letters to my friends back at school. Just to have a writing assignment, I wrote a graduation speech. It was a lofty spiel about how truth and love would set us all free.

I relished the experience of living with Henry. I had never been able to closely observe a lover over a period of time and I was fascinated with the mechanics of masculinity. I would sit on the closed toilet in the bathroom and watch him shave, aroused by the casual, almost mindless way he expertly handled his own face. I marveled at how his penis floated like an anemone in the bathtub. Lying beside him, I would watch his veins pulse and his lavender eyelids flutter with dreams as he slept.

One afternoon, while napping, Henry's eyes blinked open and he smiled at me. "Wow," he said, reaching for his glasses, carefully wiping them on the bed sheet before putting them on.

"A dream?"

"Balloons," Henry said, smiling. "There was this big, green, rolling field, and there were hundreds of huge, gorgeous hot-air balloons taking off and floating away. People were dressed in white Victorian clothes. They were pulling up in antique cars and in buggies. It was beautiful and just...so happy and free."

I kissed him. He was such a miracle, this sensitive, profound man who dreamed of hot-air balloons. His happiness was my own. All I wanted was to be able to live up to the sacrifices we had made to be together. We would prove everyone wrong with our love, just like John and Yoko. We would show them.

Henry had a history of gastrointestinal problems and had been seeing a Chinese healer in town. I knew about his colitis because at Buxton Henry would disappear, missing meals and canceling his classes. It would hit him like a tsunami, and he would be laid out for days, eventually returning to the dining hall days later, paler and thinner.

He told his doctor about the balloon dream and the old man told him air was the symbol of health and he declared Henry recovered. Henry came home with a bouquet of real florist flowers for my coffee can. We had won. Our love had healed him.

Two weeks after I left Buxton, Pilar came to see me. She said that the school had decided that if I wanted to come back, I could, on the condition that I stop seeing Henry. Once again, I was being asked to make an important life decision without the guidance of either of my parents. I could not imagine, at that point, abandoning Henry and returning to school. I was in way too deep to give up. I turned the offer down.

I monitored the end of the Buxton school year from the futon as I whiled away May and early June, packing on weight from all the Grape Nuts, deli meat, and potato salad we brought home from the Price Chopper. Everyone at Buxton was preparing for Spring Arts Weekend and would be finishing up the yearbook, I thought, spreading mayonnaise on white bread, peeling slices of dried roast beef like old scabs off wax paper, bringing a plate to my beloved, who lay stretched out on the futon, looking over sheet music but really fretting over money. He used my Olivetti to type cover letters and mailing labels, sending tapes, scores, and résumés to other schools, trying to get work for the fall.

I got a job washing dishes at an inn in Shaftsbury. Henry couldn't always drive me, so I often rode my bike there and back, a twenty-mile trip on the 7A. As I pumped over the green hills of Vermont, I thought about how the seniors back in Williamstown, just on the other side of the Massachusetts–Vermont border, would be taking over the New Building for a round-the-clock weekend of yearbook editing. The yearbook was top-secret, with one faculty member advising. They spread layouts out in different rooms and set up mattresses so people could crash, and they worked at all hours, the darkroom going full tilt all day and night. I had been shooting all year and had dozens of images that would have been perfect, but the negatives were packed into boxes that had been shipped to my dad's house in New York. Years later I would learn that Chad Baxter, who was the faculty advisor that year, had tried to have me erased from the yearbook entirely. The senior class was divided on the matter, and a bitter fight ensued. But in the end my friends prevailed and the photograph CJ had taken of me in front of the Clark Art made it into the 1982 Buxton yearbook.

On June 13, around the time the Buxton School senior class of 1982 was lining up in the Williamstown Presbyterian Church to accept their diplomas, I was scraping cold eggs and sticky French toast crusts into the garbage at the Shaftsbury Inn. The dining room was busy with cyclists out enjoying one of the first truly summery weekends of the season. I was bussing tables and loading the dishwasher as fast as I could.

All the girls would be wearing white, and the church on Main Street would be decked out in garlands of flowers, I thought as I filled the rack and sprayed the hard stuff off the dishes. The pews would be full of parents, including Dad and Carol, who were in Williamstown to see Ali graduate. Henry and I had gone to see them at the Treadway the night before. We sat in the lobby for an awkward half hour of drinks. My father would barely look at me or acknowledge Henry's presence, and Carol tried to make up for his rudeness by being overly nice. We finally said our goodbyes and as we were headed out the hotel doors Carol called out, "Good luck!" On the car ride home Henry had ranted, "Good luck?! Why would she think we need luck? She might as well have issued a curse."

Later that night Henry's moaning woke me up. He writhed on the futon beside me like a hooked fish. I brought him ginger ale and I pressed a cool washcloth to his brow, but he shrugged me off. He was far away in a world of pain. The miracle of the hot-air balloons was only temporary. His colitis was back. I sat up beside him all night trying to summon the magic in me that had cured him the first time, but it was gone.

I brought the steel doors down on the load with a wet *thunk* and hit the button that started up the washer.

Every senior gave a speech at graduation, a distillation of their deepest truths, a declaration of Self. I had spent hours sitting on the futon back at Rat Land, writing draft after draft of the senior speech I knew I would never give. What did I stand for? Truth.

Love. I had but one belief: that the application of truth and love could clear up any misunderstanding. I wanted to be understood. I wanted to write a speech so beautiful, so naked and true that everyone in the church would have risen to their feet and applauded. And it wouldn't be like Buxton was taking me back. It would be as though they had never let me go.

Winter 2008

S pade was an instrument of my own destruction, but he was not its catalyst. To find the moment my adult life first came apart, I'd have to go back to the winter of 2008, more than a year before our fateful friending on Facebook. I had been sitting in my trailer, not working, when my phone lit up with a call from an unknown New York number.

"Hello, sweetheart, it's CJ."

We hadn't spoken in over a decade and we had lost track of each other, but within minutes we were talking as comfortably as when we were seventeen.

Ben Fincke had once described CJ as "an ambulatory bubble bath." Even in middle age, he was still lilting, effulgent, and wafty. But now there was also a ragged edge of cynicism beneath the foam. I had heard, through a mutual friend, that CJ had come out of the closet, and I tried, somewhat ham-handedly, to congratulate him.

"Not so fast. I know it may not seem like it, but I'm not actually gay. I mean, my sexuality has always been pretty fluid, but I have always been primarily attracted to women."

"Sorry, CJ, I didn't mean to presume…"

"No, it's confusing, believe me, especially for me. My sexuality got completely screwed up because of the sexual abuse."

"CJ, what sexual abuse?"

"Darling, do you have a minute? I have some things to tell you."
My old friend told me a horror story I had never heard before.

Before he came to Buxton in 1980, CJ had been a day
student at the Indian Mountain School, a coed junior boarding
school in Connecticut. There was an old printing press in the
school's basement, and a charismatic and beloved English teacher,
Christopher Simonds, who ran "Print Club" as an extracurricular
activity. But rather than lining up type, the teacher liked to line
up his pupils and have them perform unprintable sex acts upon
him and one another. It was a nightmare that went on for many
years unchecked, and CJ, my tender young friend, had been
caught up in it for three of them. He left the school and came
to Buxton, where he would be safe at last, but the abuse had
destroyed his puberty and left him ravaged with PTSD and sexually
scrambled.

CJ's voice barely wavered as he filled me in on his adult life. His
pain led him to drink, drug, and fuck his way through much of his
twenties and thirties. He had married, fathered two beloved daughters, then divorced. Finally, he reported his abuse to the authorities,
which resulted in a court case. This was how CJ had found out that
he was the only member of Print Club left alive. The other kids
had all died of overdoses or suicide. "There had only been one girl
in Print Club," CJ said, ice cubes rattling in the background. "She
lived in town, so I knew her family. She shot herself in the head."
We both fell silent, letting the immense sadness of that girl's brief,
tragic life filter through us.

CJ had settled and signed a nondisclosure agreement that he said
he deeply regretted. He had been paid for his pain, but he was
discovering that money was no cure for a psychic wound. The only
viable currency in the world of trauma is being able to tell your
story. The teacher who abused him was still teaching, and CJ was
still broken.

CJ did most of the talking during what turned into a four-hour
phone conversation. He wasn't shy about talking about anything;
modesty had been scorched out of him long ago. Our conversation

meandered through our shared memories. Our friendship with Henry and Eileen, our burgeoning love for each other, and how we tried and failed to consummate our love one night at his house in Connecticut, so long ago. We had been tripping on acid and had become transcendentally knit together; having him inside me felt like the cosmically correct thing to do. But he couldn't stay hard, which I chalked up to the drugs, or his unacknowledged homosexuality, or both.

"I loved you so much that night, Erika, and I wanted to make love with you, but I couldn't have fucked you any more than I could have climbed Everest," he said. "I had so many bad associations with penetration then, I would have had to go through all of that trauma, and there was no way I was ready."

"Jesus, I am so sorry, CJ."

"It's okay. I can see how you might have thought I was gay. But I like women, and I have always loved you."

"Why didn't you tell me any of this back at school?"

"You were involved in your own passion play." I thought back to that night on the driveway, when he had confronted me about the affair.

"I've always wondered, how you knew about me and Henry."

"I was pretty well sensitized to the vicissitudes of teacher-student dynamics. I always suspected Henry and Eileen were some kind of construct. I had to stay close to you. That's why I agreed to play courier for you."

"Oh my God, CJ, I'm so sorry."

"Sweetheart, you didn't know. And I wanted to protect you from Henry."

"What do you mean?"

"Henry was like a little worm. He was a succubus. We were all being groomed for adult consumption—reading the shit we were reading; Georges Bataille, Jacques Prévert—it was all way beyond our maturity level.

"Think about it, Erika, Buxton was a repository for the families of the East Coast elite. Sure, we all dressed like a bunch of dirty hippies, but it was old money mixed up with the nouveau riche. We were brilliant garbage left out in the woods to rot."

I heard CJ dig into his freezer for ice cubes in Brooklyn. I heard the scuffle of dog toenails in the background. "Fellini! Sit!" CJ commanded without conviction, and I heard the toenails skitter off into another room.

"The Administrative Committee should have vetted Henry and Eileen better and known they weren't really married. But they didn't, and the trustees went crazy. There was a lot of money at stake, old money from the old families that sent their kids there. They were trying to build an endowment. They couldn't have you stay. It was bad for business."

I thought of all those goofy kids with their ripped jeans and flannel shirts, identifying with Frank Zappa and Emma Goldman. True, there had been a pair of Roosevelt cousins in the class below me, but it had never occurred to me they might be *Roosevelt* Roosevelts.

"How did I not know any of this?"

"You're not a classist. You're nouveau riche, darling."

True, I had been raised to pay attention to people's careers, not their family trees.

"The future of the school was at stake. Ben was getting ready to retire, and who was going to run Buxton came down to a fight. You were in the middle of it."

I could hear CJ take a sip of something. I was aware that he was becoming more and more drunk during our conversation, which was nearing the three-hour mark. We were both self-medicating, alcohol on his end and weed on mine. I took a deep hit off my pipe and let the cloud hang in my chest before I exhaled.

"Anyway, that was pretty much the end of the Administrative Committee at Buxton," he said with a sigh. "The school changed forever that year. It abandoned its Humanist/Socialist tenets and became just another fancy New England prep school with an endowment. It was the Reagan era, so it probably would have happened sooner or later, but Erika, you should know that you were the catalyst for it."

I took a moment to digest this bizarre news. Suddenly the circumstances surrounding the single most defining event of my life had changed radically. Could there really have been forces at work other than my own misbehavior? "How did I not know any of this?"

"Here's another thing I don't think you know, Erika: you were raped by Henry."

In the thirty years that I had lived with the story of what had happened to me at Buxton, no one had ever once said those exact words. It came not as a revelation, but more like I had just been told the Loch Ness Monster had been sighted in my bathtub. It felt fantastical.

"No, I wasn't a victim. I was willing. We were in love."

"You were a child."

"I was eighteen. By two months."

"A technicality. You had no agency."

I had always believed I was a fuckup who had brought shame to her family and my expulsion was the price I paid for my heedless ardor. But I had formed that opinion as a child. Now I was an adult, with two daughters, the eldest of whom was almost the age I was when I had been sent away to school. I suddenly looked at my past in a new light. What would I have done if this had happened to Grace or Mae? I would have called the cops on the teacher, sued the school, unleashed the full fury of my maternal rage. But I could not muster an ounce of umbrage on behalf of my own teenage self.

"Something was taken away from you," CJ said. "Henry took your youth and he knew he could do it because the school was set up to let him get away with it." He sighed. "They always find a way."

Winter 2011

Spade and I went to New York on book business, and CJ came to meet us at our suite at the Lowell. I was nervous Spade would try to alpha-dog him, but maybe because he thought CJ was gay, he didn't perceive him as a threat. Spade had a lunch with Sonny Mehta at Knopf, and he hustled off, glad I had someone to spend the afternoon with.

It had been a long time since I had seen CJ. Now in middle age, he hid his still boyish good looks behind an impressive beard that made him look like a Cossack. Underneath, he was still his same sweet self, and since getting back in touch in 2008, we had become close again.

We went for a long, nippy ramble around the Upper East Side. CJ didn't waste any time cutting to the chase: "I see why you love him, Erika, but the man is obviously living in a constant state of terror."

I told him about all the therapies I had tried. I had ordered Spade a weighted blanket and hired a yoga teacher to give him private sessions.

CJ laughed. "This is way beyond yoga, honey. I hate to say it, but there is probably nothing you can ever do to make him feel safe. You, my darling femme fatale, are what's freaking him out."

When he dropped me at the door of the hotel he said, "I genuinely like the man, and I see why you love him, but he *will* destroy you, my dear."

★   ★   ★

In the winter of 2011, Spade hustled up a contract for a cable TV show: *Sam Spade's City of Dead Women*. He was the writer, producer, and star of this series, in which he would do his usual banter: talk about dead women, crime, and Los Angeles history.

I was excited for him. The project focused and energized him. He churned with the tremor of intent once more, attacking his notebook paper with renewed vigor, hatching crazy ideas for the show. He wanted to have an animatronic talking dog named Bunko. Nothing delighted him like talking animals. "It's funny shit, right?" I would nod and smile. "You can be on the show too, baby. You can be Big Red, my woman, and you can wear boots and boss me and Bunko around, yank our chains. It'll be great!"

"It sounds awesome, babe," I said, wondering how it could possibly be any good at all.

"C'mon, laugh, baby, laugh! It'll be a gas!"

He brought an early edit of the first episode home to show me. It was a smash-cut mishmash and thematic rehash of everything he had done before. It was all slanting shadows; jazzy, foreboding music; and shabby re-creations of murders using non-union actors. And in the middle of it was Spade and his talking dog. My beloved looked like a bespoke kook with his bow tie on way too tight. He was all fedora and stabby pointer finger, a caricature of a caricature of himself. He ranted about honoring dead women while hosting a show that did lurid reenactments of their murders. His false teeth rattled in his head. He had an angry rash around his mouth, which he blamed on my vagina, and no amount of pancake makeup could cover up.

The first episode was called "Dead Women Haunt Me" and featured three murdered women—his mother, the Black Dahlia, and an homage to my friend's daughter Lola Barnes.

After Lola was murdered, Spade wrote an elegiac piece in *Newsweek*, connecting Lola's death to the story of his own murdered mother, expounding on how the dead claim the living, with grief as a usurper. It was beautifully written, and I was proud of him. Lola's parents seemed fine with it. We were all grappling with our own experiences of grief then, and Spade had struck a solemn, dignified tone in his piece.

When he told me nearly two years later he was using Lola in his show, I asked if he had run it by her parents, guessing they might not appreciate the memory of their beloved daughter's last moments being used for sensationalist cable fodder. Spade flew into a rage.

"I don't ask for permission! I'm Sam Spade! I can do whatever I want!" He didn't care who he hurt.

I wish this was the point in the story where our protagonist finally sees the light. Where the heroine claws back her self-respect, dumps her abuser, grabs her purse, and walks out the door never to return.

I did actually do that. So many times. I fought with him. I drew lines in the sand. I walked out. But I always came back. The abyss of life without each other was too dark and infinite for either of us. We couldn't agree on anything except that we couldn't be apart. "We are insoluble," he would say.

My world shrank further. No matter what low level Spade descended to, no matter how hard he tried to push me away I clung to him. At one point he flat-out said to me, "I will never ever be comfortable letting you be yourself. You should leave me."

I didn't leave him. I missed my former self: my career, my friends, my family. I missed going out at night, having friendly conversations with men. I missed laughing, writing, dancing, wearing sleeveless tops, smoking joints. I missed mimosas and bathing suits and Democrats. I missed having the courage of my own convictions. But I didn't leave him.

If I left him, that would mean that the only thing I had ever believed in, the restorative power of truth and love, was just a shuck.

Idyllwild, Fall 2011

Grace sat in the backseat of Paul's car, wearing a beret and clutching Fluffy, her stuffed dog. Mae sat beside her, moody, headphones in. We drove east across the Inland Empire and up into the San Jacinto Mountains. The landscape morphed from pavement to scruff to pines as we gained altitude. I thought about the day three decades earlier when I had been the kid in the backseat, heading deep into the trees of western Massachusetts, being driven away from home. Now I was the mom in the front seat, getting ready to drop her kid off at boarding school.

By 2011 the family drama had become too much for Grace, and being around me and Spade wasn't helping. Grace had been to two different schools for her freshman and sophomore years of high school. Neither had been a good fit. In her wisdom, she found an arts boarding school in the nearby mountains and begged me to help her apply. It seemed like a long shot; between her iffy grades and our iffy financial resources, I didn't see how we could get her in. I helped her with her transcripts, her application essay, her audition material. By some miracle, it all worked, and she was accepted with financial aid. My father and Spade generously split the remaining tuition between them and that is how I found myself driving my daughter to boarding school, once more astonished by how meticulously my past was repeating itself.

The Idyllwild Arts Academy was not housed on an old summer estate but was a collection of buildings on a warm and woodsy campus that appeared to have grown out of the mountainside. The school had been founded by idealistic, humanist artistic hippies, naturally. I felt like I had traveled back to 1978. Not much had changed in the decades since my own freshman arrival at school. Kids in peasant skirts and shit-kickers wandered the campus laughing extravagantly, leaping into one another's arms, acting out the never-ending passion play that is adolescence. I felt so much affection for these beautiful, awkward children playing dress-up inside their own bodies. I knew my daughter would fit right in.

We found Grace's dorm room and got her settled. Her roommate had already arrived and had left Grace the bed under the window. I discovered that teenage girls still decorated with Indian tapestries and fairy lights, and music poured out from every door of that dormitory. I helped Grace make her bed. She had picked out her own bedding—a soft, bright quilt with a fleecy zebra throw blanket to snuggle up in. I plumped her pillow and set Fluffy up firmly against it so he wouldn't list over. And that was pretty much it. Time to say goodbye. Time to do the one thing I had sworn all my goddamn life I would never, ever do: abandon my child in a boarding school.

The road back down the mountain was steep and winding. As I peered over the edge, down into the valley below, I felt myself lurch with panic and regret. I wanted to grab the wheel and turn the car back around. I wanted to fly out the window and swoop back up over that mountaintop and snatch my bunny back. What would happen to her up there? Would she become sexual prey to some married photography teacher in a Patagonia pullover? Would she end up following in her mother's, her grandmother's, and her great-aunt's footsteps? How could I trust the great predatory world to hold her safe?

Back home that night, I could hear Mae weeping behind her bedroom door, mourning the loss of her sister, and a new sinkhole opened up inside of me. I had been so focused on Grace's needs I had forgotten to consider what the outcome of all my efforts would do to Mae. I had made an incalculable mistake. I had robbed a sister of a sister, just as I had been robbed of my own sister when I was sent away to school.

No matter how hard I tried to avoid it, I had managed to replicate every step of my own adolescent story in my daughters' lives. I had created a circumstance in which my eldest needed to go away to boarding school. I had separated two sisters. My girls needed each other, if for nothing else than to bear witness to the insanity of their parents.

After a while, Mae's sobs quieted and she finally fell asleep. I lay awake wondering what this night had been like for my mother thirty years before, when she came home from dropping me off at Buxton. I had never considered how my own absence might have affected my family. Was my sister bereft? Did my mother have any second thoughts? Or did they all just go out to dinner and share a dessert without me?

I imagined Grace, up in her new dorm room, under her zebra blanket, and I thought back to my first night, up under the eaves of the Main House, beneath my scratchy army blanket. I had clutched my Snoopy and listened to all the strange new sounds, the quiet of the country night, the creak and hum of the big old building, stuffed full of strange sleeping girls.

The accordion of my life squeezed inward and every part came together in a great groaning wheeze of sadness.

PART IX

A BRIEF FAMILY HISTORY OF TEACHER-FUCKERS

Frances, Seattle, 1918

My great-aunt Frances was born in Seattle in 1903, the granddaughter of Methodist ministers who had settled the Pacific Northwest and established the first school and church in Ballard, Washington. Her own father had been a Methodist pastor who had raised his daughter to be a Jesus-loving, obedient child. But in her freshman year of high school, Frannie read John Stuart Mill's *On Liberty* and decided, "It is better to be an agnostic, to say, 'I don't know.'" Blind faith suddenly felt impossibly dishonest to her. She declared her agnosticism to her father, upon which the old man retired to his bedroom for two full days, refusing food or the ministrations of his fretful wife. "I was fifteen then," Frannie wrote. "He never took it out on me in any way, but he was deeply, deeply hurt. I can't tell you how generous my parents were with me, considering what a willful person I was, in doing what I thought I should."

Frannie told me that by her sixteenth birthday she had outgrown her father's religious library and wanted but one thing: a copy of *Leaves of Grass* by Walt Whitman. Her parents, not knowing much about Whitman, found a secondhand copy of the book, which Frannie read and reread. One afternoon her mother was knitting in the front room, and her father was reading to her from his religious newspaper, when they paused to observe their daughter, out on the porch, once again engrossed in her book.

"Frances," they asked her, "what is it you like so much about this Whitman book?" Frannie, excited to share her passion with her parents, began to recite to them, from memory, "Out of the Cradle Endlessly Rocking," a somewhat odd but acceptable poem for a girl in 1918 Seattle. But when Frannie put the book down in her lap it fell open to her favorite poem, the poem she had cracked the spine reading over and over. It was "A Woman Waits for Me," a decidedly sexual ode with its "seminal milk" and the pressing of slow, rude muscles. It must have been a tense moment. Frannie braced for parental rebuke, but her parents didn't chastise her. Their liberality and love for their daughter prevailed over what must have been considerable Christian fantods.

I believe this was the moment the last true Christian strain on that side of my family was forever snuffed out, and a loose, lusty, humanist precedent was set. A humanism I inherited and have successfully passed on to my own children.

When Frannie's family moved the next year to West Seattle she enrolled in West Seattle High School, where the second important event happened. She met Orrin Forsyth, a twenty-seven-year-old scholar, intellectual, and graduate of the University of Colorado. He taught English, literature, and journalism, and served as advisor on the student newspaper. Frances started working on the paper and helped him publish it on—what else?—a small printing press housed in the school's basement. Orrin, at least, was an honorable pedophile, and he took his sixteen-year-old lover to wife. The marriage lasted all of two years before Frances broke free to live the rest of her astonishing life.

Jill, Bronxville, New York, 1954

My mother was raised in an environment of emotional neglect as she grew up between Los Angeles and New York. Her father, John Whedon, was a workaholic writer, given to rages, dismissive of his children, often away on show business. Her mother, Carroll Whedon (née Angell), was unhappily married, alcoholic, and a frustrated writer, to boot. My mother's older brother, Tom, was too distant in age and gender for them to be very close as kids, though they became very close in adulthood. The Whedon family was "bicoastal" long before the term had been coined. Carroll kept an apartment in Manhattan while John flew between New York and L.A. for radio, television, and theatre work.

When my mother was about ten, her father brought her along to a business meeting with Richard L. Simon, of Simon & Schuster Publishing, at Simon's Westchester home. It was there she met and befriended Joanna Simon, the eldest of four Simon siblings, the youngest of whom was Carly Simon. The two girls became immediate and inseparable best friends.

The Simons were a big musical family that featured fun uncles, fond servants, friendly neighbors, and frequent, glamorous parties. In addition to their Westchester house the Simons had a sixty-four-acre country estate in Stamford, Connecticut, over which the Simon kids and their friends had free rein. There was a swimming pool, a bathhouse, a tennis court, an orchard, a vegetable garden, and a big barn where the kids would put on plays. Presiding over this household was Andrea Simon, a warm, frolicsome matriarch who liked to dress colorfully and include everyone in the fun, whether it was Jackie Robinson, Bennett Cerf, or the lost children of their acquaintances.

Jonathan "Jonno" Schwartz (the longtime WNYC radio host) was another informal adoptee of the Simon family. He described the Simon home in his 2004 memoir *All in Good Time*: "The grand front door opened into a nineteen-room labyrinth of a large family in the full swing of music and dogs, tomatoes and guitars, peonies and peanuts, tchotchkes and vodka, footsteps and surprise appearances, laughter and tantrums, poison ivy and chocolate cake, mosquito bites and bubble gum, orange juice and wet towels, crayons and tennis balls, comic books and Hershey bars and all the colors of Andrea's skirts distributed on the walls and rugs and coffee tables and in bathrooms and down hallways and up the stairs: orange, purple, dark red and touches of blue and gold. The colors of music."

Like Jonno, Jill was welcomed into the Simon family as a kind of ersatz foster child. If my mother had a happy childhood, I believe it was, in some part, because of the Simons. She loved music, tennis, board games, word games, dancing, and convivial groups of people, and these were the areas where she was most generous and at ease. In spite of her sadness and her wounds, she loved fun and had a real gift for it. There never was a better Boggle opponent, Christmas caroler, beachgoer, or storyteller than Jill Whedon.

Joanna Simon's voice on the phone was exactly as I remembered it, rich and round. I think the last time I had seen her had to be in the late 1970s. Joey featured heavily in my young life as a glamorous figure. The fact that she was my mother's best friend from childhood automatically enthroned her in my mind. A tall, leggy mezzo-soprano opera singer, Joey had big, fluffy blond hair and full, glossy lips that she outlined with a maroon pencil so that her mouth looked like a drawing that needed to be colored in. Sometimes she would be prevailed upon to sing at dinner parties and the bigness of her voice in our small living room frightened me a little. As I grew older I became aware of tension between Joey and Mom, but I had never known what it was about. By the time my mother died, they were completely estranged.

Joey was happy to get my call and eager to reminisce. "We were inseparable, we did everything together. Your mother was so much fun."

Jill spent every weekend at the Simon home, and eventually, she joined Joey at Riverdale High and essentially lived full-time with the Simons. Joey told me she rarely spent time with Jill's family in the city. Carroll made her nervous. She described my grandmother as "a physically big presence, vivacious and unpredictable." It fits with everything else I've been told about the woman who died before I was old enough to remember her. She was legendarily the life of the party, quick-witted and good with a story, but a bad drinker who could turn toxic on a dime.

"I remember one night I did stay at Jill's apartment in the city," Joey recalled. "We were in bed and asleep when Carroll came crashing into our room, flipped on the lights, and screamed at us." Someone had used her hairbrush and not put it back.

Later, I told my sister this story, and Jessica summoned a memory that I had buried with the general wreckage of the 1970s. This was post-divorce, and Mom had gone out for the evening and left us alone in the house. We made ourselves dinner, watched TV, and put ourselves to bed. We had been asleep for a while when Mom came thundering into our rooms in a white-hot rage. We had left the kitchen a mess. She frog-marched us down to the kitchen in our nightgowns to clean it all up.

We do to our children what was done to us.

Jill flourished during her Riverdale High School years. She had a handsome, preppy boyfriend named Andy Drexel, who matched her perfectly in both wit and beauty. They were a dynamic and popular couple. "Everybody just loved them," Joanna said. "Your mother was just so much fun."

After their sophomore year of high school, Joey spent a summer with Jill at her Los Angeles house and bore witness to mounting tensions between Carroll and Jill. "Jill was becoming very attractive. She was funny and beautiful and truly had the loveliest figure. Carroll was clearly in competition with her."

Was my grandmother so fragile that she would be galled by her own daughter's pulchritude? And was beauty the crime that I, in turn, committed in puberty against my own middle-aged mother? It felt too stupid and simple. More likely my mother was just unconsciously feeding me the same tainted formula of self-loathing that she herself had been fed on without knowing she was doing it.

Jill and Joey both applied to and were accepted as freshmen into Sarah Lawrence College's graduating class of 1958. Sarah Lawrence was in Bronxville, not too far from the Simons' Westchester home. They elected to share a room in Westlands, the central building on campus, and coincidentally, the same dormitory that I would come to live in my freshman year at Sarah Lawrence, three decades later.

The two friends had a lot of fun the first six months of their freshman year. Andrea Simon had clean laundry and fresh flowers delivered to the girls' room every week, and they were free to pursue their mutual interests, friends, and fun.

"But suddenly, in the middle of our freshman year, Jill cut herself off from me."

I asked Joanna what happened and got a wry chuckle, "Oh, George Goethals is what happened."

My mother was a psychology major and George Washington Goethals II was her professor. "Your mother began sleeping with George and his wife, Natalie, sometime toward the end of the fall semester."

"How do you know this?"

"Because she told me. I had to pry it out of her. When she finally confessed the affair to me she said, 'He told me not to tell you.'

"At first I couldn't believe it. I mean, she was so attractive and George looked like a lizard, with slow-blink eyes," Joey continued. "I could feel her withdrawing from our friendship as she became more involved with the Goethalses." I could hear the hurt in Joey's voice, all these years later. I thought about how I had withdrawn from my own best friend, Diana, as I came under Spade's thrall, and how that vital friendship was the first casualty of my affair with him.

"The affair permanently changed her," Joanna said. "She cut herself off from everyone. She spent so much time with Goethals and his wife it was amazing that she got anything done in school. He turned her into somebody she wasn't, that she hadn't been before. She became sarcastic and uncaring. The word, actually, is 'mean.' She became mean."

The word "mean" passed through me like a shiver. It felt electric to hear someone say it out loud.

By the end of the year Joey had had enough. She found a new roommate for sophomore year, and the two friends were never close again, though they remained lifelong frenemies, dipping in and out of each other's lives, for both good and ill.

The Sarah Lawrence archives show that Goethals was my mother's Don, or academic advisor, her sophomore year. In her junior year, Goethals returned to Harvard, where he had a three-room office suite on the top floor of the psychology department. Mom followed him there after graduation, getting a Woodrow Wilson Fellowship in psychology in order to be with George and help with his study. This is an achievement that impresses me on both a romantic and an intellectual level. Much of it squared with what she had told me back on the Cape in the summer of 1982. The relationship had foundered, but she had discovered her love of writing while transcribing those interviews.

I had asked Mom about Goethals back in 2014, two years before she died. In my mother's telling, she was a bold heroine, in control of her own wild heart and destiny at all times. She told me it was she who ended the affair with Goethals when her fellowship at Harvard concluded. She knew she was not a psychologist, and she walked away from Goethals and psychology to be a writer in New York. It almost sounded like a happy ending.

"I think Jill was permanently injured by George Goethals and never got over it. Then she met your father," Joanna said. "I never thought Jill was in love with Dick, but it made sense. He was smart. She put her ambition aside for her children and husband. Jill was never a physical person, so I never saw anything like total devotion or motherly love. She was much more intellectually motivated. She liked the idea of being a mother. But in the end, housewifing wasn't enough and she went back to writing."

Mom didn't see or speak to Goethals for twenty-five years. As she and David Vale moved around in the ten years they were together, Cambridge, Massachusetts, was one of their stops. One day while in Harvard Square running errands, Jill found herself walking across the Harvard yard and straight up to George Goethals's corner office. She found him right where she had left him: beloved by his students, still married to Natalie, and winding up a long and illustrious career. My ears pricked up at the mention of his wife, but Mom never mentioned having slept with Natalie and I didn't ask. She told me they talked for a while, caught up, and she left his office that day with a sense of closure. It sounded almost too good to be true.

"Those were the days when a lot of girls had affairs with a lot of teachers," Joanna said toward the end of our call. "They often got married."

I hung up and thought about Frannie marrying her professor. Had it conferred the legitimacy that I and my mother had been denied in our affairs, thus sparing her a lifetime of shame? I wondered who my mother might have been were it not for her professor. Who even was George Goethals?

I found Professor Goethals in the West Chop Cemetery, which maintained a memorial web page for him. There is a photograph of him in late middle age; he stands with his hands on his hips, squinting into the sun, his shirtsleeves rolled up and a tin of chewing tobacco clearly outlined in his breast pocket. I could see what Joey meant by his lizardly looks, but wondered why she hadn't mentioned that he looked unsettlingly like my father.

The *Harvard Crimson* obituary confirmed that Goethals taught at Sarah Lawrence from 1952 to 1956. From there he went on to teach in Harvard's department of psychology, where he was colleagues with luminaries like B. F. Skinner and Erik Erikson during the department's zenith. The obituary concluded, "Goethals was the author of *The Role of Schools in Mental Health* and *Experiencing Youth*. His teaching and research focused on adolescents."

I gasped and drew back from my laptop.

Was it possible that the man who had been sleeping with my mother, his student, and possibly been having a threesome with her along with his wife, had been an expert in the fields of education and adolescence? It was more irony than even I could bear.

I searched for copies of Goethals's two books online, and a few days later, I was holding both of them. Julia Whedon is acknowledged in *The Role of Schools in Mental Health*, a monograph published in 1962. It was a collection of transcribed testimonials and case studies of adolescents, just like she had said. I remembered the boy who thought she was Miss Sweden. This was the project that had made my mother a writer. I paged through the book to find some hint of her writing voice, one I knew so well, but it was all heavily edited and fairly clinical.

I also googled Natalie Goethals, but all I turned up was an article in *Harvard Magazine* from 2002 about life after retirement that featured a photograph of her. Strong-jawed with close-cropped hair, Natalie holds a tree pose. Natalie looked to be a formidable woman who was no doubt striking in her youth. Joanna had suggested more than once on our call that it was Natalie whom my mother was into all along. She suspected my mother of homosexuality, and offered up a couple of my mother's other lifelong female friends as evidence. It is true that my mother forged fierce attachments with women that often ended in dramatic breakups. But it is also true that my mother worshipped masculinity. Other than her few close female friends and her daughters, she had little interest in or affection for the world of women.

They are all dead now and I have to accept that I will

never really know the truth about what transpired between my mother and the Goethalses, or how much she may have been hurt by them.

A few days after my call with Joanna, something else occurred to me: in the loss of her friendship with Joey, my mother had exiled herself from her adoptive family, the Simons, in much the same way I was exiled from Buxton, and later from the family I built as an adult. What was this mechanism within me that I could trace back into my family tree?

Whatever she may have felt about George Goethals, by the time she arrived in New York, my mother was permanently damaged by the affair. Sadness was the dowry Jill had brought to her marriage with my father. I had been conceived in a classic attempt to distract from that sadness, to transact the alchemy of the okey-doke as a stand-in for love.

PART X

GROUND TO DUST

North Bennington, Summer 1982

Driving across covered bridges is scary. You can't see what's coming until you are all the way inside, and then it is too dark and close to turn around and go back. The day winks out as the bridge engulfs you in a thunderous rattle; the boards, spaced wide enough that you can see the water beneath, feel like they can't possibly hold you.

I didn't even have a learner's permit, but Henry had been teaching me to drive on the country roads of Bennington. The roads would unfurl like ribbon beneath the small wheels of his Renault. Henry sat barefoot beside me, talking me through the gears. I learned to negotiate the tension in shifting between first and second, the sweet ease of third into fourth that made me feel like a real driver. But inside the bridge I panicked.

We burst out into sunlight and I was surprised by an oncoming Jeep and braked suddenly, stalling the car. The Jeep swerved and passed us. "Let's take a break," Henry suggested.

We found a field that was edged with black-eyed Susans and Queen Anne's lace. I picked some flowers for our coffee cans back home. Henry spread out the car blanket and we stretched out. The midsummer sun was soft and drowsy on our backs.

"We need to talk." Henry looked at me with sad, resigned eyes, and I felt my throat clench. I sat up.

"I'm not having any luck finding work from here, just sending out tapes and scores. I need to go to Boston and New York to look for work. I need another teaching job. I need to be mobile. I need to take the car and go deal with my life. And you can't be here without a car."

"So I'll go with you."

"No, it just won't work. I can't afford hotels. I need you to go back to New York and stay with your father for a little while."

"No, I can't do that. Don't worry, I can stay here and ride my bike to work."

"You can't ride out fifteen miles to Shaftsbury and back every day on that thing. You have to go to New York."

"No."

"You have to. This is how it has to be. I have thought about it. There's really no other way."

"Please, Henry, let's think of another plan."

"It's too late, I've already called your father. He's on his way here now."

I had been in a covered bridge all along.

Henry drove us back to our apartment. There was a rental car parked out front and Dad and Carol were standing on the porch.

"Pack everything," my father said, "you're not coming back here."

Carol smoked and looked fretful.

They waited downstairs while I sobbed and gabbled at Henry and threw everything I owned into my silver trunk.

"When did you call my dad?" I asked. We didn't have a phone in the apartment.

"Yesterday, from school." He had slept next to me all night knowing this was going to happen and had not said anything until it was too late for me to object. I had been set up.

I had to stop to gasp for air. I was crying so hard I couldn't breathe. I threw myself against Henry's shirtfront and begged him to reassure me that he would come get me as soon as he could.

"Don't worry," he said, "this is only for a week or two." But we both knew in a few weeks I would be starting college.

I reached for the plastic lid for my Olivetti, but he stayed my hand. "May I keep this for you? I really need it for my résumés. I promise I will take good care of it."

I looked into his deep brown eyes for a long time. I had to trust him. I couldn't afford to be wrong about him. "Okay, but I love this thing and I'll need it for school. And I'm also coming back for my bike. They are important to me."

"Of course. I'll take care of them both. Thank you, Erika."

"You will call me from school on Monday?"

"Yes. Don't worry."

"I love you."

"I love you too."

Dad and Carol had bought a Federal house in TriBeCa, on Harrison Street. The four stories of the house had been remodeled so none of the floors had interior walls. My bedroom was on the third floor, separated from my father's study by a bookcase. Ali was in L.A., at her father's house on Dicks Street, the same house my father would later buy from Arthur when he and Carol moved west in 1986. The tension in the house was unbearable.

Thankfully, Mia called me and invited me to a party some Buxton kids were having on Long Island, so we took the train out together that weekend.

I don't remember whose party it was, just that it was at a big, modern house near the beach and CJ was there. He was drunk and stoned. We took our beers out to a bluff on the beach. I told him what had happened that summer, and none of it surprised him. "Are you all right?"

"Sure, I'm going back to Vermont as soon as Henry figures out work."

He took a deep drag off the cigarette we were sharing and passed it back to me. "I wouldn't let that be your only plan." Something had toughened in him. I felt an odd distance between us and wondered if he were mad at me for something. He had been partying hard that summer, going to parties at Grace Jones's house in the city, going to clubs, doing lots of blow. He told me he was sleeping with men and liking it. He was off on his own debauched interregnum before he headed to St. John's College in New Mexico in September. I assured myself that everything was fine between us, but in fact, it wasn't, and I wouldn't hear from him again until that phone call out of the blue, almost thirty years later.

The following Monday I waited all day for Henry to call. He didn't. On Tuesday I called the Bennington College Music Department and left a message with the secretary. I called twice the next day, and three times the following day. On Friday the secretary said, "Stop calling. Mr. Baker has gone back to his wife."

I never spoke to Henry or saw him again. I wonder if he still has my typewriter.

Los Angeles, Summer 2012

I knew Spade was calling to end it before I picked up the phone. We had broken up several times already, but even I could feel we were nearing the bitter end. We were "insoluble." That was the word we kept returning to. We couldn't be together and we couldn't be apart—we were lashed to the wheel of our mutual need for each other and his inability to trust me. Every conversation was about him pushing me away and me hanging on. We had broken up and gotten back together so many times over the last four years that I had lost track. But this time, I knew things were different. His need to be rid of me was palpable. Every other woman had dumped him in disgust, but not me. It was starting to piss him off.

He was obsessed with his own mortality. He had long planned to be interred in a vault with his stuffed animals and his coin collection. Over the course of our relationship the vault had been an ongoing point of contention between us. He wanted me to sign a contract that after he died I would never be with another man and I would go into the vault with him after my death. I said I would, if he put me in his will. Alas, he said, the terms of his divorce dictated that it all go to the Cougar. I wondered whether the Cougar would end up in the vault with us.

These issues roiled and haunted him constantly, erupting into fights more and more frequently. He had become completely dissociative with me. When he fucked me he had to narrate a fantasy of me being gangbanged by a roomful of college students in order to stay aroused. He could not bear to be with the real me, nor did he have any interest in the old projection of me that he had once so adored.

The end came when the Cougar published her second novel in the spring and asked Spade to do an event with her at one of our local bookstores. He told me that I wasn't invited to the reception or the reading.

"What do you mean?"

"Your presence will make her uncomfortable and I won't have it."

"What about my discomfort at being banned from your event? I am your fucking girlfriend!"

"It doesn't matter, I won't have you creating an awkward situation for her."

"I wouldn't be anything but completely gracious with her." I had always advocated bringing his ex into our "Circle of Love," as I called it jokingly, but I really meant it. In better times the three of us had even had an awkward lunch at the Pacific Dining Car. I knew how much she meant to him, and I had hoped, fatuously, that we might all be friends one day.

"She doesn't like you."

"But why? On what grounds?"

"It doesn't matter. She just doesn't like you. She told me so."

"Why don't you defend me? Whose side are you on here?"

"I am on my own side! I will not be inconvenienced by you. This is how it has to be." His voice had shifted; I could almost hear his teeth gnashing.

"My God, you are a monster!" I sobbed, stunned, once again, by his capacity for cruelty.

"Yes, I am a monster! A monster!"

I hung up on him.

The next morning he called. "I am ground to dust," he said. "I can't do this anymore."

"Please, babe, I am scared. Don't leave me."

"This is how it has to be." I wept so bitterly, he was moved. "I will call you exactly one month from today, and that will be our final conversation."

I wish I could have done what my mother claims she did with her big love: walk away, dignity intact, blocked his phone number, turned off my Google alerts, but instead I counted off those thirty days. He called at exactly the hour he said he would.

I had thought all month about the things I would say to him, but when I heard his voice I became sleepy; I forgot what I wanted to say.

"What am I to you?" I asked him.

"You are my ex-love." He was resolute.

"It was the sweetest shit ever," I said, shamelessly calling back the line we used back when we were so in love, when I was Her and all of this horror was unimaginable to either of us. I sounded pathetic even to myself.

"It was great sex, big yuks," he said, reducing me even further at the last.

He was silent for a long moment. "We brought each other through some shit," he said a trifle more warmly. "Go out in the world and be your wonderful self." I could hear him wanting to wrap the call up.

I was the witness to his worst shame and the embodiment of his vulnerability, and that was the crux of the problem. He would never have peace from his demons as long as I was in his life. He needed to start over, write a new draft of himself that starred someone else. It was time for me to go into the archive with his other loves. If I was lucky I would be boxed up and put into storage with all the hundreds of letters I had written to him, the scarves I had knit for him, and the mementos I had collaged together. More likely, I would end up in a Hefty bag on the curb.

"We will not be friends after this," he told me before finally hanging up. "We will never speak again."

We never have.

Bronxville, New York, Fall 1982

I cannot recall much of my freshman year at Sarah Lawrence. I was in a state of emotional pain so acute and experiencing panic attacks so severe that a couple of times I nearly blacked out from hyperventilation. I wept at inopportune moments. I thought about Henry all day and dreamed about Buxton every night.

I took a poetry class with Tom Lux, a somewhat notable poet, and a handsome, cocksure guy with elbow patches and wire-rimmed glasses. There were two wildly gifted poets in our class—Celia Bland and Lucy Grealy—to whom I constantly compared myself. I had never taken a poetry class, and I brought in a couple of poems I had typed on my Olivetti at Buxton. They were quickly torn apart in workshop. I tried to generate new work, laboring to put my gargantuan heartbreak into words and images, but Lux scolded me for alliteration and lazy metaphor and cured me of writing poetry forever.

Little did I know then, as I suffered the throes of heartbreak, that the second great heartbreak of my life was just down the road. A thirty-five-year-old Sam Spade was also living in Bronxville, on Siwanoy Boulevard, holed up in an old lady's basement writing what would be his most famous novel. He and Lux were pals and would go out carousing after hours, drinking in the local bars, bedding Sarah Lawrence girls. Decades later Celia Bland reminded me that Lux once brought Spade into our class as a special guest to talk about novel writing. He had made a lasting impression on her. I have absolutely no memory of him.

Pasadena, 2013

Thirty years later I found myself right back in the goo of heartbreak. It was all so familiar: the ennui, the sudden stabs of longing, the perils of memory.

For a while I was the "Adele H." of my local Starbucks, pale and dim-eyed as I tapped out love letters to my beloved that he would never read, wandering the streets of Los Angeles, my bonnet askance, wondering why I had been so forsaken. But I didn't have the luxury of disappearing into my heartbreak the way I had done back in 1982. This time I had children who needed me whole.

In a stroke of luck, Ali's job was transferring her to Asia for two years, and she asked me to housesit her enormous, hundred-year-old Craftsman in Pasadena. Grace, Mae, and I moved into Ali's house that July, giving all three of us a fresh start.

Ali and I had become very close in adulthood. Her mother had died suddenly of colon cancer in 1991. Carol and my father had been married for ten years and the marriage, my father confessed to me in the hospital, was on the rocks. He was wracked with guilt over it. I was by Ali's side, early one morning, as her mother passed away. The experience had turned our somewhat ironic, circumstantial friendship/reluctant stepsisterhood into a lifelong bond.

The four of us overlapped in the house for a few weeks before Ali pushed off for Shanghai, and those weeks, with the four of us living in the old house together, felt like being back in the dorm at Buxton.

When Ali left for Asia, I let Grace move into the big upstairs master bedroom with its spa bathroom and walk-in closet. Mae got the big second bedroom off the back porch. I took the tiny, almost monastic, cell of a room off the kitchen. I wanted to sequester myself, lead the life of an ascetic, remaining chaste and unbesmirched by another man in case Spade came back for me one more time. I would awake with the dawn, do my chores, and then sit at the kitchen island and try to write, but every word I wrote was a wail beseeching him to love me again.

In addition to the house, I was looking after Ali's ancient bullmastiff, Charlotte, and a flock of chickens. I was no longer a mink-stole girl, I was a chicken-farm woman, which felt like a return to form. I was done with day spas and luxury suites; instead I mucked the coop, hauled bags of feed down the flagstones, pulled weeds, and grew chard. It was Work Program all over again but on a much smaller scale. I made batches of granola, as I had done at Buxton. If only I had had a pile of logs to split, I could have ripped through a cord with the fury I felt.

Pasadena felt rural compared to Los Angeles. It was Mayberry RFD with its diagonal parking and drive-through milk stops. Girls in jodhpurs picked at salads at Le Pain Quotidien, and towheaded families drifted like taut-limbed, distracted gazelles through Old Town. Pasadena was Squaresville—Spade would have loved it.

The book Spade had started in rehab was published, and I found a copy in a Barnes & Noble. I opened it to the title page, and looking at it I felt a surge of rage, and I grabbed the page and crumpled it up. On the other side was the dedication page—he had dedicated the book to Lisa. I smoothed out the crumpled page and lowered the cover.

Being in love with a semifamous person isn't easy. Being their ex is hell. For a few weeks Spade was everywhere: doing bookstore readings, giving interviews, popping up on my local NPR station and endlessly through the Google alert that I didn't have the strength of will to turn off. This is how I heard about his next girlfriend. This is how I knew when he left Los Angeles and he and the Cougar moved to a mountain town where they now keep separate apartments in the same building.

I hatched some baby chicks. We kept them in a plastic storage bin in the kitchen with a heat lamp clipped to the side. Mae and I watched them tumble over one another, going *Eep! Eep!* and we fawned over them. One chick was so flossy we named her Beyoncé and these strange, beautiful, tiny dinosaurs grew up and laid delicate, pale-blue eggs. Those chickens felt like redemption.

One Sunday morning I plucked the *New York Times* off the front lawn and brought it into the kitchen. I shooed the chickens out the back door and poured myself a cup of coffee. I scanned the headlines and turned to the op-ed page and there, above the fold, was writer Joyce Maynard. A documentary film had been made about J. D. Salinger and revealed that Maynard had been but one of a series of much younger girls Salinger had kept and abused in his house in New Hampshire. She wrote:

> I was 18 when he wrote to me in the irresistible voice of Holden Caulfield, though he was 53 at the time. Within months I left school to live with Salinger; gave up my scholarship; severed relationships with friends; disconnected from my family; forswore all books, music, food and ideas not condoned by him. At the time, I believed I'd be with Jerry Salinger forever.

Of course, I knew all this from reading *At Home in the World*, her memoir of that time, back in 2008. Joyce was a freshman at Yale when she published a cover story in the *New York Times Sunday Magazine* titled "An 18-Year-Old Looks Back on Life." It was eight thousand rambling, precocious words in which she took stock of herself, her times, her generation. The piece sounded off-the-cuff, but I recognized the labors of a girl trying to prove her smarts while simultaneously suffering from world-weariness. I had once been a version of that girl myself.

Jack Margolin had recommended the book to me in 2008 as a way into my Buxton story. He was right to think Maynard's memoir about her affair with a much older pedagogue when she was eighteen might be helpful. But it had a much different effect on me than either of us anticipated.

The photo the *New York Times Magazine* had run on the cover was a pedophile's dream: Maynard was so young, slight, not yet fully grown into her limbs, with eyes as big as the face of the man's wristwatch that drooped off her delicate wrist. No doubt Salinger saw all of that and more and read the article over and over in his bunker in Cornish, New Hampshire. A predator's foremost skill is spotting the chink in the armor, the insecurity that can surrender itself to sadism. He picked up his only weapon, his pen, and wrote to her. When his letter arrived, Joyce was at Yale fulfilling her parents' dreams. She was anorexic, anxious, and peaking early. There was no possible way she could have resisted him. Her family and her culture had shaped her specifically for Salinger. Like mine, her own gifted childhood drama was a pastiche of narcissism, alcoholism, mixed messaging, high expectations, and benign neglect.

She dropped out of Yale to be with Salinger. On her way to Cornish, New Hampshire, she stopped at home first. "I have tried to imagine what was going on in my parents' minds as they picked me up from the bus from Yale before I made my trip to Cornish. Nobody suggests this was a bad idea or questions what might be going on in the mind of a fifty-three-year-old man who invites an eighteen-year-old to come and spend the weekend."

In fact, Fredelle Maynard made her daughter a special dress in which to meet her predator. It was a white girlish, A-line shift that could be easily lifted off her daughter's starved, defenseless body. "My mother is very proud that I have attracted the attention of such a famous and brilliant man." Her words entered me like carbon monoxide when I first read them. This was before Spade and everything else had happened. Before I would, once again, hurl myself like a virgin down the volcano of a man's passion and ego.

It wasn't Salinger who triggered me in this story, it was Fredelle Maynard. She was, in many ways, so similar to my mother. I found myself weeping at the end, when a dying Fredelle calls Joyce: "My sister puts her on the phone for a minute. My mother can barely speak. She says only one word over and over, into my ear. '*Love, love, love, love.*'" That paragraph, when I read it in 2008, kicked open the door to my grief for my mother. I had been thinking about Joyce Maynard all along my surreal journey with Spade. I read about the backlash when her book published. She had been drubbed in reviews as a coattail rider. Her life and career were a cautionary tale for me, and now she was back.

I read on:

Salinger wasn't simply brilliant, funny, wise; he burrowed into one's brain, seeming to understand things nobody else ever had....

Years after he dismissed me, his voice stayed in my head, offering opinions on everything he loved and all that he condemned. This was true even though, on his list of the condemned, was my own self.

I sat with that a minute and thought about these parasitic men, burrowing into our empty places, devouring us from the inside out, infecting us with their own hurt.

Maynard continued, arguing that artistic genius does not justify exploitative behavior. Just because he wrote nine stories and *The Catcher in the Rye* didn't mean that he should be exempt from scrutiny. But Maynard and I come from a time when girls were groomed by the culture and then offered up as the tangible, if temporary, rewards for male genius without scrutiny. We had each been one in a series of women in these two writers' lives. There was an endless supply of us.

The #MeToo movement was but two years old when I fell for

Spade and hadn't yet reached its cultural tipping point. I am so grateful that times have changed, and that a vocabulary for our experiences will be available to protect victims from the deeper harm of lasting shame.

Maynard went on to take issue with the new documentary about Salinger, and its fawning critical response:

> It is the quiet acceptance, apparently alive and well in our culture, of the notion that genius justifies cruel or abusive treatment of those who serve the artist and his art. Richard Schickel, writing of Salinger's activities, expresses the view that despite the disclosures about Salinger's pursuit of young women he lived "a 'normal' life."
>
> "He liked pretty young girls. *Stop the presses*," writes the film critic (and father of daughters) David Edelstein. The implication being, what's the fuss?

I stopped reading. The kitchen grew still around me. Coffee sat cold in my cup as I tried to swallow the article like a sideways pill.

I picked up the phone and dialed my father.

"Hey, kid. What's up? Is everything tickety-boo?"

"Not exactly. Did you see the piece in the *Times* today? Joyce Maynard's op-ed, about the Salinger doc?"

"Oh no. Is old Jerry getting the treatment again? Jesus, Joyce really can't let that one go."

"What do you mean?"

"Christ, that was fifty years ago or something. She really dines out on it."

"Do you know that she cites you and quotes David Edelstein as being okay with it?"

I could hear his office chair creak as he leaned back in it, giving himself over to deeper interest. "No shit? What does she say?"

"That you are part of a culture of quiet acceptance. Edelstein says, 'He liked young girls, stop the presses.'"

Dad chuckled. "Yeah, well, that Jerry did."

I could feel a wad of bile forming in my chest. Dad was warming up to the subject. I could almost hear him kick off his Bali loafers and rub his feet together on the other end of the line.

"Funny, all that business. I always thought it was too bad about old Joyce; she was a bright kid."

"Wait, you knew her?"

"Sure, she was one of my students. At Yale. I was guest-teaching there that year. I fucking hated the commute almost as much as I hated teaching. Those Ivy League assholes couldn't even write a simple declarative sentence."

"Dad . . . Joyce Maynard?"

"Oh yeah, well, I didn't have her very long. She dropped out of my class, presumably to *shtup* Jerry Salinger." He chuckled, then sobered. "It's really too bad. I liked her."

All the points of my life suddenly snapped together—it wasn't just artistic entitlement, it was male entitlement, period. I was just one more female life that had been thrown on the bonfire, my spark consumed by the blaze. What was a pretty, clever girl anyway? She gets called a "muse," but she was kindling.

We hung up and I sat at the table, ignoring the chickens, which had wandered back into the kitchen. I thought about my father in 1959, brush-cut and clean-shaven, taking the elevator up to the editorial offices in the CBS building to meet my sad, solitary, lovely young mother. *She was tall, she had a nice figure. She had pretty red hair. And she was a real lost soul.* It was time for Dick to find a wife. It was time for Jerry to find his next victim. Woody needed a muse. Henry needed to be understood. Spade was on his sacred mission to find the mythical *Her.* And we, the pretty, bright girls coming up through prep schools and the Ivy League, loaded up with Sylvia Plath and the Romantic poets, were prepped to be the just deserts of genius. We were milk-fed and impressionable. Privileged and heedless. We were disposable and interchangeable.

We were only supposed to last for one incandescent moment, like mayflies, then flutter off into oblivion so that the men might be free to work, to publish, and to pursue their next great passion.

PART XI

IN BLOOD AND
TO THE DEATH

January 2016

My father was in assisted living. His dishevelment and forget-fulness had bloomed into full-blown dementia. He had burned his arm on his gas burner while heating up soup, and was urinating all over himself and his house. Lillian, his longtime house-keeper, took me aside and said, "I think Mr. Schickel needs a Pamper." But Mr. Schickel wouldn't wear a Pamper. He wouldn't brook any conversation about his health or its obvious decline. It took me too long to comprehend what was happening to him, and by the time I finally got my sick and addlepated father to a doctor it was too late. His years of smoking had resulted in a series of tiny strokes that resulted in severe dementia.

I found a room for him on the memory-care floor of a Jewish Orthodox place called the Garden of Palms. It was close to his house on Dicks Street, and it was family owned by people who were genuinely kind. He hated it, and every visit he told me he would be going home the next day. I told him, yes, of course, we were just getting the house ready for him, knowing that my father would die at the Garden of Palms.

Ali came back from Shanghai and needed her house back, and so I moved, with my girls, into my father's now-empty house on Dicks Street. The house he had bought from Ali's dad back in 1986.

The 1920s Spanish stucco was in bad shape. Nearly three decades of constant smoking had tarred the walls ochre. Urine soaked the floors down to the studs. When I moved Dad's bed I found a field of dropped over-the-counter medications. His bedroom closet was infested with moths. My sister and I just slipped Hefty bags over his sports jackets, gently lifted them off the bar, and threw them out the window.

Even though the kids and I were being hammered on the anvil of big, scary life events, we had fallen into a sweet grace together. Everything that had fractured in the divorce reassembled itself into gentle, forgiving coherence. The fury of their adolescence had receded, the despair of my heartbreak had lessened, and we found ourselves grateful to be together in this house that had been home to so many members of our family.

No sooner had we unpacked our stuff and gotten settled in than my mother was diagnosed with cancer and told to get her affairs in order.

Jessica and I flew into New York to meet with Mom's oncologist. She told my mother, "Spend time with your family." The three of us walked back to Mom's apartment in stunned silence. We passed a flea market and browsed. Jessica said her husband was already getting the guest room ready for Mom back in Ohio. Everyone assumed that Mom would go home with Jess. It made sense.

My sister has always had a much better relationship with Mom than I did. She spent many more years living with Mom and David, before she escaped to boarding school, where she had a great time.

While it's never good to be the black sheep of the family, I could see, in my sister, the flipside of the coin. There was a real toll that comes with being the kept child. There is codependency and close-up neglect. Jess once told me a story that when she was living in Cambridge with Mom, she had gotten sick just as a hurricane was brewing. She spiked a fever and asked Mom to drive her to the hospital and Mom refused, telling Jess to not be so dramatic. My sister had to drag her feverish body through the hurricane to the emergency room, where she collapsed and clocked in with a 104-degree fever.

My sister was much better at sublimating her needs than I was. This carries its own heaviness, but it made her relationship with Mom slightly more functional.

When we got back from the doctor, Mom was tired and wanted a nap. We got her comfortable and I went out for a walk.

I headed west, spooked and churning with questions and images of the impossible: my mother on her death bed, her enormous-to-me life over, a world in which she no longer existed. It was a vertiginous feeling, knowing that my mother, right now, was preparing to go.

It was Halloween, and the streets were full of little costumed kids, coming home from school, excited to change out of their school costumes and into their trick-or-treating costumes. My mother loved Halloween and had a knack for pulling creative costumes together for me and my sister out of repurposed castoffs. She was particularly good with makeup and hand props. One year I wanted to be a crazy milkmaid, so I wore my dirndl, and my mother made a wig for me out of a mophead. She put enormous false eyelashes on me and gave me a milk pail to collect candy in. Then she dressed my sister as a cow, wearing Holstein-print footie pajamas and an udder made from a Rubbermaid dish glove and hung a bell from a dog collar. I got to lead my sister around on our trick-or-treating rounds on the end of a rope. We really hauled in the candy that year.

I turned down Lexington and three blocks later I found myself standing in front of All Souls Unitarian Church, where my parents had wed so very long ago. I wandered into the leafy courtyard, found a side door to the chapel open, and went inside.

The chapel was empty and quiet. I took a seat in a pew and let the calm of the chapel settle me. The room felt pure and sweet. The Georgian architecture was crisp and unfussy, with capable columns supporting solid arches down both sides of the atrium. Each arch framed a large, clear window—none of that muddling stained glass you find in a Catholic church. The light in here was almost purifying. I thought of my mother standing at the altar in this frank light,

314 ERIKA SCHICKEL

her creamy skin and auburn hair aglow, ready to cleanse herself of heartbreak through the good offices of marriage. She was ready to pledge herself to a man she barely knew and would soon enough come to hate. Her bridesmaids, Joanna Simon and Carol Rossen, looking Jackie-O chic in their matching dresses and pillbox hats. Like everyone at the start of their lives, my mother must have wondered at some point how it might all turn out. Would the marriage last? What kind of children would there be? How would she someday die?

Now we had all the answers: failed marriage, imperfect but well-meaning daughters, and a medicated death in Chagrin Falls, Ohio, in the dead of winter.

I thought of my dear sister, stretched between Mom, her still young kids, and her small upholstery business, performing one last act of selfless service to our mother. Of course Jessica, my sterling, selfless sibling, would do all of that unquestioningly and with all the goodwill in the world. But honestly, how would all that really work without affecting her family or her business?

I thought of my mother, that sun-worshipping California girl spending her last season packed in snow. And there I would be in Los Angeles, unemployed and living in my father's biggish house, with my teenage daughters, one of whom could drive, and suddenly I understood with perfect clarity what I had to do.

I had to bring my mother home with me to die.

Los Angeles, Winter 2016–2017

"I look in your refrigerator, and all I see are weird California health foods!" My mother reclined on the hospital bed I had rented and set up in the downstairs den at Dicks Street. "I just want plain 1950s foods!"

Mae was vegan, so admittedly, things could get pretty off-brand inside my fridge, but I ran to Pavilions several times a day to pick up any tidbits Mom got cravings for: Welsh rarebit, fondue, cottage cheese, and fruit cup. She sent me out to search for the prune-flavored Jell-O she had adored as a child, but she'd take peach if that's all there was, which of course there wasn't. It was all tropical flavors nowadays and I knew my mother blamed me and my generation for tropical flavors and for destroying everything she had ever held dear in this life.

I don't know what I thought it would be like to help my mother die. I thought disease might soften her into gentle acquiescence, but instead it filled us both with spitting rage.

We were making our way to her oncologist's office when she swooned in the parking garage, her body telegraphing her need to me. We had just fought bitterly in the car about my daughters, whom she felt spent too much time on their phones. A Tesla pulled out in front of us, rudely but not dangerously. My mother tightened her grip on my arm, her fingernails crawling, scorpion-like, into its crook.

Her body. My body. Both our bodies occupying different points in the death spiral. I could see her genetics in my own rapidly thinning and aging skin. She was in my upright carriage, in the timbre of my voice, the square of my shoulders. Now she wanted to occupy my body in place of her own. We were like two enemies trapped in a horse costume. We moved slowly, in pushmi-pullyu four-footed non-unison toward the elevator.

Mom was crying. We had made it to the waiting room and she crumpled under the effort of transit. The Compassionate Care Cancer Center didn't even provide so much as a box of Kleenex. Mom found a damp wad of tissue at the bottom of her battered tote bag and emptied her nose into it.

I sat beside her, fighting the gnawing desire to look at my phone, because if I did, well, that would be the last straw. So I stood up, strode over to the receptionist's desk, and helped myself to a tiny Butterfinger out of the candy dish.

"Ooh, is that a Butterfinger?" Mom asked conspiratorially, and suddenly we were no longer sworn enemies but accomplices on a bite-sized heist. She took the candy from me with childlike joy, and unwrapped it beneath her nose like a chipmunk. Here we were, left alone with each other, a pair of hungry girls looking for something to nibble on. I did not want to feel this commonality with her, so I left her with the nurse and escaped to the coffee shop in the hospital's basement, where I ate Yankee bean soup and oyster crackers, trying to maneuver the beige food past the lump in my throat.

Two days later I was awakened by a strange sound coming from downstairs. It was early morning. I tiptoed out to the landing. It took me a minute to identify it as the sound of my mother moaning. I ran downstairs to find her collapsed on the bathroom floor. The chemo had kicked in.

I called 911 and within moments my house was filled with enormous EMTs in Day-Glo fire pants and suspenders. I stood aside as they loaded my wailing mother onto a gurney and took her to the hospital.

Mom was in intensive care for three days. The chemo had allowed an overgrowth of white blood cells, and thrush had populated her throat and mouth, plunging her into a silence I had prayed for only days before. Now I sat by her bed, wishing she could yell at me again.

I ferried between Cedars-Sinai and the Garden of Palms, translating all of this for my demented father, who still nursed his hatred for my mother even though he couldn't remember exactly why.

Mom decided she didn't want any more chemotherapy. Nor did she want to go back to Dicks Street to receive more of my mitigated care. She asked for hospice in assisted living. I heard this with a mix of relief and guilt. I couldn't tell if her choice was a rebuke to me or an act of pure generosity.

I looked for a place where she might die, not knowing how long she would live. Once more I took a tour of assisted-living homes with their narrow beds adorned with sad, crocheted throws, weird smells, and sing-alongs. Big-band Christmas covers were piped into dining rooms, and in one a guide pointed to a catatonic woman resting her forehead on the communal table and chirped, "This is Myrna, she would be your mother's roommate." Later, I described the options to my sister on the phone as "ScareBnB." We laughed long and mordantly together.

I had one last place to look before everything shut down for Christmas Eve. Belmont Village, by the Hollywood Bowl, a big fake-Mediterranean building. This was no Garden of Palms, where my father, the only uncircumcised resident, was already celebrating Hannukah. There were no icy blues and tinseled stars of David here. This place was run by gentiles: a big, twinkly Christmas tree stood in the lobby, and doorways were swathed in evergreen garlands. Bing Crosby was piped into the elevator.

Maura, the manager, showed me the one room they had available. It was located at the end of the hall across from a twenty-four-hour nurses' station. It was a tiny, tasteful suite that looked out on the Hollywood Hills. It had its own little balcony so my mother could feel the sun on her face. The golden late-afternoon light coated the adjacent hillside in butterscotch. I turned to Maura, a lozenge of tears forming behind my nose. "Yes, please, this is perfect."

"You look like you need a hug," Maura said. I threw my arms around her and wept gratefully into her cashmered shoulder.

I moved Mom out of the hospital and into Belmont Village on Christmas Day. She loved her room. She loved her hospice care-giver, Jason. It was going to be all right, for now.

Jess came out after Christmas and the three of us exchanged gifts. Mom stretched out under the fluffy throw blanket I had given her. She was happy we were both there, by her side, taking care of her. This was what she had wanted all along.

Jess went home and Mom and I settled into a routine where I would come over and we would watch *Judge Judy* together and hang out for a few hours. Now that she wasn't going to die in her ex-husband's house, she was of good cheer. She liked the staff and, much to my surprise, they loved her. She knew all their names and they joked around together. I was completely stunned. I had never seen this genial, friendly side of my mother.

One day, while we were watching TV, Mom started to cry.

"Mom, what's wrong?"

"Oh God, Erika, I am so sorry!"

"Please, Mom, it's okay." She sometimes apologized to me for all the inconvenience she was causing me.

"No, I made a mistake. I made a mistake. I made a mistake." Her voice climbing upward toward frantic scales.

"What do you mean? What mistake?"

"Ah, I should never have done it."

"Done what, Mom?"

"I shouldn't have left you."

"What do you mean?"

"When I moved to Santa Fe. I just thought I didn't have any other choice. I thought I was saving my life, but I left you behind."

I could hardly believe I was hearing these words. "It's okay," I said reflexively.

"No, it's not okay, Erika. You were just a child. I am so sorry, so sorry."

All my life I had wanted this moment, without ever knowing it. I looked at my mother's drawn, worried face.

"Mom, you must know that all I ever wanted was to come home to you."

"Yes, of course you did. I am just so sorry."

Weeping, I lowered the bar of her hospital bed and bent myself toward her, laying my head on her bosom. I was back on my mother's shelf at last.

The next day she entered a waking dream state. I sat by her bed and listened as she narrated her visions to me. She saw images of Native American clay pots, flattened out and aflame. She saw a table draped in white chiffon standing in the middle of a barren desert. The wind made the fabric luff and she was my mother I first knew again, the one who taught me to see and describe what I saw.

I had taken enough psychedelics to recognize where she was. She had entered a state of cosmic consciousness. I sat quietly with her as she babbled out her visions. I kept my hand on her arm until she was done. I don't know whether she knew I was there. I wasn't frightened as I let my mother go this one last time, and neither was she.

Los Angeles, February 2017

My father's illness was more difficult and attenuated. A challenging man when he was sentient, he became more and more impossible as his dementia grew worse. He refused to acknowledge any of the things that were happening to him: the extreme incontinence, the loss of memory, the confusion, the rage. It was all I could do to keep the Garden of Palms from evicting him, he was so ornery.

I set up screenings of his favorite films in the community room. Dad would come downstairs on his walker and introduce *Yankee Doodle Dandy* and *Meet Me in St. Louis*. Even with every practical part of his brain corroded by stroke, he could rattle off the film's credit roll, remember behind-the-scenes anecdotes, and place the films in the wider context of American history. It was astonishing. In all of his brilliant career I have never been more proud of my father.

Ali was worried about my stress levels, so for my birthday she treated me to a yoga retreat in Tulum, Mexico. I checked in with all of Dad's caregivers, who all said he'd be fine. Dad said I should just go already or I would hurt Ali's feelings. The old man was frail but feisty, so I relented and went on the much-needed vacation.

Our third night in Tulum there was a huge windstorm that woke me up just before dawn. I wrapped myself in a blanket and headed down to the beach to look at the ocean and watch the sunrise. I felt my father all around me suddenly, like he was part of the wind, so I spoke to him out loud. I told him how much I loved him and how I hoped he would have an easy death, whenever it came.

Later that day as I was about to tuck into a bowl of ceviche on the beach, the Garden of Palms called to tell me my father had passed away that morning. I collapsed into the sand.

Ali somehow got us both packed and to the airport as I sobbed and blubbered, losing track of my passport for a few tense moments. Ali shepherded me onto the plane. I sat and stared into the slate of clouds out the window, gobbering with loss that I had fully expected, and yet was not prepared for. In the flow of tears and snot on the flight home I managed to pick up a case of walking pneumonia.

Five days later, as I lay in my sickbed, hot with fever and grief, my sister at my side trying to comfort me, my phone rang with an unfamiliar New York number. It was Liz, an old Buxton friend, calling to tell me that CJ was dead.

I will never understand this part of the story. How these two pivotal men, my father and my friend, were taken from me in the same week. One man had lived a long life full of luck and possibility, the other was gone in the middle of a life that was plagued by misfortune and tragedy.

CJ never really stood a chance. Despite the silver spoon he was born with, the deck was horribly stacked against him. He had had an absent father, a narcissistic mother, a murderous sister, and a molesting teacher. On top of the horrific sexual abuse he suffered in childhood, he was also the victim of a violent mugging in his late forties that left him crippled. His attacker shoved him into a standing pipe, breaking his hip. He had a botched hip replacement, followed by a second hip replacement. By his fiftieth birthday CJ had survived two suicide attempts, alcoholism, divorce, rape, assault, medical malpractice, homelessness, and Hurricane Sandy. He met his end on a sunny afternoon in Brooklyn. As a favor to a friend, he was walking a pair of dogs, and the excited pups pulled him down a flight of stairs.

The last time I saw CJ was when I was in New York packing up my mother's apartment. We met for dinner and went for a walk after. He was sober and living in a men's shelter in Brooklyn. He was as funny and wise as ever. He had an elaborate beard and mustache, curled at the tips, that barely disguised his eternal boyishness or dimmed his bright-blue eyes. CJ still off-gassed anxiety by giggling, but underneath his familiar froth was a steel plate of emotional sobriety and a healthy flame of anger. We sat on a park bench and marveled at all we had been through both together and separately over three decades of friendship. We spoke of our plans for the future. CJ was working on a project close to his heart: a website honoring the work of his photographer grandmother, Ione Robinson. We were both excited about each other's projects.

We could have sat on that bench and talked all night, but CJ had a curfew at the shelter. I walked him to the subway entrance and we held a long, deep hug. "I think the worst is over," he said. "I think we're going to be all right."

"Criminy, let's hope so." I laughed as I hugged my friend goodbye.

Epilogue

Pasadena, now

Thirty-eight years after I got on that Peter Pan bus out of Williamstown, a letter arrives from the Buxton School. The school has taken reports of sexual misconduct brought by alumni very seriously. In the interest of healing they are working with an anti-sexual-violence organization that has set up a fund to help pay for victims' therapy. It is a very carefully worded letter. I read it twice, but nowhere within its seven paragraphs is there an apology or any admission of guilt or responsibility.

I close my laptop and put on my shoes. I need to get outside. I am fueled up with rage and I need to walk it off.

I head down the driveway and cross Monterey Road. I am living in South Pasadena now, in a small apartment down the street from Arroyo Seco Park, a once-wild place that has been claimed by the municipality. It is a crazy quilt of weeds and patched-up sod, golf turf, and gopher holes. The footpath that winds between the trees is littered with lost golf balls. I pick a couple up and try to chuck them back over the fence but they fall short.

Buxton's letter is too little, too late for me. I am glad for those who can be helped by this fund, but I doubt the fund would pay retroactively for the many thousands of dollars I have already spent on therapy over the decades.

The only reason Buxton has written this letter is because I came forward with my story and forced their hand. In 2016 my sister sent me a link to a form at the *Boston Globe*. Their Spotlight team, made famous by their exposition of pedophilia in the Catholic Church, was doing a similar story focused on student sexual abuse at East Coast prep schools. Their investigation turned up more than 300 reports of sexual misconduct throughout New England private schools. I filled out their online form and they contacted me for a story that would focus on students who had suffered retaliation from their school in the wake of an inappropriate relationship with a teacher. I was one of many students who had been swept under the rug in the cleanup of scandal.

My photograph ended up on the front page of the Sunday edition. I am sitting in my father's living room, with a face that looks sad and haggard. When the *Globe* article published I hoped to hear something from Buxton. But the school remained quiet. I got the usual fundraising letters, but nothing else. Meanwhile, other elite schools who had ignored or covered up their predatory teachers were coming forward, launching investigations, and issuing genuine apologies. Still, Buxton remained silent.

In 2017 I was included by a friend in an informal Buxton alumni group email urging me and other long-distance alums to fly to New York for a winter fundraiser. Without thinking, I replied to all saying, essentially, why the fuck would I fly to New York to honor the school that threw me under the bus?

The email thread blew up. It was as though I had given everybody permission to just say what they hadn't all these years—about me, about Buxton, what they saw, how it felt. I heard from old classmates who told me that my sudden disappearance from the school had left them rattled, angry, and confused. I had never considered that my expulsion would have hurt others. But I got the impression the sudden removal of a prominent, flamboyant senior who was otherwise well respected in the community was deeply upsetting to many, even frightening to some.

A friend organized a letter directed to the school, demanding they take responsibility for a culture of abuse witnessed by all of us that was perpetrated at Buxton. We called on the director and trustees to account for Buxton's sins, using my case as the example to represent the many.

The school director quickly reached out to me through a friend, asking for a phone meeting. But I didn't want this matter settled privately, and I declined the meeting. I wanted a public apology. I wanted Buxton to say, "Yes this happened and yes, we were wrong."

The director wrote back to our group saying how terrible she felt about these "romantic" relationships between students and teachers that happened so long ago. She promised a more tangible response to the epidemic of sexual abuse in the school's history in the future, but in the meantime she hoped we could remember the good things about Buxton. It was condescending and infuriating. If there hadn't been so many things to love about Buxton, my exile from it would have hurt far less.

Just in time, I arrive at the Zen garden.

The park is a strange little corner of land that has only recently been reclaimed from chaparral and homeless encampments and put to more scenic use. It serves as a kind of outpost for non-doing. It is landscaped with native plants and a bench that looks north to the San Gabriel Mountains, with the 110 running like a rattlesnake in the foreground. I am not in nature, I am in its curated remnants. It is surprisingly pleasant.

The park features a small mandala, which I spot through the chaparral. It's a simple spiral of white stones set into the earth. It is not very big, maybe twenty feet in diameter. I usually walk past it, but I decide I probably need to walk into it today. I need to do something to center myself.

I take off my shoes and I get goose bumps all over. I forget how good being barefoot outside feels. I no longer dance naked in cow pastures, but the impulse to lay my unclothed body against the earth remains embarrassingly the same. An article I read recently explained that people are essentially batteries that need direct contact with the earth's surface to stay charged.

I know I feel electricity even more keenly these days. I feel the pull of the poles, the suck of the grave, the static of passive-aggression, a flowing, endless circuit when I fuck.

I close my eyes and take a deep breath, then look at the two paths before me, one inner and one outer. I know it doesn't matter which path I choose; they both end up in the same place, but intent matters so I begin on the inner path, since inner peace is what I'm looking for. What is it I want to walk away from? What do I want to walk toward?

I have tried walking away from the pain of the past, but as it probably says on some TJ Maxx throw pillow somewhere, the only way out is through. In the wake of Spade I understood that I had work to do. I was done running away from the past and I dedicated myself to the task of diving into the wreck. I had joined Alanon during Spade's meltdown, and I continued to find connection and understanding in those rooms, rooms my mother would have benefitted from, had she only been a joiner.

I began seeing a psychiatrist three times a week, and over the course of several years I came to trust her enough to let her see all my feelings, and help me hold them safely.

I met a shaman and drank ayahuasca and I flew into the past where I saw my mother and father and Spade as the lonely children they had all once been. I saw myself, seven years old and sitting in the window seat of my apartment at 19 East Eighty-Eighth Street, *The Family of Man* in my lap, wondering what my grown-up life would look like.

Most people vomit on ayahuasca, but my purge came in tears. I wept my heart out for those children for hours. The dawn brought an awakening into perfect, complete, resplendent love. There is nothing harder to describe than ineffability, so I will skip it. But the love I felt that morning eventually led to forgiveness.

I have survived my trauma into an age of trauma disgorgement. Stories of abuse are coming out daily. Thousands of women are coming forward with their own #MeToo stories in politics and entertainment. While it is nice to know I am not alone, I wish there weren't so many of us.

Meanwhile, at the Indian Mountain School, where CJ had been so horribly molested, full-blown investigations have taken place. CJ's abuser, Christopher Simonds, died in 2014, out of the reach of justice. But one of his student victims from the 1970s had copied pages out of Simonds's personal photo album, which featured photographs of kids having sex, masturbating, and smoking marijuana. He buried the copies in a coffee can on campus as insurance. A search is under way for that evidence. I wonder if there are pictures of CJ in that coffee can.

I reach the center of the spiral. The inward-winding circle turns outward, and I realize I am either at the end or the beginning of my path. Life isn't linear; eventually we will double back on ourselves, and hopefully we will have grown wiser, maybe we will have learned something. Maybe I will stop repeating my mistakes. Maybe I will accept that I will never get the closure I want from Buxton. "Closure is a shuck," Spade would say, and he'd be right.

I was alone for several years after Spade, and then I met a man named David—one of the kindest, funniest, most patient people I have ever known. He isn't in the least threatened by my tawdry, checkered past; he embraces all my iterations. David is also a high school English teacher, the irony of which is not lost on either of us. I guess my strange, cosmic pattern will continue, but at least it is working in my favor now.

Studies are beginning to reveal more and more evidence of the epigenetics of trauma. Grace recently told me about one study that suggested that women who suffer trauma tend to give birth to girls. My own highly anecdotal evidence confirms it.

My kids both enjoy productive, interesting adult lives. Nobody is sleeping with faculty and everybody knows they are imperfectly and completely loved. I am proud of them, they are proud of me, and nearly all is forgiven. We talk sometimes of Spade and those strange years when they were his "cubs." Mae went to a reading of his a few years ago, to say hello and reconnect with him. She reported that he was surprised to see her and offered to help her with her résumé, but of course nobody followed up and that was that.

If I do nothing else in my life, at least I have addressed the hurt in my own bloodline. My girls have their own paths before them— I know they will not spend their lives repeating my past or trying to connect with a broken mother. This is my happy ending, even though I am only three-quarters of the way through my spiral.

I thought when my father died I might hear something from Spade, but he didn't send so much as a lily to the memorial of the man he once said he loved like a father. When I press on the spot in my heart where Spade once lived, I still feel some tenderness, but the ache is gone.

Thanks to *Boston Globe* researchers I know that Henry Baker is married and that he continued to teach at Bennington College for many more years, which I assume means that Buxton never notified Bennington of Henry's predatory past. Like the Catholic Church, private schools in those days passed their predators around; it's called "passing the trash."

For years after Henry disappeared from my life, I fantasized about running into him on the street, or in a gallery. Sometimes I fantasized about driving up to Bennington and ambushing him in the Blue Benn Diner, where we used to eat breakfast. I would stand before him in that crowded place and I would ask him why he had to hurt me like that. Then I would punch him. No, I would slap him. No, I simply would turn on my heel. No. We would sit down at the table and order coffee and he would explain how he thought I deserved to be thrown away like that.

I did run into Eileen, on the street, back in 1988, right before I moved to Los Angeles. She was happily engaged to another man and living a life of art curation. She had already moved on, but I have carried these people and events with me all my life, and it's time to let them go.

I exit the mandala and stand still for a moment before I put on my shoes to go home. The Los Angeles air smells clean for once and I take a deep inhale and catch a whiff of jasmine and sage. I think back to that night I stood with my father in Piccadilly Circus, looking at the statue of Anteros and wondering if I would ever find someone to receive my love.

Now I know that Anteros never was a boy with butterfly wings. It was me: a girl dancing naked in a cow pasture, nature's darling, the most alive little spark of a creature in seven kingdoms.

Acknowledgments

My first thanks goes to my parents, Julia Whedon and Richard Schickel, who made me a reader, a writer, and a sucker for the truth. They both live in every sentence of this book, and I miss them every day.

I have been so very lucky in my agent, Laura Nolan. Fate flung us together and she has championed this book faithfully and unflaggingly since 2007 through its many ups and downs. Deep thanks to her and to everyone at Aevitas Creative.

The shape of this book was a Rubik's Cube puzzle that I struggled to solve. I got a critical edit from the talented Anna Pitoniak that helped me find a construction that worked. Even after all those drafts, it took my brilliant editor at Hachette, Lauren Marino, to finally crack the code. My deepest thanks to her for being both my ideal reader and my ideal editor, and thanks to all at Hachette who helped bring this book into the world.

I began writing this on Whidbey Island in 2008 on the first of two Hedgebrook fellowships. Thank you Nancy Nordhoff, Vito Zingarelli, and everyone at Hedgebrook for giving me time and a safe space in which to completely melt down and write my shitty first draft, then come back and write a better draft. Thanks to the Hedgebrook writing community for all the sisterhood and support.

Huge gratitude to Claire Dederer, my literary landsman, for

all the hours of craft talk, business advice, and general commiseration. This is how we do it and I couldn't have done it without her.

I would be nowhere without my talented, generous friends who gave me camaraderie, encouragement, and crucial early reads: Sandra Tsing Loh, Dinah Lenney, Meghan Daum, Caitlin Flannagan, Annabelle Gurwich, Janet Fitch, Lisa Stafford, Lori Avakian, and Laura Haynes.

Big thanks goes to Deb Drooz for an early legal read and ongoing enthusiasm for this project. Other dear friends and supporters who helped me stay in the long game: Mark Netter, Max Schwartz, David Griffin, Elizabeth Decker, Heather Swain, JoAnne Klabin, Sharon Kane, Lisa Stafford, Lindsay Mofford, Christine Ernst, Deb Vogel, and Jill Lummus.

The Buxton alumni community has been generous and invaluable in helping me reclaim some lost memories and get fresh perspectives on old stories. Big thanks to Mia Boyle, Lâle Davidson, Sheila McCullough, David Breitbarth, Cathy Burns, Kristina Lear, Chris Boyer, Virginia Hall Smith, and Pilar El Cid Gale.

Much of this book was written in public libraries, and my thanks goes in particular to the staff of the West Hollywood Library. Thanks as well to Abby Lester at the Sarah Lawrence archives and family friends Joanna Simon and Carol Rossen for their memories of Mom. Thanks to Nat Dickinson for his excellent profile of Frannie Herring.

Special thanks and eternal love to my beloved friend Gary Stewart, who I know, were he still alive, would be handing out copies of this book from the trunk of his car.

I have been blessed with two sisters—one by birth, the other by circumstance. Jessica Schickel is the reader I tried to make laugh as I wrote this sad book. Ali Rubinstein has had my back for nearly forty years. I would simply be nowhere in this life without either of these women.

Bottomless love and thanks to my partner in life, love, and literature, David H. Berry. The man fixes comma splices *and* a mean grilled cheese sandwich, and I'm a very lucky woman indeed.

Finally, to my children, who bravely shared every step of this journey with me; you two will always be my heart, my home, and my happy ending.